Congressional Women

Their Recruitment, Treatment, and Behavior

Irwin N. Gertzog

WOMEN AND POLITICS

general editors:

Rita Mae Kelly and
Ruth B. Mandel

PRAEGER SPECIAL STUDIES • PRAEGER SCIENTIFIC

New York • Philadelphia • Eastbourne, UK
Toronto • Hong Kong • Tokyo • Sydney

To Alice

Library of Congress Cataloging in Publication Data

Gertzog, Irwin N.
  Congressional women.

  Bibliography: p.
  Includes index.
  1. Women legislators—United States—History—20th
century. 2. United States. Congress. House—History—
20th century. I. Title.
JK1319.G47 1984   328.73′073′088042   84-4714
ISBN 0-03-063058-4 (alk. paper)

Material from *BELLA! MRS. ABZUG GOES TO WASHINGTON* by Bella Abzug,
copyright © 1972 by Bella S. Abzug, is reprinted by permission of the publishers, E. P.
Dutton, Inc.

Published in 1984 by Praeger Publishers
CBS Educational and Professional Publishing
a Division of CBS Inc.
521 Fifth Avenue, New York, NY 10175 USA

© 1984 by Praeger Publishers

56789 052 098765432

Printed in the United States of America
on acid-free paper

Preface

This volume began as a more modest undertaking. Its origin was a casual statement uttered in 1976 by a now forgotten source who claimed that the women elected to Congress in the 1970s were a different breed from those who preceded them. Contemporary congresswomen, according to this observer, brought more political experience with them to Washington than did earlier female Representatives. They also possessed a richer range of professional skills in such specialties as law, communications, and management—vocations whose routines readily lend themselves to lawmaking and representational pursuits. One consequence of this change, said the analyst, is that women serving today are more effective legislators than those elected to Congress from 1917 through, roughly, the 1950s.

These observations seemed reasonable enough, but they were unaccompanied by empirical evidence. Although a specialist in Congress, I was unaware of changing background characteristics of the few women who had been elected to Congress, and I could not call to mind significant changes that had come about either in the workings of Congress or in the nature of public policy which could be attributed to the arrival in Washington of a new breed of female lawmakers. Consequently, I decided to test the soundness of some of these generalizations.

I gathered information about the families, vocations, and political experiences of all women who had served in the House of Representatives from 1917, when the first woman took her seat in Congress, through the mid-1970s, and placed each into one of three time periods, 1917 to 1940, 1941 to 1964, and 1965 to 1976, depending upon the year she was first elected to the House. I then compared the combined background characteristics of the women falling within each of the three time periods. Figures were compiled determining, among other things, the proportion of women in each category who might have relied on family connections to secure election to the House, who could have exploited substantial wealth for the same purpose, and who, before coming to Congress, had secured a law degree or successfully contested a race for another public office. Inferences drawn from the comparison did, indeed, suggest that a new breed of women was being elected to the House, and the fruits of the project were eventually published in "Changing Patterns of Female Recruitment to the U.S. House of Representatives," *Legislative Studies Quarterly*, Vol. IV, August, 1979.

Information collected for this study confirmed the widely known fact that many, although not quite a majority, of the women elected to the House succeeded husbands who had died in office. But it also persuaded me to reject the popular view that widows of House members are *regularly* nominated to succeed spouses who die in office. In fact, relatively few congressional widows followed their husbands into the House. Moreover, the factors contributing to their selection were not the same for all. Widows chosen from southern districts tended to be tapped for different reasons than those nominated from districts outside the South, although there were several exceptions within each region. These findings were published in "The Matrimonial Connection: The Nomination of Congressmen's Widows for the House of Representatives," *The Journal of Politics*, Vol. 42, August, 1980.

But even while the study of widows was in its earliest stages, my interest in congresswomen became an absorbing one—primarily because they were becoming far more active and visible than they had ever been. In 1977, female lawmakers formed the Congresswomen's Caucus and national news outlets began to give these women more attention. As a result, I expanded the scope of the inquiry so that I might compare not only recruitment patterns, but the behavior of contemporary congresswomen with that of their predecessors. I soon realized, however, that changes in behavioral regularities could not be fully understood unless I also explored shifts in the ways male and female House members interacted with one another and in the treatment the latter received at the hands of the former. By the end of 1977, an undertaking once limited to the recruitment of congresswomen had been expanded into a more comprehensive examination of their entire congressional experience over time.

I went to Washington in December, 1977, and spent three months in the Library of Congress trying to squeeze out evidence about the congressional activities and treatment of women who had served in the House before World War II. An additional three months on Capitol Hill were devoted to asking male and female Representatives serving in the 95th Congress about the experiences of contemporary congresswomen. Thirteen of the 18 congresswomen and 11 of the 25 congressmen to whom I had written agreed to meet with me and, with few exceptions, the interviews were unusually rewarding. (The semistructured questionnaire appears in Appendix C.) In addition, 36 legislative, administrative, and press aides of House members, most of whom worked for congresswomen, were queried about the treatment and behavior of female Representatives. Many were asked to elaborate on observations other informants had offered. Responses from all of these interviews were relied upon while writing Chapters 4, 5, and 6, and some informed the analysis in other chapters as well.

During subsequent visits to Washington, thirty additional interviews were conducted, four with Representatives, the remainder with staff assistants. Questions raised followed no set pattern, inasmuch as respondents were chosen because of specific information they could provide. Many of the questions dealt with the workings and future of the Congresswomen's Caucus, a group later transformed into the Congressional Caucus for Women's Issues, and these responses provide much of the basis for Chapters 10 and 11. I am deeply grateful to the 24 Representatives and the scores of staff aides who patiently answered my questions and who were willing to speak candidly about the matters I raised with them. Their frank replies were encouraged by my promise to keep their identities confidential when referring to the observations and insights they volunteered. Most insisted that even the fact that we met should not be reported, and I decided, as a result, to exclude explicit, personal reference to all Capitol Hill informants. My debt to them is difficult to overstate, however.

But these Representatives and staff personnel were not the only ones assisting me on this project, and I welcome this opportunity publicly to offer my thanks to all others who helped. Several congressmen permitted me to use their offices as places to hang my hat and catch my breath during visits to Capitol Hill, and their hospitality is deeply appreciated. Congressman Stephen Solarz, his staff and his wife, Nina, were gracious hosts, as were Congressmen Marc Lincoln Marks and Tom Ridge. My debt to Congressman Lionel Van Deerlin and his wife, Mary Jo, is enormous. Our professional association and friendship began 20 years ago and, until he left the House in 1981, no trip to Washington was complete without a visit to his office. I am grateful, as well, to Mr. Van Deerlin's staff for their interest, support, and friendship over the years. Especially helpful were Alan Ciamporcero, Shirley Dave, Cindy Holson, Mona Knight, John McLaren, Sieg Smith, Carole Staszewski, and Dan Yager.

While living in Washington to conduct the research, I was fortunate to be able to count on the hospitality and companionship of many friends including Anne and Larry Pearl, and David and the late Renee Unger. Portions of the manuscript were written in the solitude and quiet of summer retreats and for the use of their homes I thank Beverly and Charles Edwards, and Barbara and Mark Kronman.

Manuscript chapters were read, analyzed and discussed by colleagues whose judgments were unusually valuable. I profited especially from the information and criticism provided by Stanley Bach, Frances Butler, Jean Dexheimer, Pat Gilmartin-Zena, Burdette Loomis, Susan Roe, Lauren Sloan, and Joan Hulse Thompson. Comments by the coeditors of this series on women in politics, Rita Mae Kelly and Ruth Mandel, were also helpful. My efforts to find details about the lives of congresswomen were facilitated by librarians in Washington and Meadville, and my special thanks for this assistance go to Marjorie Hopkins and Laurie Tynan of the Meadville Public Library, and to Reference Librarians Don Vrable and Dorothy Jean Smith of the Pelletier Library at Allegheny College. Miss Smith was meticulous in preparing the index for this volume. The skills and good judgment exercised by Carolyn Dougan, Lou Hanners, Gail Kralj, and Mary Lee McQuiston while typing drafts of the manuscript are deeply appreciated.

Gathering the data for this work was a long and tedious process and I am grateful to the many Allegheny College students whose research papers and Capitol Hill internships were so fruitful. They include Dan Auriti, Susan Devor, Kathy Dorr, Kathy Eck, Tracy Erway, Joanne Forbes, Lisa Freeman, Amy Goldsmith, Karen Harvey, Cindy LeVine, Kelly McBride, Clair Miller, Carol Morrissey, Barbara Patterson, Lisa Pepicelli, Matthew Peterson, Janet Pfieffer, Jennifer Rastro, Barbara Ross, Cynthia Saydah, Susan Scott, Nancy Seamans, Michele Simard, Michael Slotsky, June Swanson, Susan Swigart, Donna Tatro, Kevin Wegryn, and Sally Wissel. My gratitude extends to the Allegheny administration and my colleagues in the Political Science Department, as well. The moral and financial support provided by the college underscored its belief that an excellent teaching institution can retain its quality only if it encourages scholarship. The liberal reprinting policies of *The Legislative Studies Quarterly* and *The Journal of Politics*, permitting its authors to republish material originally appearing between their covers, is also appreciated.

My greatest debt is to my wife, Alice, who encouraged me to undertake this project and who commented constructively upon the manuscript as it was being written. To her this book is affectionately dedicated.

Contents

Part V: Past, Present, and Future

Appendix

List of Tables

Part I
Introduction

1 / Exploring a Small Universe

The 1982 congressional election was a benchmark for women aspiring to national office. Sixteen incumbent congresswomen running for reelection and five women seeking a House seat for the first time were successful. Together they constituted the largest aggregation of women ever to be sworn into the U.S. House of Representatives simultaneously, and they brought to an even 100 the total number ever to be elected to that body.[1]

The 100-member mark, while welcome, is hardly cause for jubilation among those who believe that more women should be holding public office. Since 1789, about 10,000 men have served in the House. But it took 66 years from the time the first woman was elected in 1916 before the 100th made it and before women became as much as five percent of the membership of a single Congress.[2] These figures are especially low when compared with the progress made by women in Scandinavian countries, for example, and they fall short of even the smaller proportions recorded in most other western countries (Vallance 1979, p. 190).

The proportion of women elected to most state legislatures is also higher than it is for Congress. In 1981, the lower chambers of thirty-two states contained a percentage of women at least twice that of the House of Representatives, and all fifty of these bodies averaged fourteen percent women. Ten assemblies reflected figures that were twenty percent or more, and voters in both Oregon and New Hampshire selected three women for every ten seats they filled.[3] While the states were augmenting female membership in their legislatures by about ten percentage points between 1971 and 1981, the national electorate was increasing the proportion of women in the House by about one percentage point.

The excruciatingly slow increase over the years once prompted Martha Griffiths to ask the Legislative Reference Service (LRS) to calculate how long it

3

would be before congresswomen became a House majority if they maintained the pace kept since Jeannette Rankin was elected in 1916. An analyst for the LRS (which has since changed its name to the Congressional Research Service) responded, presumably with a straight face, that it would take 432 years (Lamson 1968, p. 87). It is no wonder then, that scholars' interest in studying the changing character of congresswomen has been inconspicuous and that a comprehensive study of these women is long overdue.[4] Information about the factors contributing to their selection has been published from time to time, but shifts in their treatment by male colleagues and alterations in their legislative priorities have been given little attention.[5] Furthermore, the linkages among these elements—recruitment, treatment, and behavior—and their implications have never been given a systematic airing.

The pages that follow are designed to help fill the void. They begin by discussing incremental changes in the backgrounds and experiences successive congresswomen brought with them to Washington. Studies of government raise few more important questions than those which probe the characteristics of putative leaders and the criteria electors employ when they make their choices. When we analyze below some of the factors affecting recruitment of women to the House over time, we find that the structure of political opportunity has expanded for would-be congresswomen and that they have begun to emerge from a broader range of politically relevant callings than they once did.

For their part, politicians, opinion leaders, and voters have begun to give less weight to such ascriptive characteristics as wealth and family connections when choosing female Representatives and more to achievements which suggest familiarity with the tasks House members are called upon to perform. Moreover, the domestic responsibilities women normally undertake as wives, mothers, housekeepers, and helpmeets are not nearly the deterrents to service in Congress that they once were. The implications of these findings are difficult to overestimate. They mean that a socioeconomic component of our population once systematically denied access to national office has increasingly gained seats in the House and that the political recruitment process in this country has become more democratic.

When we elect to Congress groups of citizens whose entry into that body was once improbable, we increase the likelihood that perspectives and beliefs peculiar to these people as a class will be reflected in government decisions. That is, a recruitment process which links the society and the polity more intimately is apt to produce political institutions that are more sensitive to changing public values and goals and, in the long run, a political system that is more orderly and stable. But these ends cannot be realized unless the beneficiaries of a more democratic recruitment process are accepted as equals by other public officials and unless they are able to create and capitalize on occasions for shaping public policy. For these reasons, the present study looks into the treatment congress-women have received from their male colleagues, the opportunities they have had to gain access to the informal communications networks, and the occasions they have had to secure House leadership positions.

As we shall see, recent congresswomen have been integrated into legislative life more fully than were their predecessors, even though some influential informal groups have been beyond their reach and in spite of the fact that top leadership posts have been reserved for men. It seems clear, as well, that the polity's response to selected social needs has been more comprehensive because congresswomen have established a better professional rapport with male colleagues; because they developed and articulated distinctive policy orientations which both male and female members tended to ignore in the past; and because they organized their resources so as to improve the chances that their voices will be heard. These achievements were facilitated by their assignment to a broader and more influential array of standing House committees, and through formation of a Caucus whose principal focus is on the effects national laws and their implementation have on women.

Contemporary congresswomen have also formed coalitions with a new genre of congressmen, House members who are sensitive to the same social currents that nourish the values of the women with whom they are allied. Thus, emerging policy changes have been a product of a more democratic political recruitment process, more equalitarian treatment of congresswomen by male colleagues, and by the election of a new breed of women who by word and deed have insisted upon such treatment. As we shall see, these developments have been accompanied by changing gender and legislative role orientations among House members.

But Parts II through V of this book portray congressional women within a more detailed micropolitical, as well as within a macropolitical, frame of reference. The recruitment, treatment, and behavior patterns that reflect their collective careers and which have consequences for the American political system should not be allowed to obscure altogether their less abstract, more personal experiences. Accordingly, the next eleven chapters highlight some individual, as well as some collective, experiences that define their congressional identities. Chapter 2 examines the frequency and conditions under which women have replaced their husbands in the House after these men died. The matrimonial connection is employed in no other western democracy as often as it is in the United States. In fact, it seems to occur so often that speculation about the availability of a spouse almost always surfaces when a married congressman dies—sometimes before the poor man's body is cold. The fact is, however, that relatively few spouses have received the nomination to succeed their husbands and fewer still have been elected. The chapter defines the factors contributing to the selection of some widows and the rejection of others, and explores the importance of regional variations in explaining both the election of congressional widows and the length and quality of their careers. It also looks into future use of the matrimonial connection.

Chapter 3 traces the background characteristics of all 100 women who served in the House and draws inferences from aggregate information about the factors that contributed to their elections. Family connections and wealth, for example, were virtually indispensable to would-be congresswomen before World War II. Being the daughter of William Jennings Bryan, three-time Democratic nominee for President, could do nothing but help House aspirant Ruth Bryan Owen, and the stunning wealth of Republican Ruth Baker Pratt and Democrat Caroline O'Day surely strengthened their candidacies. Both family connections and money aided Ruth Hanna McCormick.

Since the mid-1940s, family pedigree and wealth have given way to advantages that derive from legal training and political experience. Congresswomen elected since the mid-1960s are younger than their female predecessors and less inhibited by marital and domestic responsibilities, qualities which promise longer House careers and the potential for influence that only House seniority can offer. Harvard Law School graduates Patricia Schroeder and Elizabeth Holtzman were blessed with neither political families nor large sums of money while trying to convince voters of their worthiness to serve in Congress. State legislators Shirley Chisholm and Barbara Jordan, city councilwomen Barbara Mikulski and Mary Rose Oakar, and county officials Gladys Spellman and Barbara Boxer also lacked these endowments. Wealth and family connections are still important, but most contemporary congresswomen exploited other resources on their way to Washington, and an increasing number (Margaret Heckler, Schroeder, and Boxer, for example) coupled political careers with those domestic obligations that accompany marriage and school-age children.

While the interaction between men and women in state legislatures has received some notice, almost nothing has been written about their relationships in Congress. Chapters 4, 5 and 6 seek to remedy that deficiency. Women serving in the House fifty years ago, for example, were hardly noticed and, when they were, congressmen smothered them with gallantry and condescension. Contemporary male Representatives, on the other hand, are inclined to behave differently, in spite of the fact that, along with virtually all congresswomen, they acknowledge that the House is a "male institution." Moreover, today's congresswomen are not prepared to suffer the conscious and flagrant chauvinism their predecessors witnessed in silence. Instead, they employ a variety of tactics to make clear that discriminatory behavior is unacceptable.

Furthermore, congresswomen are readily admitted into most of the scores of informal House groups that have formed in recent years. They have joined "the Good Guys" and the Wednesday Group, among others, and their membership in "class" groups organized by aggregations of Democratic and Republican first termers is automatic. But some groups, those which tend to be least structured and most influential, are closed to women and have been for years. No congresswoman has ever been tapped by the Republican Chowder and Marching Society and no Democratic woman met regularly with Sam Rayburn's

"Board of Education" or John McCormack's cardplaying coterie. These gaps in their experience probably contributed to their inability to obtain important party positions. And, as Chapter 6 makes clear, those who may have aspired to such posts had to be content with secondary leadership roles.

Changes in congresswomen's substantive interests are explored in Chapters 7 and 8. Female Representatives have expanded their range of concerns, maintaining a specialization in matters thought to be within the competence of members of their gender—education, welfare, children, for example—but also mastering domains once believed to be either too complicated or foreign to their natures—defense policy, business and banking regulation, and taxation, for example. At the same time, they have begun with greater frequency to obtain appointments to the House's most prestigious committees, filling vacancies on the Ways and Means and Rules Committees in the 1960s, and acquiring seats on the Budget Committee when it was created in the mid-1970s. Partly because of the proliferation of subcommittees, congresswomen have managed to keep pace with male Representatives in securing leadership positions on some policy-shaping panels. As will be demonstrated, majority party Democrats have been more successful than minority party Republican women in achieving comparable leadership roles on subcommittees.

The attention all House members, men as well as women, have given to "women's issues" and the character of the issues to which the label has been applied have undergone important changes over the years. Modest proposals to help women advanced before World War II have been replaced by more sweeping measures calculated to address modern women's basic needs. Whereas the earlier bills were fashioned to reinforce women's traditional roles, contemporary legislative proposals are designed either to secure greater equity for women or to affirm their worth after decades of deprivation suffered in a society whose values and goals are defined largely by males. Accompanying the changes in the nature of women's issues have been changes in congresswomen's representational role orientations. And most who serve in the House today are prepared to support at least some portions of the feminist agenda.

The increasingly feminist orientation of congresswomen is partly due to the formation in 1977 of the Congresswomen's Caucus. One of the curious features of the group's development was the delay in its appearance. Women's caucuses in a few state legislatures and in local political and quasi-political settings had been operating for several years before a comparable organization was established in Congress. The crucial roles of Leonor Sullivan and Bella Abzug in inhibiting its formation have never been fully explored, and the parts they played in this regard are discussed in Chapter 9.

Once under way the Caucus provided the support and momentum for scores of legislative proposals introduced in the 95th Congress. The creative energies of Elizabeth Holtzman, Margaret Heckler, and Shirley Chisholm, among others, fueled the Caucus engine. Chapter 10 makes clear that its members sought not only to leave their imprint on the political agenda, but to impose their will on those who interpret and implement policy in the executive branch, as well. As we shall see, the rightward shift of the country's political predispositions, along with the election of Ronald Reagan, strained and then tore the social and political fabric into which the Caucus had been woven. The organization's survival in the 1980s required a fundamental alteration in its composition and character, a transformation explained in Chapter 11.

Changes in the resources, skills and interests of congresswomen have had an impact on their integration into House activities and the contributions they have been able to make to that body's decisions. Contemporary congresswomen are being accepted as equals by male colleagues, not least because of the legislative skills they bring with them and the gender orientations held by the more liberated males currently being sent to Washington. Thus, the House has undergone subtle changes, just as the experiences and frames of reference of its members have changed. Chapter 12 sums up these developments and describes gender and legislative role orientations adopted by congresswomen over time. As we shall see, there would have to be a substantial increase in the number and the acquired seniority of women serving in the House before its character as a male institution is significantly affected.

Nonetheless, changes that have already taken place are both interesting and important. The stories of the first 100 congresswomen are as instructive as any that can be told about political women in the United States. Though they constitute a small universe, their frustrations, incremental successes, changing orientations, and institutional integration are surely worth exploring.

NOTES

1. Twenty-one women served in the House during the lame-duck session of the 97th Congress, November and December 1982, but only eighteen had been sworn in when that Congress convened in January, 1981. Barbara Kennelly and Jean Ashbrook won special elections in 1982 to fill vacancies created by the deaths of incumbents, and the number grew to twenty. When Adam Benjamin of Indiana died in September, Katie Hall was nominated by Democrats to fill out the remainder of his term, as well as succeed him for the next full term. Hall won and, when she was sworn in at the start of the lame-duck session, she brought the number of women to twenty-one. Thus, that number had been in the House simultaneously once before, but the 98th Congress was the first in which more than twenty women began a full term together.

Mary E.P. Farrington, a nonvoting delegate representing the territory of Hawaii from 1953 to 1957, is not included among the 100. Jeannette Rankin and Chase Going Woodhouse were elected for two nonconsecutive terms, but each is counted only once. In the analysis of recruitment patterns in Chapters 2 and 3, however, each of their nominations as nonincumbents is treated separately. The principal sources used to identify women Representatives are Chamberlin (1973), "Women in Congress, 1917–1976," published by the U.S. Congress' Joint Committee on Arrangements for the Commemoration of the Bicentennial, 1976, and Schwemle (1982). For a list of the first 100 women elected to the House, see Appendix A.

2. The more precise figure is 4.8 percent. The number of women Senators selected over the years is too small to invite the kind of analysis given here to women House members, especially since ten of the fifteen who served were appointed to fill sudden vacancies and spent less than one full term in Congress.

3. These figures were gathered and made available by the National Women's Political Caucus.

4. The two most cited volumes on women in Congress are Chamberlin (1973) and Engelbarts (1974). The first is an unintegrated collection of biographies. Its goal is to highlight the positive contributions each woman made while in office and it often exaggerates the value of these contributions. The background data are useful, nonetheless. The second offers biographical information about each congresswoman and cites sources in which additional material may be found. Chamberlin provides little analysis, Engelbarts none at all.

5. Works dealing with the recruitment of congresswomen include Amundsen (1971), Bullock and Heys (1972), Ferraro (1979), Lamson (1968), Lee (1977), Lynn (1975), Mandel (1981), Rule (1981), Tolchin and Tolchin (1974), Van Hightower (1977), and Werner (1966). The few studies touching specifically on their treatment are Driefus (1972), Gehlen (1969), Tolchin and Tolchin (1974), and Werner (1966). The brief piece by Gehlen (1969) does the best job of discussing their shifting priorities.

Part II
Recruitment

2 / The Matrimonial Connection*

Mae Ella Hunt was a quiet, purposive young woman. She was devoted to her Irish Catholic parents who had settled in San Francisco when they arrived in the United States from County Mayo, and deeply committed to her neighborhood and church. She attended St. Vincent's Convent and later enrolled in Ayres Business School. Mae was a diligent student and when she completed the business program, she found a job as a stenographer with the Wells Fargo Express Company.

It was during her employment with Wells Fargo that she met John Ignatius Nolan, and soon the politically active, muscular iron-moulder and the small, slender brown-haired office worker were married. The year was 1913, and, just months before, John had been elected to the House of Representatives on the Bull Moose ticket. The couple left California and spent their honeymoon aboard a steamer bound for Washington, D.C., via the Panama Canal. John took the oath of office soon after they arrived, and he began a career dedicated to the needs of people who worked with their hands. The San Francisco lawmaker was regularly reelected, and became chairman of the House Committee on Labor. He also became one of the most respected members of Congress, a reputation that made the grief all the more painful when he died in 1922, at the age of 49, days after his fifth reelection to the House.

Stunned business, labor, and civic leaders met in his district to decide how to fill the vacancy and agreed, in the end, to ask Mae Nolan to run to succeed her husband in a February special election. She accepted the offer, won the contest, completed the remainder of her husband's term in the 67th Congress, and

*This chapter is a revised version of an article appearing in the August, 1980, edition of *The Journal of Politics*. The author is grateful to the editors of that publication for permission to reprint it here.

served the entire period for which he had been reelected in 1922. But Mae was unhappy with political life in Washington, and before the 68th Congress finished its work, she announced that she would not seek another term. "Politics," she said," is entirely too masculine to have any attraction for feminine responsibilities." She longed to return permanently to California, where she and her ten-year-old daughter, Corliss, could have a "normal home life" (quoted in Chamberlin 1973, p. 50).

Mae Nolan was too modest to claim significant legislative achievements during her short stay in the House. But she nevertheless deserves recognition for beginning a Washington tradition. She was the first woman to participate in the curious practice by which a congressman's widow succeeds her husband when he dies in office. The pattern began little more than six years after the first woman won a seat in the House of Representatives and only three years after the Nineteenth Amendment legalized female suffrage in all forty-eight states.

*   *   *

The matrimonial connection is not a phenomenon peculiar to the United States, although its incidence in Congress has been greater than that exhibited in any other western democracy. The British House of Commons comes closest to the House of Representatives in this regard, although wives of MPs occasionally replace their spouses for reasons other than death. The first woman to serve in Parliament was Lady Nancy Astor, who succeeded husband Waldorf when her father-in-law passed away and left a vacancy in the House of Lords that Waldorf was obliged to fill. The second and third women to serve in Commons also followed their husbands, Mrs. Margaret Wintringham, because her husband had expired, and Mrs. Mabel Philipson, because her spouse had been barred from seeking a seat in Commons for seven years. Mr. Philipson's campaign agent had been found guilty of fraudulent dealings during his successful election contest. As a result, the victory was nullified, and, in a by-election his wife was selected to replace him. Her performance in the post was exemplary, and her constituents retained her services even after her husband regained his eligibility to run for the office.

Some observers find little wrong with use of the matrimonial connection, suggesting that, on the contrary, it has notable advantages. One British political commentator refers to the practice as "male equivalence," and argues that a woman who replaces her husband under these circumstances is better able than a stranger to pursue the policy goals he had already charted. Moreover, because she already knows the constituents and they know her, she is more likely to provide a brand of representation that district residents find eminently suitable (Currell 1974, pp. 58–59). And few would cavil at the variation on the matrimonial connection adopted by widows of World War II resistance leaders in France immediately after the end of hostilities. Their springboard to the National Assembly was the wartime underground activities of their husbands rather than prior legislative service. At the time, six percent of the Assembly was female, a figure that has never again been as large (Currell 1974, p. 170).

American students of the practice have not been as charitable, perhaps because it is employed more regularly on this side of the Atlantic, but also because there was a time when it seemed as if almost all women serving in the House were widows of former Representatives. In the nine Congresses from 1927 to 1944, at least one-half of all women members had succeeded their husbands. Democratic party activist Emily Newell Blair was neither satisfied nor dismayed by these developments but she believed that suffragists would have taken consolation from them and would have responded to critics of the practice by saying:

> . . . Inheritance of a man's political assets by a woman is a great step forward. Why in our day a woman did not even inherit her own money or her own child, let alone the opportunities and the responsibilities that she and her husband had built up together (Blair 1925, p. 516).

The sarcasm of a political scientist who took a different view is more characteristic of feminist reaction. She suggested that one cause of this "sentimental nepotism" resided in the belief that any woman who survives the refractory and willful personalities of the men we usually send to Washington deserves her constituent's approbation. The widow's mandate may also be a form of a sentimental tribute, " . . . of the kind we offer when we subscribe to a memorial window: something to please the family" (Comstock 1926, p. 384).

The practice continues to generate comment, even though the number of widows benefitting from it has declined in recent years and in spite of the fact that an increasing proportion of women elected to the House have pursued a different path to Washington. But much less is known about the "connection" than is warranted by professional and popular curiosity.[1] Questions about its incidence, the circumstances under which it is employed, and the future of the matrimonial connection need to be addressed more fully than they have been.

THE INCIDENCE OF WIDOWS' SUCCESSION

When a married congressman dies in office, speculation about his successor often touches on the availability of his wife. Mention of the spouse is partly based upon what many believe is the high frequency with which wives have replaced congressmen-husbands. This belief is understandable, after all, because women have been named to succeed their husbands in Congress on more than a handful of occasions, and, even when they were denied the opportunity, it was often not for lack of trying.

During the 96th and 97th Congresses (1979–1982), for example, five married male Representatives died in office. Among the surviving spouses, at least three displayed a reasonably sustained interest in the seat that once belonged to their husbands.[2] One, Patricia Benjamin of Indiana, was endorsed by the Lake County Democratic Chairman at a meeting called to name a replacement for her late husband, Adam. Mrs. Benjamin lost out, however, when other Democratic party leaders, including Mayor Richard Hatcher of Gary, threw their support to Katie Hall, a black state senator. A second widow, Dorothy Runnels, sought the Democratic nomination in New Mexico's second district, but was unsuccessful. When denied a place on the ballot, she ran as a write-in candidate. Runnels received twenty-eight percent of the vote and finished third behind a victorious Republican write-in contestant, Joe Skeen, and David King, the choice of Democratic Governor Bruce King.[3] The third spouse, Republican Jean Ashbrook, received her party's endorsement and was easily elected to succeed her late husband, John.

But recent instances of widow's succession, actual or abortive, should not obscure the fact that the great majority of Representatives' widows have *not* succeeded their husbands. During the period from 1916, when the first woman was elected to the House, through the elections of 1982, 381 Representatives died in office.[4] Among this number, 105 could not have been replaced by wives because they were bachelors or widowers, or because the timing and circumstances of their deaths made succession by a spouse unlikely if not impossible.[5] This leaves a total of 276 women who could have conceivably filled House vacancies created by the death of a spouse. Of these, only forty-one were nominated to run for the office, little more than one in seven.

Even this ratio is as high as it is because the term "widow's succession" is broadly defined. Among the women included as having been affected by the matrimonial connection are a Representative's daughter (Winnifred Mason Huck) rather than his spouse; the wife of a House member who did not die but was jailed during Prohibition for bootlegging (Katherine Langley); two wives of nonincumbent men who died after being nominated but before the November elections, and who were replaced by spouses who went on to win House seats (Charlotte Reid and Marilyn Lloyd); one widow who, following her husband's death, was denied her party's nomination, but who contested and won both the nomination and election two years later (Leonor Kretzer Sullivan); and one widow who appeared to be nominated and elected to follow her husband into the House but whose victories were successfully challenged (Lallie Connor Kemp).[6]

Observer's inflated perceptions about the incidence of widow's succession are probably fueled by three factors. One is the incredibly large proportion of widows who, once nominated, were, indeed, victorious in the general election. A second is the lengthy period congressmen's widows have served in the House, relative to the average tenure of other congresswomen. A third factor is the productive legislative performance turned in by a handful of unusually visible widows—women whose celebrity status has led many to believe that congressmen's spouses are regularly chosen to replace them.

The success rate of women nominated to follow their husbands into the House has been unusually high. Thirty six of the forty-one widows won the general election contests for which they were nominated, an incidence of eighty-eight percent. Of course, some of these women had only token opposition, and a few had none at all, but a good many were challenged by skillful, well-financed adversaries.[7] The figures in Table 2.1 help highlight the extraordinary rate of success congressmen's widows experienced over the years. Since 1916, only fifteen percent of the nonincumbent women who were not Representative's widows won their elections, a far smaller proportion than the eighty-eight percent recorded by widows. The decrease in the number of widows nominated in recent years and the simultaneously sharp increase in the number of women candidates who were not widows have brought little change in the rate of success experienced by each group.

Of course, a comparison between them is not entirely appropriate because an unusually large proportion of widows ran in special rather than biennial November elections, and they competed in districts where their names were well known and where their parties (and their husbands) had prevailed in the last House election. When acquiring their perceptions of widow's success, however, most observers are unconcerned with such distinctions. They know that women nominated to succeed their congressmen-husbands face unusually appealing odds, and they do not have to make too great an inferential leap to conclude that more widows secured their parties' nominations than has, in fact, been the case.

The average number of House terms served by those who capitalized on the matrimonial connection, compared with the number recorded by other congresswomen, also contributes to the illusion that widows have been frequent successors to their husbands. Between 1917 and 1940, the average for each group of women was about the same, two and one-half terms. But between 1941 and 1964, women who succeeded their husbands spent an average of five-and-one-half terms in the House compared with three-and-one-half terms for other congresswomen. The difference has narrowed in recent years, but from 1965 to 1982, the former continued to record a longer average tenure, four-and-one-half to three-and-three-fourths terms. Thus, the fact that wives who replaced their husbands have been around longer than other women may have given some people the impression that more of them run for House seats. This perception, in turn, feeds public expectation and media speculation about who a deceased Representative's successor could (or should) be.

Finally, the matrimonial connection is probably perceived as more common than it is because several widows who had long and distinguished careers acknowledged their initial dependence on it. Margaret Chase Smith, for example, had no compunctions about articulating the importance of her spousal role. She said: " . . . I am a product of nepotism—a living symbol of nepotism—for I would not be in the Senate today had I not been a $3,000-a-year secretary to

Table 2.1. Nonincumbent Widows and Nonwidows* Nominated and Elected to the House, 1916–1982

	Years (Congresses) and Status							
	1916–1940 (65th–76th)		1941–1964 (77th–88th)		1965–1982 (89th–97th)		1916–1982 (65th–97th)	
	Widows	*Nonwidows*	*Widows*	*Nonwidows*	*Widows*	*Nonwidows*	*Widows*	*Nonwidows*
Number nominated	15	69	17	130	9	238	41	437
Number elected	14	11	14	21	8	29	36	61
Percent elected	93	16	82	16	89	12	88	14

*The very small number of nonwidows contesting special elections are omitted.

Sources: Congressional Quarterly, Inc. (1975); Gertzog and Simard (1981); and *Congressional Quarterly Weekly Report* election results, 1978, 1980, and 1982.

my late husband when he was in the House . . . " (Lewis 1972, p. 299). Leonor
Sullivan's views about her own election to Congress were the same.

> I won on the strength of John's name and reputation. John Sullivan had a
> program I wanted to carry out. He believed in good government and that you
> had to fight to get it. In time I hope to build a reputation of my own. Then I
> can run as Leonor Sullivan (*Washington Star* September 3, 1967).

Both Smith and Sullivan did, indeed, establish reputations of their own, the
former mainly through her contributions to national defense policy, the latter
primarily as a champion of consumer rights. Others, such as Edith Nourse Rogers
and Frances Payne Bolton, also acquired a celebrity status. Their legislative
accomplishments, coupled with unusual success in general elections and
comparative House longevity, have contributed to the belief that widows are
nominated to succeed their husbands with a regularity that cannot be supported
by the facts.

Whatever the popular conception, the incidence of widow's succession has
not been reflected uniformly throughout the country. Party leaders, activists, and
voters have been more apt to nominate spouses in some regions than they have in
others. The practice has been common in southern House districts, where one of
every four deaths of married congressmen has been followed by the nomination
of their wives. On the other hand, use of the matrimonial connection in western
states is considerably less frequent, as is made clear in Table 2.2. Incidence of
the pattern in the other two regions comes closer to the national average. The
importance of this regional variation, especially the high rate recorded in the

Table 2.2. Regional Use of the Matrimonial Connection, 1916–1982

Region*	Number of married congressmen who died	Number of widows nominated to fill vacancies	Percent of vacancies for which widows were nominated
South	72	18	25
Northeast	88	11	13
Midwest	76	9	12
West	40	3	8
Total	276	41	15

*The distribution of states among regions is as follows: South includes Alabama, Arkansas,
Florida, Georgia, Kentucky, Louisiana, Mississippi, North Carolina, South Carolina, Tennessee,
Texas, and Virginia; Northeast includes Connecticut, Delaware, Maine, Maryland, Massachusetts,
New Hampshire, New Jersey, New York, Pennsylvania, Rhode Island, Vermont, and West Virginia;
Midwest includes Illinois, Indiana, Iowa, Kansas, Michigan, Minnesota, Missouri, Nebraska, North
Dakota, Ohio, South Dakota, and Wisconsin; West includes Alaska, Arizona, California, Colorado,
Hawaii, Idaho, Montana, Nevada, New Mexico, Oklahoma, Oregon, Utah, Washington, and
Wyoming.

Sources: *Congressional Record*, 1916–1982; Schwemle 1982.

South, cannot be overestimated, for there is not one, but two sets of explanations for selection of a spouse to succeed her husband in Congress. One accounts for a preponderant percentage of the cases in the South, the other for most of the instances of widow's succession outside the South. Put another way, widows have followed not one, but two different routes to their party's nomination, with each route a product of the regional political culture that defines the role of women in public life.

TWO SIDES OF THE MATRIMONIAL CONNECTION

Just why some women were nominated to succeed their husbands and most others were not is a question that has not been confronted systematically, although several writers have offered possible explanations. It has been suggested, for example, that widows whose husbands enjoyed considerable seniority and influence in the House were nominated to succeed their spouses because the latters' formidable reputations were expected to benefit their widows' standing with the voters and with their former colleagues (Amundsen 1971; Gruberg 1968; and Tolchin and Tolchin 1974). When a congressman serves his district for many years and acquires power in the process, he is more likely than a House newcomer to leave his mark on the district—in the form of post offices, better roads, larger military installations, and more federal money, for example—and thereby make his spouse a better-known, more appealing candidate.

Among additional factors that might have contributed to decisions to nominate widows is one which is related to the degree of competition within a district. It has been argued, for example, that party leaders are more likely to support congressional widows when their party dominates elections within the district than when it sometimes loses House contests, and when factional disputes within the dominant party are far more threatening than the candidate nominated by the opposition (if, indeed, an opponent is even nominated).

These conjectures seem reasonable, but they are supported by available evidence only when regional distinctions are observed. House seniority and leadership, and the degree of district competitiveness alone tell us little about why some widows are nominated and others are slighted. Only after southern and nonsouthern districts are treated separately are they serviceable explanations for the widows' succession phenomenon.

Table 2.3 shows the relationship between seniority and widows' succession. It reports the percent of wives of deceased House members who succeeded their husbands and groups these women into those whose husbands served three terms or less, those whose husbands served from four to seven terms, and those whose spouses were in the House for eight terms or more. Taking all the states together, relatively few widows (sixteen percent) were nominated to succeed

Table 2.3. Widows' Succession and Seniority, 1917–1982

	Districts in all states: Terms of service			Districts in 12 southern states: Terms of service			Districts in nonsouthern states: Terms of service		
	1–3	4–7	8+	1–3	4–7	8+	1–3	4–7	8+
Percent widows nominated	7	19	16	14	18	31	6	20	7
Total number of widows	82	83	109	14	17	39	68	66	70

husbands who had served for sixteen years or more. This means that seniority has not been anything like a sufficient condition for securing the nomination.

When we examine the columns distinguishing southern from nonsouthern districts, however, a regional difference in the relationship emerges. In the South, slightly more than three of every ten wives (31%) who survived husbands serving eight terms or more were nominated to succeed their spouses, as compared with fourteen percent and eighteen percent nominated to follow spouses who had served respectively one to three terms and four to seven terms. In districts outside the South, on the other hand, widows of the most senior House members were no more likely to succeed their husbands than were wives who survived junior congressmen. The twenty percent figure for women whose husbands had served between four and seven terms suggests that, outside the South, a moderate amount of tenure has been more closely associated with widows' nominations than has either extended or abbreviated House service.

The relationship between the matrimonial connection and leadership is revealed in Table 2.4 and is similar to the association found between widows' succession and seniority. Although the acquisition of a leadership position and seniority are linked, they are not one and the same (Polsby et al. 1969, p. 788). And if the term "leadership" is defined to include House Speaker, floor leader and whip, chairman and ranking minority member of a committee, chairman of an Appropriations Committee subcommittee, and chairman of congressional and national party committees, the hypothesized relationship is not immediately in evidence.

Table 2.4 reports the percent of congressional widows whose husbands were House leaders and those whose spouses were simply rank and file members. Nationally, almost one-quarter (24%) of the women married to House leaders succeeded husbands in office, as compared with one in ten of nonleaders' wives. But when wives who survived their husbands are again divided between those from the South and those representing districts elsewhere in the country, the figures portray marked regional differences. Almost two of every five widows

Table 2.4. Widows' Succession and Leadership, 1917–1982

	Districts in all states		Districts in 12 southern states		Districts in nonsouthern states	
	Husbands were not leaders	*Husbands were leaders*	*Husbands were not leaders*	*Husbands were leaders*	*Husbands were not leaders*	*Husbands were leaders*
Percent widows nominated	10	24	14	39	9	16
Total number of widows	188	86	37	31	151	55

(39%) of the southern House leaders were selected by their parties to succeed their husbands as compared with only fourteen percent of southern widows whose husbands were rank and file congressmen. The first of these percentages seems to be an unusually large proportion and it takes on even more significance when it is contrasted with sixteen percent of leaders' widows outside the South who received their party's nominations.

Finally, when these same women are divided into those whose husbands served districts which were safe for their party and those representing politically competitive districts, the anticipated relationship is borne out once again only when a regional distinction is made. Table 2.5 divides the districts into "safe" and "competitive" and, as was done in the two preceding Tables, groups the districts further into South and non-South categories.[8] Nationally, there is little difference (six percentage points) between the percentages of widows nominated from safe and competitive districts. The regional variation is made clear in the remainder of the Table, however. Slightly more than one in four (27%) of southern widows in safe districts were nominated to succeed husbands as compared with about one in seven southern widows whose husbands represented competitive districts. Outside the South, there was virtually no difference in the frequency with which widows from safe and competitive districts were nominated.

What seems to be apparent from these findings is that there is not one but two paths along which congressional widows have traveled to obtain House nominations. Many whose husbands represented southern districts seemed to have had their nominations affected significantly by the seniority or leadership roles of their husbands, or by the degree of competitiveness reflected in district elections. Among the seventeen widows from the South, sixteen followed spouses who served eight terms or more, or held a party leadership position, or were elected from a safe district. The one woman whose husband could be described in none of these ways, Elizabeth Pool, lost the special election that followed her nomination. Widows' nominations outside the South, on the other

Table 2.5. Widows' Succession and Party Competition, 1917–1982

	Districts in all states		Districts in 12 southern states		Districts in nonsouthern states	
	Competitive	*Safe*	*Competitive*	*Safe*	*Competitive*	*Safe*
Percent widows nominated	12	18	15	27	11	10
Total number of widows	165	109	20	51	145	58

hand, seem to have been unrelated either to the length of service or House status of their husbands. Furthermore, these women were just as likely to have contested elections in competitive districts as they were to have run in safe districts. (See Appendix B for a list of all widows nominated between 1916 and 1982 and identification of their spouse's seniority, leadership, and district characteristics.)

If the nomination of widows outside the South cannot be accounted for in terms of the characteristics of their husbands' service or districts, how, then, might it be explained?[9] Some answers to this question materialize when five additional distinctions are made between southern and nonsouthern women who were named to succeed their husbands. First, relatively few of the former (31%) faced serious opposition in either the primary or general elections, whereas almost all of the widows outside the South (96%) had to deal with a primary or general election challenge. (See Appendix B.)

A second important distinction between southern and nonsouthern widows is that, among the former, few received the party's nomination for a second term, while most of the latter were selected for at least one additional term. Almost two thirds (65%) of the congresswomen who succeeded husbands whose districts lay outside the South were renominated at least once. By contrast only nineteen percent of the widows from the South were awarded their party's nomination after completing an initial term.

Third, southern widows who thought about running again, were probably discouraged by the fact that so few women who were not wives of former congressmen had represented southern constituencies. Among the sixty-four female Representatives who served from 1917 to the beginning of 1983 and did not succeed their husbands, only five were from the South—Eliza Jane Pratt of North Carolina, Helen Mankin and Iris Blitch of Georgia, Ruth Bryan Owen of Florida, and Barbara Jordan of Texas. Pratt worked as a secretary to Congressman William Burgin. When Burgin died in office in 1946, she was nominated and elected without opposition to serve out the remainder of his term. She neither sought nor was encouraged to seek reelection.

Helen Mankin, on the other hand, tried to run again. Although she won a majority in the Democratic primary, she was denied the nomination when the court upheld Georgia's "County Unit" system—a system which had the effect of over-representing rural voters (and which was declared unconstitutional by the Supreme Court eighteen years later). Mankin's popular vote majority was nullified by the fact that she had failed to carry two of the three counties embraced by the House district. As a result, among nonwidows elected in the South, only Owen, Blitch, and Jordan successfully sought reelection, and southern widows have had few role models upon whose experience they could build their own reelection attempts. Congressional widows outside the South, by contrast, had many such models.

A fourth distinction between South and non-South widows is in their average ages when first elected to office. Age is of concern to men as well as to women who compete for elective office. But it is normally important to voters and party leaders only when a candidate is perceived as being either too young or too old for public office. Age may also limit the length of time a candidate serves once elected and it is relevant to the present discussion because of the considerable difference in the mean age of widows nominated to succeed husbands in each of the two regions. The average widow nominated outside the South was forty-nine years old, a figure substantially lower than the fifty-four years of the average widow nominated in the South.[10] Only three of the widows outside the South (16%) were over sixty when nominated for the first time and three were younger than forty. On the other hand, seven of the seventeen southern women were at least sixty years of age (41%) and one was younger than forty. (See Appendix B.)

The fifth difference between widows falling in each regional grouping has to do with the extent to which members of each played a part in the political lives of their husbands. Information about these relationships is fragmentary, but it would appear that a smaller proportion of southern than nonsouthern widows were an integral part of their spouses' political careers. Among the thirty-four women about whom evidence is available, fourteen represented (or still represent) southern districts, twenty nonsouthern districts. (See Appendix B.) Five of the former, but none of the latter, played little or no role in their husbands' Washington or district activities.[11]

The degree to which a wife is familiar with the political affairs of her spouse is among the most important factors affecting the matrimonial connection. If a widow is awarded a complimentary nomination, one which sends her to Washington to complete only the remainder of a spouse's term, her understanding of the people, places, and things that were important to him is of little consequence. But if a woman is looking beyond the current term, close friendships with activists upon whom her husband relied, and an understanding of the problems salient to the district become necessary, even if not sufficient, conditions for nomination and renomination. She is in a position to capitalize on the contacts and financial support that aided her husband and to speak and act in ways which do not violate fundamental constituency values. A wife who knows little about her husband's work and who has no rapport with his political and financial supporters is far less likely to be able to aggregate the resources needed to succeed him for more than the unexpired portion of his term.

The close ties between Margaret Chase Smith and her husband Clyde is a case in point. An associate of the former congresswoman described the relationship in this way:

> Margaret was an active wife, in fact, Clyde Smith's top staff member. . . . They campaigned as a team. Clyde was the candidate, Margaret the manager. She drove the car and she maintained a current blackbook of maps of all the routes in the district with the names of key people and their residences and offices along the routes. In Washington she handled the correspondence, which was the backbone of the operation keeping the political fences mended back in Maine. Many times she typed until midnight or later (Lewis 1972, p. 65).

A contemporary congresswoman who was similarly well connected when her husband died is Lindy Boggs, a woman reputed to have been as much a part of husband Hale's political life as any wife could be. Perhaps so intimate a political relationship was required to persuade Louisiana's Democratic leaders to ignore tradition and support a congressional widow beyond the expiration of her husband's term. The experience of Peggy Begich, widow of Congressman Nick Begich, was very different. Her husband was in the same plane carrying Hale Boggs when it was lost during the 1972 campaign. Mrs. Begich had not been active in her husband's political career, however, spending much of her time bringing up their six children. When she announced an interest in running for the vacant seat, Democratic leaders in Alaska were astonished. Most withheld their support and a party convention denied her the nomination. Said one party leader who was sympathetic to her new found aspirations: "The response to her candidacy was not good. But how could it have been good? The party people had no feeling for her; they just didn't know her. They could not relate to her as part of Nick."[12]

Finally, there is the case of Katharine Byron of Maryland, wife of Congressman William Byron, who succeeded her husband after he was killed in a 1941 plane crash. Following a hard-fought special election campaign, featuring visits to the district by celebrities of both parties, she managed to win by little more than 1,000 votes. Byron had worked closely with her husband as a confidante and aide, and, once in the House, she established good rapport with Democratic leaders. She filed for reelection in 1942, but was unacceptable to some district Democratic leaders, notably Montgomery County chairman E.

Brooke Lee. The County leader had supported her nomination for the special election with the understanding that she would not seek reelection.

Lee, a scion of the most powerful political family in Maryland, told Byron that she would receive no support from the party if she persisted in her reelection bid. He prevailed upon her to withdraw from the race and secured the nomination for himself. Byron's public explanation centered on her need to care for five fatherless sons—a face-saving gesture that most could accept. Perhaps she believed that the score was settled when, thirty years later, her middle son, Goodloe Byron, won the House seat that had once been hers. But he died suddenly in 1978, and was succeeded by spouse Beverly, thereby making the Byron family the only one to have twice exploited the matrimonial connection.

These examples make plain, first of all, that not all southern widows fit the pattern described here, with Boggs an important exception to it. Complete immersion in her husband's career and her unusual political skills probably explain much of the aberration. Smith's success and Begich's failure, on the other hand, suggest that, outside the South, widows normally must demonstrate political virtuosity—acquired in most cases while serving their spouse's professional needs—if their battles to secure nominations are to be fruitful. And Katharine Byron's experience indicates, first, that southern widows are not the only ones muscled out of a reelection attempt; and, second, that a close working relationship with a spouse may be necessary for triggering the matrimonial connection, but it is not a sufficient condition for perpetuating it.

The lessons to be drawn from this evidence are clear. Widows' succession cannot be treated adequately in unidimensional terms. The factors contributing to the recruitment of widows were not the same for all. Selection of southern women to fill spouses' seats seems often to have been influenced by the venerable status of the men who died and the safeness of the seats their husbands had vacated. Most wives chosen were those whose spouses had served long enough and well enough to have left a demonstrable legacy in their districts, a legacy upon which wives could capitalize while ambitious males in the district vied for long-term control of the seat through established nomination processes. Widows selected in districts outside the South, on the other hand, were usually required initially to confront serious primary or general election opposition. They were also expected to secure renomination and, unlike their southern counterparts, they could look to a number of successful female House members in their region—women who had not succeeded husbands—as models by which to define their own political identities. Furthermore, these women were younger than southern widows and more likely to have been an integral part of their husbands' political careers.

It seems fair to conclude that, with a few exceptions, the selection of widows in southern districts had less to do with the personal or political identities of these women and more to do with their husbands' reputations and the nature of their districts. Their nominations seem to have served as a part of a holding action until a real (i.e., male) successor emerged from the interstices of more orderly, more deliberate internal party conflict.

Widows outside the South, on the other hand, were chosen under considerably different circumstances. Most were selected close to their prime of life—a time when they could do more than simply serve out the remaining months of their husbands' terms. They were, as a group, more politically vigorous than their southern counterparts, more likely to have been active in their husbands' careers, and young enough to look forward to careers of their own. Thus the qualities of their own candidacies, more than the characteristics of their husbands or of their districts, seem to have contributed significantly to their receiving the nomination.

There is another perspective within which to interpret these findings. Prewitt (1970) maintains that, when discussing recruitment to public office, it is useful to think of the population as comprising four politically relevant groups. He calls these groups the "dominant social stratum," another name for which is "eligibles"; the "politically active stratum"; "recruits and apprentices"; and "candidates." As a rule, "political activists" emerge out of a pool of "eligibles" (so defined because of their high socio-economic status), and "recruits and apprentices" come out of the ranks of "activists." "Candidates," in turn, are selected from "recruits and apprentices."

There are exceptions to these patterns, however. An eligible need not necessarily become an activist or a recruit in order to secure nomination to office. According to Prewitt, some people who are neither may, nonetheless, be inducted directly into the political arena, usually by political parties, but by interest groups, friends, and extraordinary events and circumstances, as well. Entry into electoral politics, in short, need not be a product of a long-standing interest in public life. Indeed, a person may not evidence serious aspirations for office until he or she actually secures a major party nomination and is elected (Prewitt 1970, p. 59).

Over the years, virtually all congressional spouses, including the scores who never dreamed of running for office, possessed the characteristics that qualified them as eligibles. If they did not have them before marriage, then they acquired them afterwards, when they were part of the lives of men destined for a seat in the most prestigious legislative body in the land. Having committed themselves to roles as wives of aspiring public officials, it was extremely unlikely that they would engage in self-promoting activities normally pursued by ambitious political activists and apprentices. Of course, many performed politically relevant chores to help their husbands' careers, but it is difficult to imagine them doing so in a way which anticipated a candidacy of their own.[13]

When their husbands died suddenly, a great majority had neither the political skills nor the ambition sufficient to justify a race for Congress. Most had no reason to adopt patterns of behavior followed by Prewitt's eligibles who became activists and recruits before advancing to candidacy. Even if they decided to seek a House seat, opportunities to succeed their husbands were threatened by the ambitions of other candidates, almost always male, whose compelling claims to the nomination were based upon experience in public office, established political connections, abundant financial resources, and the support of opinion leaders. Many of these men had been waiting for the incumbent to retire or commit a serious blunder so that they could advance their own candidacies for Congress. Some, in fact, were prepared to run against him at the first opportunity. Death gave them an unexpected head start, and they became the principal adversaries to congressmen's widows who aspired to replace their husbands. It was this point in the widows' recruitment process that regional differences helped determine which of the two routes to the House widows would employ.

In the South, wives who seriously considered replacing spouses over the long term were almost always discouraged from running or defeated, usually by the men who had been waiting in the wings for the seat to become available. These women simply could not compete with resource-rich, ambitious males in a region disdainful of political women. Widows who did secure their party's nomination were expected, if not required, to hold office only for the remainder of their husband's terms. In the meantime, an election system fashioned to accommodate the needs of established party leaders was permitted to work its will. Districts that were mostly one-party Democratic witnessed a primary election followed by a run-off primary. The process normally produced a consensus choice, a person already well known to constituents and almost certain to reflect the basic values of district leaders and voters. These steps were taken while the southern widow acted as a caretaker of her husband's seat. To have conferred the vacancy on someone else might have given him too big an edge in the battle for control of the seat.

The real choice, then, was selected through political machinery that had been legitimated by long use and which made authentic widow's succession unlikely. As Prewitt points out, entree to candidacy in the political recruitment process is influenced significantly by established legal arrangements and by the prevailing political culture. Of course most male leaders in the region found all female candidates unacceptable, but they were prepared temporarily to elect a congressman's spouse, the wife of a late friend, perhaps, because she could be persuaded to abide by the norms limiting women's roles to peripheral and auxiliary political activities. An independent, politically ambitious woman was anathema.

Outside the South, cultural limitations were not quite as detrimental to the candidacies of women, although the difference was probably more a matter of degree than of a kind. Still, widows securing nominations to succeed their husbands could anticipate a congressional career that exceeded the remainder of an unfinished term. The elaborate system of primaries and one-party politics that vouchsafed control of candidacies to orthodox aspirants in the South was not nearly so well established outside the region. And the resources and skills of nonsouthern widows, including the benefits derived from working closely with their spouses, could be exploited more effectively. In Prewitt's terms, their transition from eligibles to authentic candidates was less likely to be inhibited by cultural and legal constraints.

True, nonsouthern widows also had to contend with the aspirations of people who had been eying their husbands' seats. They often had to fight for party recognition, face formidable opposition in the general election, demonstrate that they had acquired political savvy from association with their husbands, and exhibit the qualifications and vitality that constituents expected in an effective Representative. But, if this alternative form of the matrimonial connection meant a greater investment of resources than was expended by successful southern widows, it also meant greater political rewards.

THE FUTURE OF THE MATRIMONIAL CONNECTION

Precisely how often the connection will produce future nominations of congressional spouses is, of course, difficult to say. Nevertheless, it is possible to draw some inferences from past and present patterns of widows' succession and to rely on these inferences to speculate about the future.

Although the percentage of widows among women in the House has declined,[14] there has been an increase in the proportion of widows selected to contest their husbands' seats when vacancies caused by death have been created. As is reported in Table 2.6, twelve percent of Representatives' widows were nominated to succeed their husbands during the pre-World War II period. This figure increased to eighteen percent during the twenty-four years between 1941 and 1964, and to almost one in four between 1965 and 1982. The Table also makes clear, however, that the increase cannot be described as a national trend as much as it can be explained as a development common to southern districts. Little change is recorded among districts outside the South, but from 1965 to 1982, four of the nine southern districts turned to wives of deceased members when House vacancies were created by an incumbent's death.

In spite of the small number of cases occurring in recent years, it is worth noting that the circumstances under which southern widows have been nominated in recent years have begun to resemble more closely the conditions under which widows outside the South have been selected. In 1968, for example, Elizabeth Pool was chosen by Texas Democrats to succeed her husband in spite of the fact that his district was a competitive one and apparently without regard to either his low seniority status or the absence of his hold on a leadership position.

Table 2.6. Widows Receiving Nominations as a Percent of House Vacancies Created by Married Members' Deaths, 1917–1982

Time Period	Total		South		Non-South	
	%	N	%	N	%	N
1917–1940	12	141	17	42	7	99
1941–1964	18	97	28	18	14	79
1965–1982	24	34	44	9	16	25

Furthermore, the last two congressional spouses nominated in the South, Lindy Boggs and Marilyn Lloyd, had both worked closely with their husbands; both faced credible opposition when they sought their husbands' seats; both were renominated following their first term in office; and, in choosing Lloyd, Tennessee Democrats nominated a woman considerably younger than the average widow elected from a southern district—a woman who could conceivably provide more than just a few years of House service.[15]

If the analysis conducted earlier in this Chapter is accepted, increased party competition in the South, together with a decline in the seniority and leadership roles of southern House members, will limit the special form of the matrimonial connection so often employed in that region to date. This may mean either an end to the nomination of southern widows, or party designations linked to their political skills and qualifications rather than to characteristics of their husbands' incumbency. To the extent that future widows seek the nomination in that region, they can expect stiffer competition. Moreover, the careers of Boggs and Lloyd suggest that, except for isolated instances, there may be no turning back to the old ways.

But these findings should not obscure the strong probability that the matrimonial connection is likely to be less serviceable in the future. There are three reasons for forecasting this decline. First, fewer Representatives are dying while in office. Between 1917 and 1940 an average of seventeen members died each term. This figure declined to eleven during the period 1941 thru 1964 and to below five from 1965 to 1982. Furthermore, this reduction seems to have picked up momentum, reflecting a much larger percentage decrease during the latter years than between 1941 and 1964.[16]

This is not to suggest that the matrimonial connection will necessarily disappear as a pathway to Congress. The percentages reported in Table 2.6 for the most recent period may remain constant or even increase, especially if more congressional wives become better integrated into their husbands' careers. What the declining mortality rate suggests is that with continued decrease in the number of House deaths, there will be fewer opportunities for widows to gain their party's nomination. But that does not mean that a smaller *percentage* of these women will secure that nomination.

A second reason for a likely decline in the incidence of widow's succession is that party leaders, voters, and candidates themselves seem to have altered the criteria they employ to evaluate potential female nominees. As will be made clear in the next chapter, where nonwidows, as well as widows, are discussed, professional training, campaign experience and prior public office seem to have become far more important than the matrimonial connection when assessing the qualifications of women for House office.

This development, in turn, may be viewed as both a blueprint for and a confirmation of a recruitment process based on merit and achievement rather than one anchored in status and ascription. However able and resourceful many congressional widows have been, most have had little opportunity publicly to display their political skills *before* securing their party's nomination. That such a display is more of a requirement for women today than it was in the past may be a compelling reason to expect fewer nominations of congressional widows in the future. Increased attention to merit and achievement, moreover, may very well encourage a larger number of politically experienced women to seek House vacancies created by incumbents' deaths.

Finally, we should expect fewer widows to succeed their husbands because recent years have witnessed a gain (small and irregular though it may have been) in the number of women serving in the House. Judging from recent increases in the number of women nominated for House seats by the major parties, there is likely to be little, if any, retrogression in the number of female Representatives and it is possible that they will soon make up an even larger proportion of the House than they do at this writing.[17] The larger the number of female Representatives, the smaller the number of male members—and the fewer the number of men whose deaths would occasion succession by a wife. Of course, the death of women House members may produce opportunities for "widowers succession," but the number of congresswomen has not increased so much as to suggest that this alternate form of the matrimonial connection will claim much attention in the immediate future.[18]

NOTES

1. Professional analysts who have studied the phenomenon include Amundsen 1971; Bullock and Heys 1972; Gruberg 1968; Kincaid 1978; Tolchin and Tolchin 1974; and Werner 1966. Popular treatment of the subject appears almost every time a married congressman dies, especially if his wife is nominated to succeed him.

2. Wives of the other two, Congressmen Tennyson Guyer and John Slack, may also have thought about succeeding their husbands. If so, reports of their interest were not carried in the national media.

3. Harold Runnels died three months before the general election, but after New Mexico had held its primary. The Democratic state committee chose David King to run in his place, apparently at the urging of King's uncle, Governor Bruce King. Dorothy Runnels received about one-half as many votes as King among committee members, in spite of claims by her supporters that David King's change of residence from the first to the second congressional district immediately after Congressman Runnels' death was patently opportunistic. Mrs. Runnels' attempt to appear on the ballot as an independent was rejected by the courts, as were efforts of Joe Skeen to be listed on the ballot as a Republican. No GOP candidate had sought the party's designation in the primary, giving Congressman Runnels a free ride in the November election. But after he died, Republican leaders met and nominated Skeen. The court held that since no Republican had filed in the primary, the party was not entitled to field a contestant in November. Consequently, both Skeen and Dorothy Runnels ran as write-in candidates against King, with Skeen receiving thirty-eight percent, King thirty-four percent and Runnels twenty-eight percent of the popular vote. For a fuller account of the controversy, see *Congressional Quarterly Weekly Report*, Vol. 38, October 11, 1980, p. 3043.

4. Two of the 381, Frank Reid, Jr., and Mort Lloyd, were not incumbents, but major party nominees who died while campaigning for a House seat. They were replaced on the ballot by their wives, both of whom were elected.

5. Other cases excluded from the analysis are those in which congressmen had announced their retirement from the House, or had been defeated in a primary election before their deaths. It seemed reasonable to omit instances in which incumbents had relinquished a claim to a House seat, voluntarily or otherwise, before they expired. The wives of six suicides were considered unlikely to succeed their husbands, and seventeen congressmen followed by a son, brother, or nephew were also defined as special cases. It seemed reasonable to infer that their widows would be required to defer to a male member of the immediate family (whose surname was the same) whatever their ambitions.

6. Kemp was a victim of one of the most bizarre controversies in the history of the matrimonial connection. She was caught in the middle of a bitter factional dispute between pro-Long and anti-Long forces in Louisiana. Senator Huey Long wanted her to fill her husband's vacancy, but local community and county leaders in the district had other plans. The latter boycotted an election in which Mrs. Kemp received 99.8 percent of the vote and managed to get the result thrown out. A second election was held a few months later, but she did not contest it.

One "widow" who might have been included in this analysis but was not received the nomination to replace her son. Curry Ethel Coffey, mother of Representative Robert Coffey, Jr., and a women's group activist in Pennsylvania, was persuaded by Democratic party leaders to contest a special election after her son was killed on a 1949 training flight. The much-decorated World War II pilot was thirty at the time of his death. Curry Coffee lost the election, but she was a much more likely choice than her daughter-in-law, Eileen Mercado-Parra Coffey, who was still in her twenties, had two children under the age of five, and was a native of Puerto Rico.

Two other women who did not quite fit the criteria are Ruth Hanna McCormick and Clare Boothe Luce. McCormick's husband had been a member of the House from 1917 to 1919, before moving to the U.S. Senate. He was defeated for renomination in 1924 and died in 1925, before the Senate term expired. His spouse did not win a House seat until the 1928 election. It was Luce's stepfather, Albert E. Austin, rather than her husband who preceded her in the House, and he did not die in office. Austin was defeated for reelection in 1940. Two years later his stepdaughter won the House seat.

Congresswomen who came to the House as widows of men who never served in Congress were not beneficiaries of the matrimonial connection and, consequently, are considered "nonwidows" for the purposes of analysis in this and remaining chapters.

7. See Kincaid (1978) on this point. Her treatment of widows' succession corrects some commonly accepted factual inaccuracies, disputes some myths implicit in the literature on the topic, and interprets the phenomenon within a fresh perspective.

8. "Safe" seats are defined here as those which were won by the deceased incumbent's party by

twenty-five percentage points or more in each of the last three elections. All other seats are considered "competitive."

9. Some nonsouthern widows were nominated to replace husbands with high seniority, a House leadership role, or a "safe" seat, but this was not the case nearly as often as it was among wives who replaced southern Representatives. And, as Tables 2.3, 2.4, and 2.5 indicate, the proportion of nonsouthern widows succeeding husbands who did not have these characteristics differed little from the proportion of those widows whose husbands possessed them.

10. The median ages of the two groups are the same as their mean ages.

11. Sources for this information include Chamberlin 1973; *New York Times* and *Washington Post* stories; sketches appearing in *Current Biography*, 1940–1976; and biographical information reported by *Congressional Quarterly Weekly Reports*.

12. This statement was made to the author by a Democratic Party activist from Alaska who had been a close associate of Nick Begich. The subject was explored in our conversation only after assurances were given that the source would be kept confidential.

13. One possible exception that comes to mind involves the congressional ambitions of Pat Lear, a former spouse of ex-Congressman James Corman. While Corman was still representing a southern California district, his wife, Mrs. Lear, considered the possibility of running for a House seat in a neighboring district, represented at the time by Republican Barry Goldwater, Jr. Her initial interest in the election was whetted when Goldwater was toying with the idea of mounting a race for the Senate, a promising development for Democrats who could then try to capture an open seat rather than tackle a well-known incumbent. But even when Goldwater decided to stay in the House, Lear persisted in her candidacy—against her husband's wishes. She lost the 1976 election, as well as the one two years later, after her marriage had ended in divorce.

14. The proportion of congressmen's widows among all women elected to the House has gone from fifty-four percent between 1916 and 1940, to thirty-seven percent from 1941 to 1964, to twenty-one percent from 1965 to the election of 1982.

15. Lloyd remarried after her first term and assumed the name of her new spouse, Bouquard. She took the name Lloyd again at the start of the 98th Congress, however, and she is referred to as "Lloyd" throughout these pages to avoid confusion, even though she was known as "Marilyn Lloyd Bouquard" from 1979 through 1982.

16. Decline in Representatives' deaths from the pre-War period to the 1941–1964 period was thirty-one percent. The decrease between 1941–1965 and 1965 through 1982 was sixty-five percent. This change can be explained in several ways. Earlier recognition of debilitating illness, more effective means of prolonging life, and other developments in medical science have surely permitted a larger number of ailing Representatives to complete their terms and withdraw from public life before their deaths. Representatives also seem to be retiring from the House and seeking other offices at a younger age, thereby reducing the probability of incumbent death. And recent improvements in retirement benefits for congressmen, along with stricter limitations on the wages they may earn outside of their House service, may be additional inducements for members to leave Congress while they can still do so under their own power.

17. During the 1940s, the average number of women receiving major party nominations every two years was approximately sixteen. The number increased to between twenty and twenty-five during the next twenty years, with the average in the 1970s close to forty. In each of the last two elections, 1980 and 1982, the number exceeded fifty. There were about nine successful female candidates each election during the 1940s. The number increased to fourteen during the 1950s, decreased to twelve in the 1960s, and increased again, to sixteen, in elections held between 1970 and 1978. Thus far in the 1980s the average has been slightly more than twenty.

18. The first attempt by a husband to succeed his wife in the House occurred in 1981, after Maryland's Gladys Spellman was reelected in November 1980, but was prevented by catastrophic illness from being sworn in. When the hopelessness of her condition was beyond doubt, the seat was declared vacant, and a new election called. Spellman's husband, Reuben, was narrowly defeated in the Democratic primary.

3 / Changing Patterns of Recruitment*

Decline in the number of congressional widows and their decrease as a proportion of the female population in the House are reflections of more fundamental changes in the characteristics of the women we have been sending to Washington. Most commentators recognize these changes, but they are understandably prone to highlight more obvious verities about the female presence in Congress. They note that women are grossly underrepresented in both houses, that the recent gains made in their numbers have been barely visible, that increases in the number of female state legislators are outstripping by far changes in Washington, and that, in spite of achievements recorded by the modern feminist movement, the future promises only incremental improvement.[1]

These are important observations, but, when emphasized, they obscure consequential changes that have taken place in the *qualities* of congresswomen. The number of women elected to the House may not have increased dramatically, but the pool of eligibles from which they emerged and their preparation for office have.[2] Shifts in the treatment they have received from male colleagues and in their policy and legislative role orientations have also been recorded. These changes have occurred largely because we have elected women with more impressive political skills than were possessed by their predecessors and because they adopted less inhibited gender and legislative role orientations. These developments will be dealt with in subsequent chapters. Here we will

*This chapter is a revised version of an article appearing in the August 1979 edition of *Legislative Studies Quarterly*. The author is grateful to the editors of that publication for permission to reprint it here.

trace changes in the socioeconomic and political backgrounds congresswomen have brought to the House over time.

Change in these background characteristics means that there has been change in the social, economic, and political resources that successful female candidates have been able to aggregate and exploit. For example, a decrease in the number of congressional widows elected to the House and in their percentage as a proportion of all congresswomen indicates change in the value of the matrimonial connection. The intimate association women have with their congressmen-husbands is no longer as serviceable a resource as it once was. Wives who share the name, the offspring, the values, the lifestyle, the friendships, and the organizational (or auxiliary) affiliations of male Representatives are still prime recruits for House seats, but they have lost the dominance they once had in their access to House portals. Today, female aspirants to Congress are capitalizing on other resources to carry them to Washington, and party leaders and voters seem to be more inclined than they once were to support women who offer something other than a matrimonial affiliation with men who were Representatives before they died.

Change in the precongressional experience of congresswomen and in the resources they are capable of exploiting, means that the process by which women are recruited to the House has been transformed.[3] The criteria people use to evaluate candidates and the political opportunity structure through which candidates pass as they proceed, in Prewitt's terms, from eligibility to public office, have been altered substantially. To the extent that the opportunity structure expands, for example, women with a broader range of experiences are elected to the House. At the same time, more women may become "available" for candidacy, in that they are ready to assume the risks and costs associated with conducting a professional campaign (perhaps because their chances of winning have improved); they are predisposed to subordinate other (personal and domestic) interests to those of holding a legislative seat if they win; and they are prepared to return to private callings with a minimum of disorientation should they lose (Czudnowski 1975, p. 200).

Six background characteristics of congresswomen are traced, aggregated, and analyzed below. Each of the six tells us something about the advantages and impediments these women could have experienced by virtue of the fact that they possessed or did not possess that characteristic. One of the six is great personal wealth, a second is a family with an impressive political pedigree. The importance of money in politics needs no elaboration here, although too much of it indiscreetly employed can be a liability. The value of having relatives, including fathers, brothers, uncles, and husbands who have emblazoned the family name on the hearts and minds of voters is also obvious. Legal training and experience in elective office, the third and fourth characteristics, may also be useful resources for those who can boast of them. The first acquaints the recipient with the language of the law, and transmits the skills useful for conducting a credible campaign and for projecting a productive legislative career. The second means that the candidate has already been a winner, that she has had experience working with constituents, and that she has compiled a presumably enviable record upon which to run.

Age at the time of first election to the House is important because it says something about a congresswoman's vitality (although no formula has yet been devised to establish the relationship between chronological age and performance), and because it gives us some idea of whether she will serve in the House long enough to wield more influence than is denoted by a "yea" and a "nay." And marital status, a characteristic all but meaningless for gauging the political assets of males, is important for women because of the distribution of traditional gender roles. A married woman, much more than a married man or a single woman, is expected to assume family responsibilities which frequently clash with goals defined by her political ambition.

There is, of course, no necessary relationship between any one of these characteristics (or all of them taken together) and electoral success. On the other hand, a woman who is not a lawyer, for example, is unable to exploit law school credentials and legal experience in order to win a House seat. A person who has legal training may use both to advantage. Potential command of a resource then, is an important attribute of candidacy. First we will report on the extent to which congresswomen possessed these qualities over time. We will then infer the criteria party leaders and voters employed to select congresswomen and the resources congresswomen relied upon to promote their candidacies. The patterns revealed will be interpreted in terms of changing boundaries of the opportunity structure and changes in the availability of women for House office.

CONGRESSWOMEN FROM POLITICAL AND WEALTHY FAMILIES

Being the wife of a former House member is not the only family link congresswomen have had with the world of politics. The parents and other close relatives of many of them held public or prominent party office both inside and outside of Washington. Of course this linkage is not limited to women. Between twenty and twenty-five percent of the men elected to the first five Congresses had had relatives who preceded them in the Continental Congress or who had served in the House or Senate (Clubok et al. 1969, p. 1043). This figure has declined considerably since those early years of the Republic, but family connections continue to be serviceable springboards to the national legislature.[4]

Substantial wealth also seems to be characteristic of many representatives, a far larger proportion than one would expect if seats in the House were filled randomly from among the adult population over twenty-five years of age. This should come as no surprise since money, like family connections, is a valuable political resource and often, even more than family ties, contributes significantly to the electoral success of those who have it. The wealth controlled by well-to-do congresswomen was not always their own, but whether it came from affluent parents, generous husbands, or their own enterprise, it must surely have been put to some use when they sought office.

One might assume, then, that the affluence and the active political orientations of families of congresswomen are useful in explaining the recruitment of women to the House of Representatives. We would expect affluence and activism to have affected the social development of these women early in their lives and, at the same time, to have reduced the impact of gender role prescriptions to which they were almost certainly exposed. These prescriptions tend to discourage women from taking an active part in politics, let alone consider a political career, and to reserve the world of politics for males (Kirkpatrick 1974, p. 15).

It would follow, then, that congresswomen who were members of wealthy or politically well-connected families, more easily than women whose families were politically inert or without significant financial resources, ignored or coped well with the social and psychological penalties that are often the consequence of nonconformity. In spite of gender role constraints, they sought and won national office. Intimate exposure to politicians and wealth probably offset, if it did not supersede, their status as females.[5]

A systematic examination of the backgrounds of congresswomen suggests, however, that while family wealth or roots in electoral politics may have once contributed significantly to their recruitment to the House, such factors are not as important today.[6] The evidence for this inference is presented in Table 3.1. The Table groups all women into three time periods, categorizing them according to the years in which they were initially elected. The columns divide them into those whose families were politically active and those whose families were wealthy, with congresswomen having both characteristics included in both columns. Representatives falling under each of these headings are divided further into "all congresswomen" and those who did not benefit from the matrimonial connection.

As the Table makes clear, decline in the potential importance of family connections and private wealth in securing a House seat is precipitate. In the earliest period, about four of every five congresswomen (81%) were able to capitalize on family connections. Most were widows of former members, but, of the nonwidows, one-half were able to take advantage of the reputation of a relative. Many Floridians, for example, knew that Ruth Bryan Owen was the daughter of William Jennings Bryan, and, in Illinois, a large number of voters were aware that Ruth Hanna McCormick was the daughter of President-maker Marc Hanna, as well as the wife of the late Senator Medill McCormick.

Their successors were considerably less able as a group to take advantage of a family name. The percentages for all congresswomen drop sharply, from a little

Table 3.1. Congresswomen from Political and Wealthy Families, 1917–1982

Congresses (years)	Women from political families				Women from wealthy families			
	All Congresswomen	N*	Non-widows	N	All Congresswomen	N*	Non-widows	N
65th–76th	81%	26	50%	12	27%	26	33%	12
(1917–1940)	(21)		(6)		(7)		(4)	
77th–88th	47	38	17	24	11	38	8	24
(1941–1964)	(18)		(4)		(4)		(2)	
89th–98th**	34	38	17	30	3	38	3	30
(1965–1982)	(13)		(5)		(1)		(1)	

*The total number of congresswomen exceeds 100 because Jeannette Rankin is counted twice, once in the first period, once in the second, and Chase Going Woodhouse is counted twice in the second period. Each served two nonconsecutive terms.

**Includes women elected in 1982 to the 98th Congress.

less than one-half (47%) between 1941 and 1964 to one-third between 1965 and 1983. Most of the women in the last group were congressional widows, but many were not. For example, Barbara Kennelly's father, John Bailey, was Democratic State Chairman in Connecticut and a one-time Democratic National Chairman. Helen Meyner's husband had earlier served two terms as Governor of New Jersey. Thus, the decrease in the proportion of women able to rely on family connections to gain a seat in the House does not mean that the resource is no longer usable. It is apparent, however, that many recent congresswomen found other resources upon which to build a successful campaign.

Significant wealth has been a scarcer commodity than family connections for female Representatives, although between one-quarter and one-third elected between 1917 and 1940, depending on whether we refer to all congresswomen or only to nonwidows, had access to it. Among the widows whose supply of funds was abundant were Edith Nourse Rogers and Frances Payne Bolton. Among nonwidows were Ruth Baker Pratt and Caroline O'Day, both of New York and both privy to fabulous wealth from oil and other investments. Decline in possible reliance on enormous financial holdings was more gradual than the decline in potential use of family connections, but the former seems to have reached rock bottom. The one authentic millionaire among the women elected since 1965, Millicent Fenwick, came to the House in 1975. No other multimillionaire congresswoman has been sent to the House since then.

THE INCIDENCE OF HOUSE LAWYERS

One of the more constant features of the American political system is the legal training of so many of its politicians. The law degree has clearly been the most common professional credential acquired by public office holders, particularly those who rise to the highest levels. There is no shortage of explanations for this phenomenon (Czudnowski 1975, pp. 204–210), and the House of Representatives, at least as much as any legislative body in the country, has had its share of attorneys.[7]

The paucity of legal training among women who came to the House before World War II would probably come as a surprise if the special character of so many of these early congresswomen had not already been explored here. As has been pointed out, many were women who were elected to succeed their husbands and had no professional or political ambitions. A number seemed to owe their visibility and election more to family connections or private wealth than they did to other factors. It is possible to conclude, therefore, that women lawyers and, perhaps, career women in general were considered insufficiently attractive politically to warrant the support of party leaders and rank and file voters.

In recent years, however, lawyers have begun to capture a larger share of the House seats held by women. The information in Table 3.2 indicates that whereas only eight percent of all congresswomen elected before World War II had acquired legal training, about one in four (26%) fit that description between 1965 and 1983. When the group of thirty-six widows is excluded from consideration, the same pattern, a demonstrable increase in the proportion of congresswomen who are lawyers, emerges. During the most recent period, one of every three nonwidows elected to the House held a law degree, with the bulk of the increase coming between 1970 and 1978, when eight of the seventeen new women coming to Washington had been to law school. In 1983, however, at the start of the 98th Congress, only three of the twenty-one congresswomen were lawyers. Obviously the proportion fluctuates within each time period, but it seems evident that the percentage of female attorneys in the House is approaching the share of male Representatives who are attorneys.[8] In the meantime, female lawyers as a proportion of all lawyers throughout the country has increased from 2.4 percent in 1940, to 4.8 percent in 1970, to 14.1 percent in 1982.[9]

PRIOR POLITICAL EXPERIENCE

Although prior experience in a state, county, or local public office is not a prerequisite for service in Congress, more representatives have included than have excluded at least one of these way stations en route to the House. Observers may differ about what exactly constitutes a "public office," but if we define it strictly as any government position to which one must be elected, we have a reasonably well-delineated, even if not comprehensive, definition of the term. And although this more specific meaning reduces considerably the number of

Table 3.2. Lawyers among Congresswomen, 1917–1982

Congresses (years)	All Congresswomen		Nonwidows	
	Lawyers	N*	Lawyers	N
65th–76th	8%	26	17%	12
(1917–1940)	(2)		(2)	
77th–88th	13	38	21	24
(1941–1964)	(5)		(5)	
89th–98th**	26	38	33	30
(1965–1982)	(10)		(10)	

*The total number of congresswomen exceeds 100 because Jeannette Rankin is counted twice, once in the first time period, once in the second, and Chase Going Woodhouse is counted twice in the second time period. Each served two nonconsecutive terms.

**Includes women elected in 1982 to the 98th Congress.

House members who may lay claim to prior public office, the figure is not reduced to less than a majority.[10]

A number of reasons have been offered to explain this pattern (Czudnowski 1975, p. 187; Lasswell 1954, p. 222), but, whatever their bases, the high incidence of representatives who held prior elective offices has only recently begun to manifest itself among congresswomen. Table 3.3 reports the percentages of these women who had been elected to government office before they went to Congress. It further divides them into "all congresswomen" and "nonwidows" and groups these women according to the three time periods established above. Before World War II, less than one in five (19%) of all congresswomen had been elected to a public office before they were elevated to the House. Over the years this percentage has increased, with more than one-half (53%) of the women elected to the House during the last eighteen-year period able to claim prior service in an elected office.

A similar pattern is revealed among congresswomen who did not succeed their husbands, although, as is evident in the Table, the percentages of previously elected women is considerably higher during each of the three periods when widows are excluded from the analysis than when they are included in it. Among the thirty nonwidows elected to the House for the first time between 1964 and 1982, sixty-seven percent had successfully sought voter support in a previous campaign for office—a proportion approximating the comparable figure for all contemporary House members.

This figure is somewhat larger than the corresponding figure for "all congresswomen," a finding which, given the sudden incumbency of widows, should not be surprising. However, it is important to acknowledge here that elected office is not the only position in which would-be House members might learn and demonstrate the range of qualities making them putative candidates for

Table 3.3. The Incidence of Prior Election to Government Office among Congresswomen, 1917–1982

Congresses (years)	All Congresswomen		Nonwidows	
	Held Elective Office	N*	Held Elective Office	N
65th–76th	19%	26	42%	12
(1917–1940)	(5)		(5)	
77th–88th	32	38	50	24
(1941–1964)	(12)		(12)	
89th–98th**	53	38	67	30
(1965–1982)	(20)		(20)	

*The total number of congresswomen exceeds 100 because Jeannette Rankin is counted twice, once in the first time period, once in the second, and Chase Going Woodhouse is counted twice in the second time period. Each served two nonconsecutive terms.

**Includes women elected in 1982 to the 98th Congress.

Congress. Experience in appointed office, as well as leadership positions within the major political parties, may be just as likely as occupying an elective office to provide would-be representatives with the appropriate skills, political orientations, proximity to decision-making centers, visibility, and credibility.

But the elective experience is clearly in a class by itself. Normally it means that one must appeal for public support and counter the competition of stipulated antagonists. Far more than almost any other experience that could conceivably lead to membership in the House, elections require public exposure; they involve greater psychic and material risks; they normally demand more time, energy, and sacrifice of private, nonpolitical goals; and usually the rewards at stake are more desirable. For these reasons, an increase in the proportion of congresswomen who have had prior experience in elected office is noteworthy, and, as will be suggested below, this development has important implications for the treatment they receive from male colleagues and for the legislative behavior in which they engage.

AGE AND MARITAL STATUS

Among the few studies that touch on the age of women in politics there is general agreement that females normally seek elective office later in life than do males. The phenomenon of "older women running against younger men is especially common at the local level where male candidates in their late twenties are not unusual but where women candidates under thirty-five are virtually unknown" (Smith 1976, p. 67).

The same pattern may be observed at the national level, as well. First-term congresswomen as a group have tended to be older than first-term House members generally. The median age of all new Representatives from the early years of this century until 1960 was forty-five (Oleszek 1969, p. 101). The comparable figure for congresswomen was forty-nine, an age which does not change even when women who succeeded their husbands are excluded from the calculation.

What these aggregate figures mask, however, is the fact that the median age of beginning congresswomen is declining in both relative and absolute terms. From 1965 to 1982, for example, the median age of all first-term female Representatives who were not congressional widows was forty-three, while that of all House members was about forty-one.[11] These findings suggest that congresswomen have been closing the gap between themselves and male Representatives. The data in Table 3.4 also make clear that the decline in the ages of new congresswomen has been a steady one. The Table includes only those female House members who did not succeed their husbands and groups them in the same time periods established in previous tables. Among the women who served in the House before World War II, one-half were above and one-half were below the age of forty-nine at the time of their initial election. The median age of the second group of women was somewhat lower, forty-six years, with the decline continuing to forty-three years among women elected to the House between the 89th and 98th Congresses.

A second pattern revealed in Table 3.4 is the sharp increase after World War II in the proportion of congresswomen who were married, although the numbers falling into some of the Table's categories is not so large as to inspire great confidence in the percentage variations. Before the War, only two of the twelve women unable to rely on the matrimonial connection were married with living spouses when first elected to the House. Two of every three fit that description after the War, which suggests that conflict between political and traditional family obligations has been less of a deterrent to would-be congresswomen in recent years than it had been in years past. This inference is reinforced by the fact that more than one-half (eleven of twenty) of the married women elected between 1965 and 1982 had at least one child under the age of seventeen. Two of the women who were divorced when elected to Congress, Bobbi Fidler and Lynn Martin, also had school-age children. That divorced women are being elected to Congress at all, moreover, suggests modification of the criteria party leaders and voters are employing when evaluating would-be congresswomen.

IMPLICATIONS OF CHANGING RECRUITMENT PATTERNS

The findings presented here have accented changes in the backgrounds of congresswomen who have come to Washington during the last sixty-five years.

Table 3.4. Median Age and Marital Status of Congresswomen Who Did Not Succeed Their Husbands, 1917–1982

Congressess (years)	Median Age	Marital Status					
		Married	Single	Widowed	Divorced	Total	N
65th–76th	49	17%	33%	50%	0%	100%	
(1917–1940)		(2)	(4)	(6)	(0)		12
77th–88th	46	67	17	17	0	101*	
(1941–1964)		(16)	(4)	(4)	(0)		24
89th–98th**	43	67	17	7	10	101*	
(1965–1982)		(20)	(5)	(2)	(3)		30

*Exceeds 100 percent because of rounding.
**Includes women elected in 1982 to the 98th Congress.

The House has witnessed a gradual reduction in the proportion of women who succeeded to the seats of deceased spouses. There has been a decline, as well, in the percentage of congresswomen who could capitalize upon enormous family wealth or upon their identification with family members who had already made their way in politics. In the meantime, legal training and prior election to state and local office have become more significant components of the credentials congresswomen have relied upon to fuel their ambitions. Recently elected congresswomen have also been younger than earlier female representatives, and more likely to have living spouses.

The aggregate figures upon which these conclusions are based, however, provide neither direct nor comprehensive insight into the changing recruitment patterns of female House members. Only a detailed, case-by-case analysis of the factors contributing to these women's candidacies could provide that insight. Still, we can draw some conclusions on the basis of circumstantial evidence. Changes over time in typical social and political characteristics of congresswomen permit generalizations to be formulated about the nature of these changes and about their implications.

A More Inclusive Structure of Political Opportunity

Even the casual observer of American politics is aware of the nonrandom quality of the process by which public offices are filled. While virtually all adult citizens are legally eligible to hold these offices, few have an effective political opportunity to do so. Most people simply do not possess either the advantages associated with high social status or the abundant resources by which Seligman et al. (1974) define effective political opportunity. By effective political opportunity these authors are referring to the extent to which would-be candidates possess sufficient resources realistically to seek and secure elective office. They are concerned here not with whether citizens may legally run for public office but whether they can do so practically.

The authors state that " . . . the boundaries of *effective* political opportunity" correspond with "the characteristics of those nominated and elected compared with the characteristics of the excluded." These characteristics are defined by the social structure, with such factors as family background, occupation and education influencing the process by which people are made aware of and encouraged to capitalize on political opportunities. They also have an impact on the extent to which people have the wherewithal to pursue their opportunities effectively. These factors, in short, affect predispositions to political involvement and aspiration. The competition among party leaders and political groups, in turn, "creates vacancies that attract the predisposed to run" for office (Seligman et al. 1974, pp. 16–17). When this frame of reference is applied to the groups of women who have held House seats, it seems clear that the structure of effective political opportunity has become more inclusive over the years.

Among the range of social characteristics and resources that a candidate may convert into political success, money, family connections, professional training, and political experience are among the more important. The extent to which each of these characteristics contributes to victory is likely to vary in time, place, and circumstance. But when successful candidates possessing one combination of these characteristics are systematically replaced by candidates who possess a discernibly different set of characteristics, it is reasonable to assume that an important change has taken place in what Seligman calls the boundaries of the effective political opportunity structure. And the information presented above indicates that such a change has indeed occurred.

In many and perhaps most respects, recent congresswomen do not differ markedly from earlier female House members. Almost all experienced a degree of financial security and educational training that was inaccessible to the vast majority of their female contemporaries. Almost all grew up within a milieu of social activism, if not political activism, and, if members of the earlier Congresses were initially uninterested in politics, they were at least interested in and knowledgeable about the world around them.

Where contemporary congresswomen tend to differ from their predecessors is in the nature of the resources that contributed significantly to their election to Congress. Most earlier congresswomen seem to have been elected to office partially on the strength of their enormous wealth or their families' political connections. These connections may have been established by either marital or kinship ties. But whatever the basis of the nexus, the resources these attributes generated called attention to both the candidacies and the qualifications of these would-be congresswomen.

Although a number of women have been able to convert family connections and wealth into a House seat in recent years, most contemporary women have relied on a quite different set of resources. They have depended upon legal training and intimate elective experience, career assets that promoted opportunities, habits of thought, and patterns of behavior valuable both to the candidate appealing for public support and to a House member interested in expanding upon support already mobilized.

In sum, it seems reasonable to conclude that, in the past, women Representatives relied upon those attributes of their candidacies that were linked to ascribed characteristics—wealth, family affiliation, and social standing. More recent female House members, by contrast, have relied more upon discernable vocational and political achievements, merits suggesting virtuosity in such political skills as organization, communication, bargaining, and policy expertise (Seligman et al. 1974, p. 14). The shift from a recruitment pattern that places a high value on achievement at the expense of ascribed characteristics both reflects and presages a democratization of the recruitment process. In Seligman's terms, we have an effective political opportunity structure today that is accessible to a wider range of women than it was in the past.

Increased Availability of Women

The great majority of Americans are not available for recruitment to public office. They are unable either to accept full or part-time political office or to return to their occupations after filling that office temporarily because their principal occupation does not permit them sufficient flexibility to do so, or because the economic or psychic price they must pay for doing so is unacceptable (Czudnowski 1975, p. 200). The findings presented in this chapter indicate that the process by which women have been recruited to House office has undergone important change not only with respect to the structure of effective political opportunity open to them, but in the extent to which they have become available for congressional office as well. Women have become available for a seat in the House from a wider range of pursuits.

We have already noted that female lawyers, although only recently becoming a significantly larger percentage of the profession than they were in the past, are nonetheless capitalizing on the expertise and the flexibility made possible by their vocation. More important, however, is the fact that married women with young children are not necessarily being dissuaded from seeking office by the constraints imposed by their roles as wives and mothers. Before World War II, congresswomen did not have to assume the obligations normally borne by the female adult in a traditional, nuclear family. Almost all were either unmarried or widows. After the Second World War, however, the proportion of married congresswomen increased significantly.

One might conclude, then, that the male monopoly on the flexibility needed to seek and hold office has been eroded in recent years and that the availability of House office is now devolving on larger numbers of women. The whole range of maternal and domestic obligations until recently performed almost exclusively by women has apparently come to be shared, delegated, hired-out, or indefinitely postponed by would-be congresswomen far more than was possible in the past. And the conditions under which women may become available for office have expanded no less dramatically than has the effective political opportunity structure through which they must pass.

Both of these developments are important because the recruitment process serves as a critical link between society and the polity. When a process that systematically discriminates against persons possessing clearly definable social and economic characteristics is altered to permit their inclusion in the political system, the fidelity of this link is likely to be improved. And, to the extent that the newly included citizens harbor perspectives and beliefs rarely expressed in national politics, the altered recruitment pattern is likely to be a more serviceable channel for orderly change in a democratic political system.

Gaining seats in Congress by the formerly dispossessed is only the first step, however. There is no assurance that once in the House they will be treated as equals by other members, that they will aspire to and gain positions of influence, and that they will use that influence to articulate values and beliefs that had been ignored because people like themselves were once excluded from Congress. In the chapters that follow, attention will be given to the way in which male Representatives have responded to their presence in the House over the years, and to the patterns of behavior in which they engaged while fulfilling legislative responsibilities.

NOTES

1. These points are developed in Amundsen 1971; Buchanan 1978; Bullock and Heys 1972; Diamond 1977; Gehlen 1969; Lee 1977; Lynn 1975; Mandel 1981; Rule 1981; Tolchin and Tolchin 1974; and Werner 1966.

2. One of the few recent treatments of congresswomen's changing background characteristics is Thompson (forthcoming). She compares these changes with shifts in the experiences of male Representatives.

3. Czudnowski (1975) provides a comprehensive and stimulating treatment of political recruitment and Prewitt's (1970) and Seligman's (1974) discussions and applications of the concept are extremely useful. The term is defined here as those experiences undergone by members of a society that contribute to their induction into the specialized roles of the political system, their training in the appropriate political skills, and their acquisition of political cognitive maps, values, expectations, and affects. Almond and Coleman (1960, p. 31) give this meaning to the term when applying it cross-nationally.

4. Hess (1966) reports that 700 families have had two or more members serve in Congress. These families account for seventeen percent of all senators and representatives who served from 1774 to the mid-1960s.

5. On these points see especially Kelly and Boutilier 1978, Chapters 4 and 5.

6. The sources for this information include Chamberlin (1973); *Current Biography Yearbooks*, 1940–1982; Edward T. James (ed.), *Notable American Women, 1607–1950*, 1971; *Biographical Dictionary of the American Congress, 1774–1971* (1971); and *New York Times'* stories about these women. The amount of wealth controlled by each congresswoman is, of course, impossible to document precisely. But it can be demonstrated that the following House members, grouped according to the time periods stipulated in Table 3.1 and in order of their initial elections, were "millionaires" (the criterion by which "wealthy" Representatives were distinguished from other congresswomen):

65th–76th Congresses—Rogers*, McCormick, Pratt, Greenway, O'Day, Gasque*, and Bolton*;

77th–88th Congresses—K. Byron*, St. George, Church*, and Weis;

89th–98th Congresses—Fenwick.

Among those who emerged from "political families" and listed in the same order are:

65th–76th Congresses—Rankin, Huck*, Nolan*, Kahn*, Rogers*, Langley*, Oldfield*, McCormick, Owen, Wingo*, Eslick*, Clarke*, Greenway, Honeyman, Gasque*, Bolton*, Smith*, Sumner, McMillan*, and Gibbs*;

77th–88th Congresses—Rankin, K. Byron*, Boland*, Fulmer*, Luce, Hardin, Kelly, Church*, Kee*, Buchanan*, Sullivan*, Granahan*, Simpson*, Norrell*, Reece*, Riley*, Reid*, and Baker*;

89th–98th Congresses—Thomas*, Hicks, Andrews*, Boggs*, Collins*, Lloyd*, Meyner, Pettis*, B. Byron*, Snowe, Kennelly, Ashbrook*, and Johnson.

7. Putnam (1976) notes that the United States has the highest proportion of lawyers in national office among all developed countries. From 1947 to 1967, fifty-three percent of all newly elected House members were lawyers (Bullock and Heys 1972).

8. One reason for the convergence is that the percentage of lawyers among male House members is decreasing. In the elections of 1970 to 1976, the proportion of lawyers among first-term House members averaged forty-six percent. From 1978 to 1982, the average was forty-two percent.

9. The U.S. Census Bureau's *Statistical Abstract of the United States* regularly reports these figures. The most recent percentage is from the 1982–83 edition, p. 388.

10. During the years between 1947 and 1967, for example, about three of five new members of the House had served in some elective government office (Bullock and Heys 1972). A significant majority of first-term members coming to Washington in the 1970s and 1980s saw similar elective service. The figures are as follows: 92nd Congress, seventy-five percent; 93rd Congress, sixty-five percent; 94th Congress, sixty-two percent; 95th Congress, sixty-five percent; 96th Congress, sixty-five percent; 97th Congress, sixty-one percent; and 98th Congress, seventy-one percent.

11. The median age of all first-term House members in the three most recent Congresses was thirty-nine in the 96th, and forty-one in both the 97th and 98th.

---

*Beneficiary of the matrimonial connection.

Part III
Treatment

4 / House Perceptions and Treatment of Female Members

The changing pathways women have taken to get to the House and their improved preparation for legislative tasks have been accompanied by a more respectful reception from male colleagues whose own orientations toward women in politics have come to differ significantly from those of the men who came before them. Congressmen tended to be polite and effusively deferential to congresswomen prior to World War II, demonstrating little inclination to take them seriously. Since the end of the War, female lawmakers have commanded (and male members have manifested) much more professional respect, and they have had many more opportunities than were available to the women who preceded them in Congress to carve out legislative reputations of their own. Yet, in spite of some dramatic changes in these regards, women are still not fully integrated into the House.

In the three chapters that follow, attention is given to changes in the treatment congresswomen have received from male Representatives. They describe the extent to which these women have been accepted by congressmen as equals—that is, the degree to which women have been integrated into House routines, made privy to deliberations in informal groups and caucuses, and given access to formal leadership posts. This chapter explores changes in the way congressmen have perceived and related to female colleagues during the course of their daily activities. It deals, as well, with the perceptions congresswomen have had of male behavior toward them as women, and the responses they exhibited to discrimination based upon gender. The next chapter traces the progress congresswomen have made in securing access to informal channels of communication. And Chapter 6 discusses and documents the frequency with which congresswomen have gained entry to House leadership positions.

Before dealing directly with these matters, it is important to define the gender-related orientations that male and female House members have adopted toward the institution they serve. Although the attitudes of 435 Representatives are likely to be exquisitely varied on both organizational and public policy issues, those interviewed agreed that the House of Representatives is essentially a "male" institution.

PERCEPTIONS OF THE HOUSE AS A MALE INSTITUTION

Several years ago, Jeane Kirkpatrick and coworkers at the Eagleton Institute's Center for the American Woman and Politics interviewed a group of women legislators then serving in state capitals throughout the country. On the basis of these women's comments, she concluded that state " . . . legislatures share the macho culture of the locker room, the smoker, the barracks." Among the folkways of these bodies, she said, " . . . none appears to be more widely shared than the tradition of the *masculine* legislature" (Kirkpatrick 1974, p. 106; emphasis is Kirkpatrick's). Other studies of state political systems also characterize legislatures as "male clubs" (Epstein 1958; and Sorauf 1963).[1]

Interviews with twenty-four members of the House during the 95th Congress leaves little doubt that contemporary Representatives, male as well as female, are inclined to define their legislative body as did their state legislative counterparts.[2] A majority of the respondents stated that the House was becoming less "male" in many respects and that women were excluded from fewer activities and discussions than they once were. Some said that women were being accepted as equals more than they had been in the past, and several noted that an increasing number of men were apt to define the House in ways that had nothing to do with gender. However, all but a few felt that, in spite of these changes, Kirkpatrick's characterization of state legislatures applied with almost equal force to the Congress, and that the House of Representatives, too, can be defined as a "male" institution.

A congresswoman who had been a state legislator before coming to Washington compared her experiences in the state and national capitals:

> I was assigned to Finance and Insurance Committee in the Assembly and there had never been a woman on that Committee. It held its meetings in a men's club and they wouldn't let me in to attend the meetings. And once we got into a caucus meeting, they didn't want to hear from you. I think it is still that way in Washington.

The comments of another congresswoman were perhaps the most representative female response:

> It is there. I don't feel it that much, but there are indications that it is a male club. But that is true of most institutions that have so many men and so few women. I don't think it affects my service, but I don't think there is any

question that many of the men sort of assume that Congress belongs to them. But this is probably more true of a state legislature, where members are without their families and spend so much time at night together. Here members live with their families and there aren't as many occasions where you can be one of the boys. There is less likely to be that kind of legislative camaraderie and therefore women are less likely to be excluded or dismissed.

Bases for Perceptions

The reasons respondents offered to explain the House's "maleness" vary, but among these explanations, four were offered often enough to warrant explicit mention. A majority was inclined to cite the large numbers of men and the small number of women as a principal reason for the House's male orientation. When they look around at the members on the House floor, they see an "army" of men and barely a "squad" of women. In committee, subcommittee, or state-delegation meetings, the lone female members are simply "lost in the crowd," although one male representative said that a congresswoman is so conspicuous that "when your eye comes to rest on her" you are startled at how unique a figure she is. Other males pointed out that many of the official and unofficial meetings they attended included no women at all, and women members noted how often they were part of groups in which they were the only female present. It would seem, then, that by simply being around so many men and so few women, members of both genders cannot help but come to think of the institution as essentially male in its orientation, as well as in its composition.

Many of the House members also suggested that the attitudes and behavior that make the House "male" were rooted in "the culture." Implicit in their remarks is the view that the American culture embodies behavioral norms which significantly influence the way in which members of society define themselves as men or women. These norms encourage members of each group to engage in different sorts of activities, just as they impose limitations on what members of each gender may do. According to these respondents, political decision making in the United States has been and continues to be an essentially male enterprise. When men get together within a predominantly male legislative setting, a friendship or camaraderie develops based upon a common purposiveness and sense of mission, as well as upon other shared "male interests." If and when women enter that environment, they are considered intruders or outsiders and they may be ignored, treated courteously but dismissed, or treated with contempt or derision. In the view of many of the House members interviewed, therefore, the House is a male institution in the same way as business organizations, industrial labor unions and other predominantly male, political and economic organizations are male. A congressman who strongly agreed with this characterization of the House asserted that " ... we are *representative* of the country in the *worst*, as well as the best sense of that term" (the emphasis is his).

A half-dozen House members, both male and female, had an additional culture-related reason for the masculine character of the House, attributing the warmth and sense of camaraderie that men develop for one another specifically to "male bonding." One congressman said that he would not dream of asking most congresswomen to have a cup of coffee with him to "get away and simply talk shop," even though he was very friendly with a number of them. On the other hand, he would not give a second thought to asking any one of twenty-five or more different male members to take the same coffee break. Another male respondent put it this way:

> Friendships bind men together in a way that women do not experience. There is a bonding, a male bonding that does it. The language we use, the drinking we do, make it very difficult for women to enter this world.

And a congresswoman gave an even more explicit and detailed response:

> In an institution so dependent on bonding—that's where women are really not part of the process. And I'm not sure I want to be. There is a line between getting accepted and being one of the boys—a line between being included and part of the group on the one hand and being an unwelcome member and an embarrassment to yourself and the group on the other.

Finally, several male House members and two female members suggested that the House is a male institution because the behavior of many of the female members leaves observers inside and outside Congress little alternative but to perceive it as such. The behavior referred to takes several forms. Some women, these respondents asserted, overcompensate for their being women. Others define themselves as "mavericks" and act accordingly. And some women, including several in each of the first two categories, take up feminist causes. All three of these approaches to the congressional vocation call attention to the minority status women hold and thereby reinforce the belief that "maleness" is the norm. Each of these adaptive strategies attributed to congresswomen warrants both brief elaboration and a discussion of the rejoinders offered by House members who rejected explanations based upon female behavior.

Congresswomen overcompensate for what they perceive to be weaknesses associated with gender, said some respondents, because they fear that their constituents see them as "soft," "unassertive," and politically "ineffectual." They try to counter the image of "weakness" by projecting "firmness," "certainty," a "seriousness of purpose," and a cold "rationality." They compete with and try to destroy the stereotype of women that has been accepted by female as well as by male voters. In the process, they overcompensate for what they believe is an important political deficiency—their "femaleness."

Women who cast themselves in the role of "maverick" often seem distrustful of party leaders and of senior members of the House, against whose records they may very well have campaigned. They appear less willing to adhere to carefully balanced bargains struck in the House because of reservations about one or two decisions which they believe involve "matters of principle." And they are determined not to be co-opted by the system. From the perspective of many males, these women are unreliable, inflexible in the beliefs they hold, and incapable of engaging in the give-and-take that leads to compromise. They are also perceived as humorless, disloyal to their parties, and too apt to violate House norms.

A few male respondents, but no female interviewees, noted that some of the women elected in more recent years have demonstrated an "unfortunate tendency" to identify themselves as "women" and to become too intimately associated with "so-called women's issues." According to these informants, this inclination has diminished congresswomens' standing in the eyes of some members and has had the added effect of jeopardizing the potential influence of other women who become too closely linked to these feminists. One congressman who was critical of this behavior said: "You don't see men defining themselves consciously as men. And this permits us to concentrate on other, more important, things."

Debunking the Stereotypes

To some of the male and most of the female respondents, blaming continued unequal treatment of women on female behavior is simply another instance of making the victims of discrimination responsible for the inequities they suffer. The language and styles of politicians were developed by men, not women, said one respondent, and women should not be penalized for " . . . copying a rhetoric and a political posturing that have proved to be effective over the years." Even if women sometimes "come on too strong," the incidence of such indiscretions is not any greater among women then than it is among men. Furthermore, women who sometimes depart from established political "scripts" are not taken seriously by male colleagues. Said one female Representative, "Showing uncertainty or some other human frailty means, to some men, that a congresswoman cannot make the tough decisions we all have to make from time to time."

Most respondents felt that the so-called "maverick" role attributed to many women is not limited to members of one gender. Many men also prize their "independence" from House leadership and it was asserted that a far higher proportion of men than of women can be described as ideologically inflexible, indifferent to House norms, or unwilling to engage in compromise. One congressman noted no woman member had violated House norms as often as former Congressman Wayne Hays, assuming that civility is among these norms, and none spoke as often and used as much time in floor debate as former Congressman H. R. Gross. Yet both of these men were respected by many of their colleagues and given a wide berth by others.

Some female respondents also alluded to the frequency with which male members appear as parts of minuscule minorities following lopsided roll call votes, as much a measure of ideological inflexibility as any they could think of. Women, they argued, rarely oppose overwhelming majorities of their colleagues, whether the issues are cast within partisan or bipartisan frames of reference. And several respondents felt that if women are perceived as mavericks, it is because the members who see them within such a perspective are predisposed to do so. Incidents which can be interpreted to support such prejudices are used by these men to reassure themselves of the "soundness" of their bias. These males are much less inclined to pin the label "maverick" on male colleagues who engage in unorthodox behavior.

This argument was sometimes coupled with a direct challenge to the alleged causal relationship between female behavior and perceptions of the House as a male institution. If there is such a relationship, one woman pointed out, the cause and effect have been transposed. Because the House is essentially a male institution, women sometimes have to remind themselves about "who they are." They have to call attention to their own identities, even if it is only for their own mental health. The patterns of social and political interaction they encounter in Congress, along with the system of rewards and punishments, the legislative priorities, and the rhetorical styles are matters with which many females feel uncomfortable when they first come to the House.

And so, if a woman occasionally feels the need to define herself as "a woman" and to act out her "womanhood," and if men do not demonstrably define themselves as men, it is because the House is already a male institution and it prescribes orientations and patterns of behavior that men have already internalized. Most women, on the other hand, are expected to "unlearn" patterns of speech, patterns of social interaction, policy priorities, and habits of thought that have grown out of the gender role they learned. "Men never need to think about their 'maleness'," said one female informant. "The frame of reference within which they operate permits them to take for granted the fact that they are male."

It would follow, then, that the women most admired by congressmen are those who have adjusted most effectively to the workways and habits of the House. They are the women who take pains to speak for their districts, their states, or some major interest groups in these geographical units, but not for other women. They are members who use the dozens of clichés that punctuate House debate, rather than employing a more individualized rhetorical style of their own. They are women who express a concern for saving money, or a strong national defense, or the importance of law and order, or a healthy business and banking climate, but they will not speak out conspicuously about part-time government jobs for women, the Susan B. Anthony dollar, or displaced homemakers, issues which are considered by many to be illegitimate grist for the legislative mill. Accordingly, those who take up feminist causes are perceived as outsiders. And, in the words of one feminist member " . . . we have to put up with an awful lot of silly remarks and nastiness just because our priorities do not happen to be high up on the legislative agenda."

It is important to reiterate here that a majority of respondents did not mention the behavior of women when discussing factors contributing to the masculine character of the House. Most said that the composition of that body and the cultural orientations members bring with them are the most prominent factors leading to the "maleness" of that chamber. But whatever the explanations, the masculine orientation of the House seems to affect the way in which contemporary congresswomen are treated. Such treatment has not been constant over time, however and, as we shall see, today's female Representatives are considerably better off than were their predecessors.

THE WAY IT WAS

Information about the relationship between male and female House members in years past is difficult to come by, inasmuch as few scholars have devoted systematic attention to the subject and Representatives themselves normally found little reason either to dwell on the subject or commit their thoughts on the matter to writing. But, based upon the scanty documentary evidence available, it appears that before World War II, female lawmakers were seen as amateurs and curiosities, rather than as authentic public figures, by reporters, male colleagues, and government officials.

The press was probably the principal purveyor of this unfortunate image, although it was almost certainly catering to the well-established preconceptions of its readers. It seemed more interested in printing information about those attributes of female House members associated with their being women than they did about women's performance as legislators. This may have been the case because only a few women compiled a record in Congress worth discussing. But it is also true that editors and writers of the period defined as oddities women who undertook what were considered to be male pursuits and they were inclined, as was most of the public, to use different criteria to explain and evaluate both the presence and the performance of females in a field for which women were expected to have little competence (Comstock 1926, p. 379).

The press simply did not cover women politicians in the same way as they covered men in public life and congresswomen were asked questions exploring purportedly "female topics," questions that male Representatives were almost never asked. Their views on most national issues and events were rarely solicited, and their unusual status was given far more attention than anything worthwhile they had to say (Blair 1927, p. 542).

Even as late as the mid-1940s, women candidates were subjected to unconventional queries. At a press conference held during her first House campaign, Helen Gahagan Douglas found attention paid to her hat (photographers said it was too large), her knees (which were revealed when she sat down in a tight skirt), the color of her eyes, and what she would wear when she addressed the Democratic National Convention. Only a few questions dealt with her political views (Douglas 1982, p. 196).

When newspaper and magazine writers engaged in the often sterile but "amusing" speculation about which women might be given serious consideration for a congressional, or even a presidential nomination, the women mentioned were rarely those who had begun political careers of their own. Named were women married (or otherwise related) to nationally known political or industrial figures (Blair 1927, p. 542). They included among them Alice Roosevelt Longworth, Anne Morgan (of the House of Morgan), and Ruth Hanna McCormick (who, indeed, did eventually serve in the House, but not before her husband, U.S. Senator Joseph Medill McCormick, died).

The image of the congresswoman as a curiosity appears to have influenced the treatment she received from male Representatives. She was patronized, condescended to, and ignored or dismissed by her colleagues, depending upon which of the House rituals was called for by the legislative "script." The swearing-in ceremony for women was greeted with considerably more applause and patronizing comment than was the case for men. Winnifred Mason Huck, the third woman to serve in the House, recalled how she received a bouquet of flowers from Alice Robertson, the only other woman serving at the time, and the happy, enthusiastic reaction of her fellow House members when she was escorted up to the Speaker's Chair to take the oath of office (Huck 1923, p. 4). Of course the effusiveness of the response could be explained by the fact that she was replacing her recently deceased father, a man well known and admired by many of her new colleagues. But it is hard to imagine so festive an air if, for example, William Mason's son, rather than his daughter, had been succeeding him.

After they began their legislative service, congresswomen were often treated to oratorical excesses which heaped lavish praise upon them and others of their gender. "To the ladies, God bless them; they lend sweetness and light to our somber legislative halls" was among the choicest bouquets tossed in their direction. On one occasion Mary Norton of New Jersey was so exasperated by these comments that she cried out "I'm no lady. I'm a congressman" (Porter 1943, p. 22). The New Jersey Democrat must have been incensed when a Republican whose position she had attacked replied: "We can, dear lady, reason with you only with our hearts, not our minds" (Davis 1943).

Many House members seemed to use the advent of women in their membership as an occasion for demonstrating just how gallant they could be. Queen Guinevere could not have been attended by a more chivalrous array of courtiers. A veteran Capitol Hill writer, Duff Gilfond, described the scene in this way:

> The courtly Speaker [Nicholas Longworth] set the precedent. Tenderly referring to the new female members as gentlewomen, he created an atmosphere in which every politician in the House turned into a knight. To greet a gentlewoman's request or recitation with anything less than applause would now cause a sensation. Some time ago . . . veterans of the rowdyish Tammany Hall actually withdrew an amendment to a tax bill so that the gentlewoman from New Jersey, Mrs. Norton, could have the privilege of introducing it; and the hard-hitting [Fiorello] LaGuardia, after a recitation by Gentlewoman Ruth Owen confessed: 'If it were not for the irresistable appeal made by the charming Representative from the State of Florida, I would object; but under the circumstances, I cannot.'

Gilfond added:

> So gallant are these rascals on the floor that nobody would think of taking them to task for the unimportant committee assignments they hand out to the girls (Gilfond 1929, p. 151).

Even if Gilfond may have overstated the case (some women did, after all, receive important committee assignments during this period), the moments of legitimate female glory in the 1920s, 1930s, and 1940s were few indeed. When the leaders of the House decided to permit a woman to preside over that chamber for the first time, they chose to make it while a roll-call vote was underway and, therefore, when the temporary "Speaker" was unable to exercise any of the powers that accompany the position. Feminist observers were outraged both by the patronizing manner with which the ritual was carried out and the inconsequential issue at stake. One wrote:

> They were calling the roll on a vote to send a representative from the United States to the Peruvian Centennial. Momentous occasion! And 'Sister Alice Robertson, the lady from Oklahoma,' was allowed to stand up like a little man and hold the gavel in her hand all by herself for one brief moment! Wonderful privilege! But before anyone could address her as 'Miss Speaker,' it was all over (Clarke 1925, p. 95).

Critics were anguished not only at the perfunctory nature of the event and the fact that Representative Robertson had permitted herself to be used in this way, but they were incensed, as well, by the fact that Robertson had been among the strongest opponents of the 19th Amendment and they believed there were women far more deserving of recognition than she.

But most of the time congresswomen seem to have been ignored or simply dismissed as unimportant by other Representatives, as well as by official Washington. Their status as House members was devalued by men as high up in the capital's pecking order as the President and party leaders and by individuals as low down in that order as House doorkeepers, guards, pages, and elevator operators. Winnifred Mason Huck could not find a place to powder her nose, in spite of the fact that she had learned all about Capitol Hill while her father was serving in the House and the Senate (Huck 1923), and leaders of her party " . . . took a dim view of lady members at the working level." These men " . . . don't dispute woman's right to run for election and serve," said one Washington observer, "But they privately believe few women possess the political savvy, shrewdness and, above all, the level-headed qualities needed to function properly as a party legislator" (Lockett 1950).

Stories are legion of congresswomen who were told that they could not come on to the House floor or enter certain elevators because they were "reserved for members" (see Wiley 1947, p. 155, for example). According to Republican leader Joseph Martin, women who were not members were sometimes inadvertantly permitted on the floor because the men guarding the doors to the chamber were so uncertain about who the congresswomen were and what they looked like that several women distinguished enough in appearance and carriage were permitted to penetrate the inner sanctum, even though they were not lawmakers. Martin describes some of what he calls the "strange things" that occurred in the House during his first fifty years in politics:

> I can see some of them distinctly in my memory: The woman dressed in pure white, who suddenly appeared in the center aisle, and walked majestically to the well of the House, hoping to deliver a message. Another mysterious woman dressed in pure black who slipped past a doorkeeper and took a seat on the Democratic side in such dignity that no one at first could be sure whether she was a member of Congress or not, even though she had not been seen there before (Martin 1960, p. 212).

Even an embattled President Franklin Roosevelt, seeking to mend his fences with a hostile Congress, forgot the congresswomen. Late in 1938, the White House arranged for the President to meet with all congressional Democrats to mark the close of the 75th Congress, a Congress that had been deeply divided over administration proposals to increase the membership of the Supreme Court and drastically reorganize the federal bureaucracy. The place chosen for the three-day bash was the Jefferson Island Club, situated on a Maryland Island retreat used by Senator Millard Tydings. There, about 400 Senate and House Democrats were expected to exchange pleasantries with the

President, smooth over personal antagonisms that had developed in the Congress which had just adjourned, and produce the kind of party unity needed to successfully contest the imminent mid-term congressional elections.

The fact that the Jefferson Island Club excluded women was either unknown to the White House or deemed insufficiently important, and a half-dozen female Democrats were unable to attend the weekend gathering. This in spite of the fact that the New Deal credentials of most of the Democratic women were among the most authentic in Congress. They kept a stiff upper lip, however, and some suggested that the slight was a blessing. "We will have a chance to give him our views another time in less crowded circumstances," one woman said, "when we won't have to compete for his attention with all those males" (*New York Times* June 17, 1938).

As the years of this early period passed, more and more women were elected to the House and an increasing proportion began to speak out in a bold, independent fashion. A few exercised some influence and their aggressiveness and power could not easily be ignored. Some of the men abandoned the gallantry exhibited earlier and resorted to harsher and more pointed means of putting congresswomen in their place. When the outspoken "gentlewoman from Massachusetts," Edith Nourse Rogers, one day during debate asked if a male colleague would yield, he responded with what he doubtless considered to be humor, as well as rancor: "Not now. It's not very often that we men are in a position where we can make the ladies sit down and keep quiet" (Wiley 1947, p. 157).

But the statement which is perhaps most revealing of both male condescension and insensitivity to the feelings of congresswomen was made during the opening weeks of the 80th Congress, the first full Congress to convene after the end of World War II. The speaker was Charles Gifford of Massachusetts, one of the more senior and, at the time, respected members of the House. The statement is all the more remarkable because it appeared in the *Congressional Record* and Gifford presumably had had an opportunity to "revise and extend" his remarks before they were published. The speech is a rambling one, covering three pages of the *Record*, but most of the relevant portions are included in the following excerpt:

> Mr. Speaker, . . . I have my anxieties about the present Congress and the future, and as an older member, I am anxious to know what the new members will bring to us in abilities and opinion. As I look to my left, I see the face of a new lady member. I wish that all other lady members were present. May I say to her, one of the great worries I have in Congress itself is lest we have too many of you. Although I say this in a somewhat jocular way, still I am a little serious about it.
>
> The lady members we have today are extremely satisfactory to us. But they, like all women, can talk to us with their eyes and their lips, and when they present to us an apple it is most difficult to refuse. Even old Adam could

not resist. Women have a language all their own. I do not like to particularize but I should. I see the gentlewoman from Ohio [Mrs. Bolton] is present. I read or listen carefully to everything she says on the floor. . . . Because I admire her so much I could hardly resist. I fear supporting any measure that she would propose, especially if she looked at me as such a woman can. The gentlewoman from Maine [Margaret Chase Smith] . . . never seems to have a vacant chair beside her that I could take and get acquainted with her . . . these ladies are so attractive. They are dangerous in that they may influence us too much. Suppose we had fifty of them. Seemingly, I note flirtations enough now, but what would there be with fifty of them? (U.S. Congress, *Congressional Record* 1947, pp. 631–32).

A contemporary feminist could not concoct a statement which would, more than Gifford's, cogently document male chauvinism in high places. His harangue makes explicit or implicit reference to virtually all of the female stereotypes embraced by his contemporaries. These congresswomen are "satisfactory" to male needs. But they are also manipulating, enticing, conspiratorial, unreliable, flirtatious, and objects of physical appeal. That Gifford could make these kinds of allusions without thought, let alone fear, of being challenged is convincing testimony to the 'all male" mentality of the House of Representatives.

A few months later, Gifford was dead, stricken while still a member of Congress. But, before long, male Representatives began to see congresswomen in a different light, in part because the qualities of the women coming to the House had changed.

TREATMENT OF CONTEMPORARY CONGRESSWOMEN

The testimony offered by two dozen Representatives of both genders and by thirty-six Capitol Hill staff members during the 95th Congress provides a rich array of perceptions about male treatment of female House members. Although there is widespread belief that the House continues to be a male institution, virtually all respondents, male as well as female, acknowledged that today's congresswoman is considerably better off than her predecessors. She is given more of a chance to participate as an equal in the legislative process and her views are more likely to be respected than were those of former congresswomen. She is consulted often, she takes the initiative on a wide range of issues, and she is valued for the efforts she brings to House tasks.

In the meantime, open condescension has diminished, fewer congressmen consciously attempt to patronize female members, and achievements recorded by many women Representatives have made it impossible for them to be collectively ignored or dismissed. Several House members noted that remarkable changes had taken place in these respects even during the relatively few years in which they had served.

On the other hand, virtually all respondents felt that congresswomen continued to labor under noticeable handicaps. In her study of women in state legislatures, Kirkpatrick found four forms of discrimination to which they were subjected. These included linguistic conventions which make reference to males only, rather than men and women collectively; a "killing with kindness" through over-protective or openly flirtatious behavior; an exclusion based upon the belief that women legislators are interested in a narrow range of issues and should not be bothered with broader, more weighty matters; and a propensity to "put women in their place" through snide or insulting remarks (Kirkpatrick 1974, p. 109). Respondents agreed that present day congresswomen experience all of these "put downs," but there was less agreement on the extent to which this treatment occurred. Furthermore, there were important differences in the impressions offered by most male Representatives and those offered by most female House members, and it is appropriate, therefore, to examine these responses separately.

Male Perceptions

While acknowledging the unequal treatment given congresswomen, most male Representatives tended to stress the infrequency with which it occurred and the change for the better that had taken place in recent years. The open discrimination they observed was relatively rare and, for the most part, unsystematic. Even covert behavior of this kind, perpetrated, for example, within an all-male setting, was not common. Furthermore, few could recall instances of cavalier or condescending behavior. Many male informants also felt that the occasional incidents of discrimination were not as flagrant as they used to be.

But some noted two sets of conditions which contributed most to the isolated instances of unequal treatment. One was the presence in the House of women who had succeeded husbands who had died while serving in the House. Another was the presence in the House of a few men, not many according to most male informants, who were disdainful of all women, but especially contemptuous of women who were assertive or who gained positions of influence.

Attitudes toward specific widows who had succeeded husbands varied considerably. Some were admired, others were thought to be incompetent or "useless," and much depended upon which respondent was doing the evaluating. But the comments of some Representatives suggested that most widows fell into a category of House members who "did not make it on their own" and who, therefore, were incapable of contributing very much to House functions. They were seen as having inherited their positions, and there was some question about the legitimacy of their credentials. Two male respondents stated that they themselves, tended to "write off" these women as of little consequence, a practice that was confirmed by a widow who said: "When I first got here, I think a number of members did not take me seriously. I was just a woman who would be gone after two years and I was not important enough to think about or get to know."

One congressman who was critical of women who had succeeded their husbands in the House remarked:

> Mrs. _____ sits there prettily and never says anything. People ignore her. She is strictly her husband's stand in and has never done anything to change that impression. . . . But she succeeded her husband and there really isn't much you can expect from her. It is different for women who come here as a result of their husbands' service.

Other male Representatives said that these women were patronized by some of the older members, perhaps because of relationships formed when the widows' husbands were alive. Respondents felt that such behavior was good neither for other congresswomen nor for the House.

Testimony provided by several male respondents suggests that there exists in the House a relatively small number of men who are scornful of most if not all women with whom they serve. They tend to be among the more senior members, although, according to most respondents, there is no necessary relationship between seniority and male chauvinism. These men are quick with a wise crack, an obscene joke, or a snide reference, utterances often delivered in a stage whisper to an all-male audience.

Sometimes the comment will be expressed within the hearing of a congresswoman in an effort to "get under her skin." The target may be a single Representative or women in general. These men may exchange a knowing look and a smile with a male colleague when a female Representative says something which strikes them as "silly," "unnecessary," "dumb," "insignificant," or "feminist." Her statement is then understood as something only a "frivolous," "disorganized," "unintelligent," "parochial," or "castrating" woman would say. According to many informants, these men believe that their insulting or derisive remarks and gestures raise their own stature in the eyes of colleagues and that their reputation as "one of the boys" is thereby confirmed.

Such House members cannot always be identified from their voting records or public statements, and even most feminists would find the roll call votes of some faultless. "At the substantive policy level," said one respondent, "many of these fellows seem as sensitive to, and as understanding of, women's problems as any member of the House." Political ideology or policy orientation, then, are not as useful a pair of distinguishing characteristics as are the basic attitudes these men have toward women generally.

One legislative assistant told a story about a congressman who had impeccable liberal credentials but who was among the males frequently criticized for insensitive treatment of women members. The aide and his congressman were working on an amendment to a bill that was coming up for debate the following week. They asked this liberal member to stop by the office when he had an opportunity to go over the amendment draft. He arrived that evening about seven o'clock accompanied by a woman, and both wore formal evening dress—she in a long gown, he in a black tie. It was clear that they were about to go out for the evening and it appeared as if he had stopped by just for a few minutes to go over the language of the amendment. The aide recalled the incident:

> He asked if our secretary had gone home for the day and when my boss said 'yes,' he told the woman he was with to sit in the outer office to take all calls so we wouldn't be disturbed. Then the three of us went into the back office and for four hours we worked on the draft. He never once went outside the room to see how she was doing or even to say how much longer he would be. At about eleven o'clock we walked out and she was sitting just where she had been sitting when we had started the meeting. And she got up and walked out with him without a word. This tells you something about how this man sees either the woman he was with or women in general, and I think it's both.

Although several male Representatives said that a decreasing number of members can be described in this way, some also pointed out that many male members, including themselves, were sometimes critical of individual women members. But they argued that their disparaging remarks were no different from those they would use about males who were guilty of similarly lamentable behavior. They pointed out that sometimes it is difficult to distinguish between criticism emerging out of male chauvinism and the same response which springs from some other orientation. They asserted that most congressmen are no more critical of women colleagues than they are of male Representatives, but that sometimes it may appear as if they are harsher on the women.

Respondents singled out specific congresswomen for their "incompetence," or their "mediocrity," or their "perverseness," or for their frequent violations of House norms, but they went on to name males who they have criticized on the same grounds. One congressman put it this way:

> It's hard to determine whether negative assessments are based on sexist or on other grounds. Some of the men here wouldn't take much of anything a woman said seriously, but it is not a general attitude. Most of us might criticize a woman for talking too much on the House floor, but that doesn't mean that we don't hold her in high regard, nonetheless. And it doesn't mean that we are predisposed to think that her weakness is a failing all other women share. And if I feel that a particular congresswoman is too 'motherly,' that feeling detracts very little from my assessment of her as an effective member.

What this and other male informants stressed is that there is an important difference between Representatives who hold the view expressed in the above quotation and those who are systematically contemptuous of female House members. The former, they argue, are not prepared to generalize about all women members on the basis of isolated indiscretions or idiosyncrasies. The latter, on the other hand, relatively small in number, perceive and use these events and personal attributes to reinforce already negative predispositions.

Female Perceptions and Reactions

The women members interviewed readily agreed that they were much better off than female predecessors and that they were working with a new breed of male—more sensitive to their needs and feelings, more willing to treat them as equals, and more apt to share responsibility with them. But most of these women felt that condescending, patronizing, and, less often, just plain insulting treatment was more frequent than most males believed was the case. Furthermore, they were convinced that instances of such treatment were more flagrant and more widespread than was acknowledged by their male colleagues. One congresswoman estimated that there were about 100 "macho sons-of-bitches" in the House, about 100 "decent, sensitive guys," and about 200 "in between." "It's a normal curve," she said. Another woman, one for whom a number of male respondents indicated a high regard, would not cite figures, but felt it wasn't "quite as bad as all that." She asserted:

> There is an unmistakably macho attitude among some males, but not that many. Sure, there are some leering, macho men. But most of the chauvinism we experience is unconscious; but you don't find these things in the House anymore than you find them anywhere else.

A third congresswoman was not quite as charitable. She observed that some congressmen were not accustomed to treating women as equals, but rather like "tables." "If you dust them off once a day, they will be kept happy." She noted that one congressman had tried patiently to explain to her that being in Congress meant Chivas Regal, beautiful women, and Lear jets. "You see," she added, "women are 'things' just like Lear jets and liquor."

Apart from confirming some "macho" behavior in the House, these statements touch on two other ideas that were referred to frequently by other female members. The first is that such behavior is engaged in by members of the House in roughly the same measure as males display it in other organizations and within society in general. The point more relevant to the present discussion is that most of this overt behavior is "unconscious." Almost all of the women interviewed noted the "unintentional" nature of many of the indiscretions they observed.

Female reactions to what they perceive as objectionable male behavior varied, depending upon the woman, the nature of the insult, and the circumstances under which it occurred. One response noted frequently by informants was simply to ignore the slight. One congresswoman said:

> I don't feel or experience most of the macho behavior. Maybe because it is not important to me. . . . Moreover, my job is to forget the irrelevancies, such as mode or form of address, or who should get off the elevator first, and focus on the things that are really important here—my committee work, legislation, and my constituents.

Several other congresswomen indicated that they had neither the time nor the inclination to make an issue of most male indiscretions. They felt that there were too many more important matters that demanded their attention and their energies. Furthermore, some felt that if you called these gaffes to the attention of erring males, many would be defensive about their behavior or feel embarrassed. These men might also feel you were blowing a minor point out of proportion, thereby jeopardizing what might otherwise be a perfectly friendly, helpful relationship. One woman noted that sometimes sexist remarks are uttered in jest and that "you have to be a good sport to get anywhere in this House." She added:

> As a matter of fact, a good deal of affection is shown through the ribbing that takes place here. Some of the jokes would drive a New York feminist up the wall, but you come to accept them. And you have to be less uptight about these things because they are meant to be funny.

Another female member reported that there was one male colleague who let out a wolf whistle whenever he saw her, adding that it was just "a little joke" between the two of them.

One legislative aide recalled an incident in which a subcommittee chairman, a courtly, southern gentleman, called upon a young, unmarried congresswoman to make an opening statement just after their subcommittee convened and he referred to her as "Mrs. _____." She ignored the slip and was about to read her first sentence when the chairman interrupted to apologize for the error and added with fatherly affection, "We wouldn't want to chase the fellas away." By correcting the mistake and adding what many felt was a patronizing comment, the chairman had made matters worse. A subsequent interview with the congresswoman involved, however, produced the following response: "But my chairman is a charming and gracious man who has behaved this way all of his life and I would be hurting his feelings more than he hurt mine if I objected to his remarks."

In this connection, another congresswoman remarked:

> Several congresswomen are patronized by male members, particularly the older members. There is one woman member who is very young and is really

a bright, energetic, secure woman. And the men treat her like their daughter. She is young enough to be their daughter, and they don't act that way to be deliberately impolite or condescending, but that's the way they feel. They say such things as 'now listen here, young lady' or 'listen here, dear' ('dear' is very often used), 'you have to understand that I've seen a lot more than you and you're so young and inexperienced.'

Some female members try to use this behavior to their advantage. About a half-dozen congresswomen insisted that there were certain positive aspects to being a woman in the House and that they are happy to take advantage of the courtesies which men of the kind described in the preceeding accounts are inclined to dispense. Most pointed out that the help they may receive from chivalrous colleagues was no substitute for the hard work, knowledge, and professionalism that they themselves had to demonstrate. But they felt that once a woman had gained the respect of a gallant male Representative, there was nothing wrong with requesting his help on, say, an amendment or cosponsorship possibilities—thereby capitalizing on his experience and gentlemanly predispositions. One woman put it this way:

In some ways the deference women receive is to their advantage. I know that many younger women here, and in every profession, dismiss any special treatment as condescending, as a kind of male chauvinism. It isn't chauvinism. This male behavior is ingrained in men of certain age. It is an act of respect and most of us, at least I, accept it and make the most of it.

Another congresswoman stated:

There are advantages to being a woman that no woman would admit. There are so few women anywhere that they stand out wherever they are. They are an easily recognizable minority. In addition, men are trained to some kind of courtesy and we benefit from that. I would never have gotten some of the bills I introduced in the state legislature passed if I were not a woman. The leadership was being nice to me.

Although most congresswomen were willing to overlook what they considered minor annoyances produced by male behavior, some were not as forgiving as others, and many were prepared to challenge what they considered serious male indiscretions. These women are not inclined to ignore discriminatory language in proposed legislation, for example. One woman indicated that she had introduced many amendments to bills which made the language apply to both males and females. She described how she once asked a subcommittee chairman who was explaining a measure and who continually used "he" and "him," whether the legislation would apply to women. He apologized and said he would make the appropriate changes. "But," she added, "you have to remind them of these things all the time."

Several women noted that there were times when male colleagues were so patronizing that they could not help but make their displeasure known. One recalled that when she appeared on the House floor for the first time, the only subject some of the men raised was what her husband thought about her serving in Congress and how she planned to run a household while working full time. "They were nice, but they treated me as some kind of strange animal—and I finally started asking them what their wives thought of their serving in the House while there was a household to maintain and children to bring up." She added: "Some laughed and a few were embarrassed or sort of sheepish, but some had no idea of what I was getting at."

Another female Representative also recalled the annoying behavior of male members during her first few months in the House.

> Several said how glad they were that I didn't wear pants suits, as if it is their business. Plenty of women wear pant suits; why should that be so important to them? To their way of thinking, a woman in a pants suit was doing something wrong. But that's changed. That was five years ago. Now its not mentioned, although some men may still think about it.

Details of an incident involving a former congresswoman were published some time ago and are relevant here. According to her account, she was riding in an elevator with a Democratic Senator whom she considered "one of God's more stupid creatures," when:

> ... with that great condescension of which the male of the species is so guilty so many times, he literally patted me on the shoulder like a small child then took hold of my dress and said: 'Myy, what a P-R-E-T-T-Y dress you have!' I couldn't stand it! ... So I turned to him and in a voice imitating his, said: 'Myyyy what a lovely suit you're wearing. You *are* handsome' (Dreifus 1972).

But the incident which received most attention in the 95th Congress, including coverage in at least one major newspaper, occurred during a committee meeting while a male member, known for his graciousness and charm, was addressing the group. A woman committee member asked if he would yield and he responded "In just a minute cutie pie," and went on speaking. The sound of his own voice probably obscured the bristling response from the woman, who was in the process of asking him just who he thought he was calling "cutie pie." He responded to what he thought was her continuing request for the floor with "just a few minutes, honey." The congresswoman then interrupted committee proceedings, referred to him as "Congressman cutie pie," objected vociferously to his language, and asserted her strong woman's liberation orientation.

Some of the women indicated that they were aware of other, more vicious and more calculating insults directed toward them and toward other women, but they are the kinds of remarks uttered less frequently today, partly because most congresswomen would not countenance them and partly because many men wouldn't either. But stories had gotten back to female members that some men felt threatened by them or that they had been characterized as "hard-nosed," or "unpredictable" or "unreliable bitches." The vulgar character of some comments made in private was revealed during the Abscam trials of House members accused of taking bribes from FBI undercover agents disguised as Arab shieks. Secret tape recordings made of the transactions had one male Representative referring casually to a congresswoman whose suggested "meanness" was a product of her " . . . never [having] been laid" (Anderson and Cappaccio 1980).

The tendency of another congresswoman occasionally to employ language calculated to shock male listeners led to a well publicized exchange between her and her committee chairman. The congresswoman in question " . . . likes to use the word 'vagina'," said one male respondent. "It stops most men cold for a moment and she slips it into conversation for effect." She used this tactic with the chairman one day when he refused to sign a travel voucher entitling her to reimbursement for committee-related travel expenses. After the argument had proceeded for a few minutes, she had become exasperated and said: "The only reason you won't sign is because I have a vagina." The chairman is reported to have replied: "Well, if you used your vagina more and your mouth less you might get someplace around here." The exchange is revealing on several counts, but perhaps the most telling is that it illustrates the alacrity with which the chairman was prepared to formulate his comeback within a flagrantly sexist frame of reference, the same framework he had doubtless employed many times before within the confines of an all male audience.

Gender-based resentment expressed by congressmen is usually directed toward women who are successful. Sponsoring a useful amendment, appointment to a desirable committee, selection for a plum by party leaders sometimes generate derisive or heated comments, comments which some respondents concluded stemmed from deeply felt jealousy. A woman Representative provided the following explanation for such a reaction:

> Some men in the House feel that they are not going to let some 'girl' get ahead of them. They feel that they are overburdened, harrassed, and overworked, and they feel that women couldn't possibly be as overworked as they are. . . . and they are not going to be out-done by a woman.

It would seem, then, that most women are inclined to look the other way when objectionable remarks and behavior occurring in their presence are unintentional or offered in jest, or perpetrated in a private, rather than a public forum, or when a response may be more self-defeating than the perceived harm done by the action in the first place. But when the comment is snide or intentionally demeaning or uttered in public, most contemporary congress-women will not let it go unchallenged. Their response may take a number of forms, including an angry retort, sarcasm, humor, or simply straightforward chastisement, depending upon the nature of the indiscretion and the personality and style of the woman witnessing it. Whatever the form, these reactions represent a pattern of responses which was conspicuously absent from the behavioral repertoires of most women serving in the House in the years before World War II.

Finally, a few of the same women who respond to unequal treatment by ignoring it, or by trying to exploit it, or by challenging it, also respond to it by behaving in a way which tends to reduce the differences between what they believe is their own perceived behavior and model male behavior. There are not many respondents whose reactions can be described in this way, and few may be willing to acknowledge such a tactic. Nevertheless, some of the things they have said and done may be interpreted as efforts to produce such a result. It would appear that they are trying to show their male colleagues that they are not only as tough, as cold, as unemotional, as infallible and as efficient as any of them, traits which most Americans think are obligatory in good public officials, but that they can also use locker-room language as casually and as naturally as most men do with one another.

Sometimes a congresswoman will do it in an open and dramatic way, as in the case of the member who surprised her colleagues and some businessmen at a committee hearing that was having difficulty getting underway. The business-men who had come to testify and some of the committee members had spent more than twenty minutes exchanging effusive and exaggerated praise for one another, a common Capitol Hill practice. The congresswoman finally interjected the remark: "Can you gentlemen please stop all of this bullshit and tell us about the problems you came to tell us about?"

Her comment "broke the ice," and the committee turned to the business at hand. Colleagues and lobbyists came away from the session favorably impressed with this fiesty female member who, as one observer put it, "has real balls." Apparently one reason male members of the committee welcomed her behavior was that they, too, were getting weary of the delay and she had expressed a sentiment with which they heartily agreed. But she did it in a way which, ironically, they would never have dreamed of doing, in the mixed company of an open committee hearing.

This example is not an isolated instance of a congresswoman employing a term not normally heard in the mixed company of House members. For there is additional evidence that male and female members have begun to be much less inhibited in the language they use with one another and it is clear that some feel perfectly free to tell a Representative of the opposite sex that he or she is "full of shit." Since Congress is an organization which has institutionalized the exchange of all shades of opinion, opportunities for making such charges are not infrequent.

Apparently there is such a thing as going too far, however. One congresswoman put it this way:

> A group of us were meeting to discuss a proposal and after we completed our formal business, we adjourned and went for a drink. A point was reached in our conversation, maybe after the second drink, when the nature of the jokes was such that if I had stayed it would have detracted from myself. You reach a point when you demean yourself and the locker-room mentality prevails. There really is a line. *We* have to do something about whether we are included and sometimes it's best to leave. There is a difference between being raw and vulgar and being saucy and spicy. [The emphasis is the speaker's.]

Change in what is considered acceptable language exchanged between congressmen and congresswomen is doubtless a reflection of what is happening in the larger society. But it is possible to interpret one of the usages to which this tendency is being put as an effort by some female members to promote their acceptance as equals and to facilitate their integration into what is still an essentially male institution.

INTEGRATION OF WOMEN INTO THE HOUSE

Among the inferences to be drawn from the testimony of contemporary House members, the most important is that the routine treatment women have received from male colleagues has changed significantly. This change has occurred in spite of the fact that the House is still perceived as a male institution by both male and female members. To be sure, women continue to be subjected to condescending and patronizing behavior. But the number of men who indulge themselves in this fashion is smaller than was the case in the past, the frequency with which such discrimination occurs is diminishing, and the seriousness of the indiscretions is less marked. Congresswomen saw less of a change in these regards than did congressmen.

Members of both groups believed that most discrimination suffered by female members by virtue of their gender is unintentional, and female members felt that much of it is either of insufficient importance to warrant a response, or that it is self-defeating to do so. None felt the unequal treatment is harmful enough to prevent them from serving as effective members of the House. Indeed, some women believed that the willingness of male members to patronize them could be used to advantage.

Both male and female respondents agreed, however, that there are isolated instances of serious discrimination in the routine interaction that takes place between male and female members. This behavior is engaged in by a comparatively small, vanishing group of men who are disinclined to take most female members seriously. They have little difficulty creating justifications for ridiculing congresswomen behind their backs, and they sometimes treat women condescendingly in face-to-face encounters. When serious indiscretions are perpetrated openly, however, contemporary congresswomen, far more than their pre-World War II predecessors, are likely to challenge such behavior.

These responses have probably contributed to a decline in overtly discriminatory behavior. Male Representatives cautioned to use "she" or "her," as well as "he" and "him" in legislative proposals and amendments are likely to recall such reminders the next time they are hammering out legislative language. The same members are also likely to think twice before they call a female colleague "honey," and they will probably show increasing respect, even if grudging, for women who have been unwilling to remain silent in the face of open condescension or male chauvinism.

Also contributing to fuller integration of female members has been the increasing professionalism contemporary congresswomen have brought with them to the House. Male members cannot help but be aware of the elective experience, legal training and political savvy more and more congresswomen are demonstrating while performing House tasks. These women command treatment as equals and as colleagues, a development explored more fully in Chapter 12, and congressmen who treat them lightly run the risk of looking foolish in the eyes of male, as well as female, Representatives.

Whatever the strategies contemporary congresswomen have employed to find a place for themselves in the House, they have been aided by an increasing number of male allies. Turnover has accelerated in recent years and more Representatives are in their late 20s, 30s, and early 40s.[3] Some attended colleges, graduate schools, and law schools after traditional gender roles and the cultural values underlying them had come under attack from the women's movement. Many matriculated with women whose educational and vocational aspirations were the same as their own and, perhaps because of the increased visibility of these women, their achievement levels were perceived as similar to their own. Some of these soon-to-be congressmen married women who were positively inclined toward the women's liberation movement. And it is reasonable to assume that these spouses raised their husband's consciousness about discrimination based upon gender. One congresswoman noted in the interview that some of the wives of younger House members had asked about the possibility of meeting with congresswomen as a group to discuss matters of mutual interest.

But for some veteran congressmen, the appropriate mode of interaction with women colleagues is not an obvious one. One older House member, a committee chairman, approached a female colleague and implored her to tell him how he should "act toward women." He had always seen himself as a "gallant gentleman" and he was uncertain how he could alter a code of behavior to which he had always adhered in his relationship with women. He wanted desperately to work effectively with younger, female members and, said the congresswoman, "He came to me to learn and do the right thing."

Another congresswoman recalled that after a particularly embarrassing exchange she had had with her committee chairman over flippant and flagrantly condescending remarks he had directed toward her, a male member of the committee came to her and said that he represented a group of congressmen who had observed the exchange and wanted to help but did not know what to do. He asked whether they should have come to her defense or let her fight her own battles. She added:

> This shows the confusion some of the men face. I asked him what he would have done if a black member of the committee had been referred to as 'boy,' and he said that he would have been insulted and come to that member's defense. And I said that if you would come to my defense because you thought I was a defenseless female, then don't bother. But if you thought that I had been insulted and that the committee process had been impaired, then it would have been proper. He then went to the chairman and I received what I felt was a gracious and sincere apology.

These incidents reveal the uncertainty some congressmen feel about the ways male and female Representatives ought to interact with one another, and about the gender and legislative roles they occupy and perform, a significant finding that will be discussed within a broader conceptual framework in Chapter 12.

For now, it is important to point out that, although contemporary congresswomen are not fully integrated into the House, they have made demonstrable gains in that direction. The routine treatment they receive from males has come to resemble more closely than in the past the treatment congressmen extend to other male colleagues. Today, it is difficult to imagine a male Representative rising to "bless the ladies," and it is all but impossible to envision a speech appearing in the *Congressional Record* similar to the one given by Congressman Gifford in 1947. If, by some stretch of the imagination, a congressman delivered one, it is safe to assume that the *Record* would also show that the gentlewomen and, doubtless, some gentlemen, presented appropriate rejoinders.

But if the treatment women receive in routine interaction with males is demonstrably more even-handed than it was in the past, the treatment they receive today on nonroutine matters has not changed quite as much. True, their access to important informal groups has expanded considerably, and few established caucuses contain no women at all. But there are some groups which women have never penetrated, and it is to these matters that we turn next.

NOTES

1. None of these works explicitly defines the term "male institution." Questions posed to House members in the 95th Congress did not ask for a definition of such an institution, but answers to other queries (see Appendix C) suggest that, for these Representatives, a "male institution" has some or all of the following characteristics: a preponderant proportion of its membership is male; its members define the institution as "male"; the routine treatment accorded to males by one another is advantageously different from the routine treatment accorded to females by male colleagues; the institution's basic and subsidiary facilities satisfy the needs of males more fully than they satisfy the needs of females; and the institution's influence structure is more accessible to males than it is to females.

2. Thirteen of the twenty-four House members interviewed were female—eighteen women were in the House at the time. A total of thirty-six administrative and legislative staff aides were also interviewed, all but six of whom served on members' office staffs. The remainder were attached to committee and House staffs.

3. One way of demonstrating an increase in House turnover is to compare the number of House members who had served three terms or less at the start of the last four Congresses with the number who had served a comparable length of time in the four Congresses preceding the 95th. From 1969 to 1975, an average of 165 House members had served no more than three terms. From 1977 to 1983, on the other hand, the number never slipped below 200 and the average for the four terms was 209.

5 / Access to Informal Channels of Communication: Women and House Caucuses

Informal discussions House members have with one another do not lend themselves to ready observation, and relatively little has been written on the subject. Representatives communicate among themselves informally in many settings—on the floor of the House, in one another's offices, and in House corridors, to mention just a few. These conversations take place on hundreds of thousands of occasions annually and they collectively embrace the entire range of matters of concern to social beings who also happen to be elected public officials.

Accordingly, congressional observers undertake a formidable task when they try to single out informal interactions sufficiently significant to warrant systematic attention, or when they attempt to analyze the patterns of informal influence Representatives exert upon one another. Those who follow the behavior of female House members must bear the additional burden of learning the extent to which variations in these patterns are gender-related. Among other things, they want to know the extent to which women are an integral part of the informal communications network and the extent to which they are excluded from these channels.

The research approach adopted here is to concentrate upon the informal groups that operate within the House. These groups were chosen as a focus because they are among the most important crucibles within which, hidden from public scrutiny, information and ideas are exchanged, legislative tactics and strategies formulated, coalitions and majorities mobilized, and confidences shared (Stevens et al. 1980). At the same time, they affect and are affected by the structure of influence within the House, the range and nature of public policy options open to the House, and the effectiveness and influence of individual House members. This approach has its drawbacks, inasmuch as some important relationships are established and decisions made in ways that have little to do with group life. The approach is appealing, nonetheless, because the House possesses an extraordinarily rich array of active caucuses, and because exchanges that take place within them often have a significant impact on the behavior and careers of House members.

Male and female Representatives in the 95th Congress were asked about their own membership in informal groups and about the extent to which one or more of these groups excluded congresswomen because of their gender. Respondents were also asked about the extent to which group affiliation had anything to do with the legislative and institutional success of group members. What follows is a distillation of the answers to these questions. In addition, inferences are drawn about changes that have taken place in the access women have had to small groups during the last twenty years, and about the disadvantages from which congresswomen suffer by virtue of their being excluded from some of these groups. But first the groups must be defined.

INFORMAL GROUPS IN THE HOUSE

The House of Representatives, like many other large organizations, contains a number of relatively small, informal groups. These groups have no sanction in law and were recognized only recently by House rules.[1] They are created by combinations of Representatives who decide that they have enough in common with like-minded members to meet with one another on a more or less regular basis and share information, common problems, law making possibilities, and ideas for improving their performance. Members are attracted to each other because of party, ideological, geographic, ethnic, or racial ties, or they may unite because of a pressing economic problem their constituents share. Some may have simply developed a personal rapport with one another, a bond which induces them to meet, compare notes, and enjoy camaraderie.

Groups of this kind have always been present in the House, but only after World War II did they begin to proliferate. Their greatest surge occurred from the mid-1970s through the beginning of the 1980s. From 1977 to 1980, for example, their number doubled, and by the start of the 98th Congress, the figure exceeded fifty.[2] Some of the caucuses formed during these years reaped membership bonanzas, with the Congressional Arts Caucus swelling to 166 in three years and the Tourism Caucus reaching 180 during roughly the same period (*New York Times* January 15, 1983).

The rise of small groups has been linked to greater heterogeneity in the composition of House districts, an increase in the number and complexity of problems which contituents have come to look to Washington for resolution, a decline in party loyalty among voters, and the absence of serviceable ideological frameworks to give order to the broadened range of contemporary issues. Decentralization of the House's power structure and continued parochial concerns of its committees also contributed to their increase (Stevens et al. 1980).

All of these changes made law making and representational tasks more difficult for individual Representatives. The larger, more varied character of their districts and the declining usefulness of formal House instrumentalities increased members' uncertainty about the problems faced by constituents and possible remedies for these problems. They were also more likely to be unsure about the impact legislative proposals would have on the nation and their districts, and about the extent to which enacted measures were, in fact, fulfilling intended purposes.

Members created informal groups to reduce this uncertainty. Among the groups' most important functions is to provide information about pending legislation. They are also a source of voting cues, and they constitute deliberative arenas for shaping legislative, political, and institutional strategies. In addition, they offer opportunities for rank and file members to place high priorities on problems they believe deserve attention, to develop a procedural and substantive expertise that is useful in Congress and in the district, and to promote integrated consideration of policy proposals—measures not likely to receive such consideration from committees shackled by narrow jurisdictional constraints (Stevens et al. 1980). Apart from vastly enriching the social and political lives of their members, these groups also tend to facilitate the congressional decision-making process (Fiellin 1962; Stevens et al. 1980; but see Loomis 1981).

Some groups are "structured" in that they possess an established leadership hierarchy, a paid staff, a well delineated division of labor among its members, a more or less exclusive communications network, a reasonably descriptive title or designation, or enough of these features in sufficient measure to warrant such a classification. Other groups may have relatively little formal structure in that they have no designated leaders, no staff personnel, no subgroups to which tasks may be allocated, and no communications' system other than that which is available to all other House members. Such a group is also less likely to have a name which defines its character and by which members and outsiders can readily refer to it. This distinction is an important one, as will be demonstrated. A reasonably comprehensive, but not exhaustive list of post-World War II groups appears in Table 5.1.

Group meetings may be carefully organized, with an agenda and list of speakers, or they may encourage a free-flowing exchange of views among members. Membership in a group may be taken seriously or viewed casually. It may be permanent or temporary; constant or intermittent. And, finally, membership may be conferred by the group as a whole or it may be contingent upon the needs of the individuals who float in and out of them, depending upon whether affiliation happens to suit their goals at given times and under given circumstances.

Table 5.1. Recent and Current Informal Groups in the U.S. House of Representatives*

Structured Groups

Bipartisan

Alcohol Fuels Caucus	New England Caucus
Arts Caucus	Northeast–Midwest Coalition
Automotive Caucus	Populist Caucus
Black Caucus	Port Caucus
Blue Collar Caucus	Prayer Breakfast Group
Coal Group	Roller/Ball-Bearing Caucus
Environmental Study Conference	Rural Caucus
Ethnic Caucus	Caucus for Science and Technology
Export Task Force	Shipyard Coalition
Federal Government Services Task Force	Ad Hoc Monitoring Group on South Africa
Great Lakes Caucus	Senior Citizens Caucus
Hispanic Caucus	Space Caucus
Human Rights Caucus	State Delegations (e.g., California)
Task Force on Industrial Innovation	Steel Caucus
Ad Hoc Committee for Irish Affairs	Suburban Caucus
Long Island Caucus	Sunbelt Council
Maritime Caucus	Territorial Caucus
Metropolitan Area Caucus	Textile Caucus
Military Reform Caucus	Travel and Tourism Caucus
Mushroom Caucus	Vietnam-Era Veterans Caucus
	Western State Coalition
	Caucus for Women's Issues

Republican

The Acorns	SOS
The Chowder and Marching Society	Republican State Delegations (e.g., New York State Republicans)
Republican "Class" Groups (e.g., the 97th, the 98th)	Republican Study Committee
The Good Guys	The Wednesday Group

Democratic

Conservative Democratic Forum	Democratic State Delegations
Democratic "Class" Groups	Democratic Study Group
Democratic Research Organization	United Democrats of Congress

Unstructured Groups

Sam Rayburn's Board of Education	John McCormack's Poker Playing group
Friendship groups	Sporting groups
Gymnasium groups	

*Based, in part, on Rundquist 1978; Stevens et al. 1980; and Brownson 1983, pp. 438–44.

CONGRESSWOMEN AND INFORMAL GROUPS

One study of state legislatures concluded that women serving in these bodies are "outside the informal communications networks" of which informal groups serve so integral a part and that sometimes female leaders are denied access to the strategy sessions and other meetings to which their *ex officio* leadership status would otherwise entitle them (Jaquette 1974, p. xxx). Until only a few years ago, women in the House of Representatives faced similar deprivations. Based upon interviews with male and female Representatives in 1962, Frieda Gehlen reported that, with the exception of such groups as state delegations and "freshmen classes"—groups to which members were granted automatic membership—and apart from the Democratic Study Group, which admits all Democrats who care to join, women were denied admission into those "informal groups made up of friends and acquaintances who meet more or less regularly to discuss current legislation, general politics, and whatever else comes to mind" (Gehlen, 1969). She pointed out, for example, that apparently no woman had ever been invited to attend "the Board of Education."

The "Board" was a House institution. It had its roots in the friendship of two future House Speakers, Republican Nicholas Longworth and Democrat John Nance Garner. During World War I, the two often met for drinks in a Capitol hideaway called the David Webster Room. Later they moved to an office on the third floor of the Cannon Office Building and began to invite colleagues there to discuss House business over cocktails (which were illegal at the time). When Longworth became Speaker, they moved their meetings to another room, this time under the Capitol dome, and the sessions began to be referred to as the "Board of Education." House members were invited to the inner sanctum, not to be lectured by House leaders, but to reveal what they knew about legislative developments and to indicate by their behavior whether they had leadership potential. Garner explained one of the Board's purposes: "You get a couple of drinks in a young congressman and then you know what he knows and what he can do. We pay the tuition by supplying the liquor" (quoted in MacNeil 1963, p. 82).

Other goals of the Board were to expedite congressional business, negotiate disputes, reach accomodations and gentlemen's agreements, distribute patronage, and provide occasions for camaraderie among men who genuinely enjoyed one another's company. Garner continued the tradition when he became Speaker, as did Sam Rayburn after Garner became Vice President. Rayburn moved the meetings to a small room on the first floor of the Capitol, H-128, and for two decades he and his intimates, Homer Thornberry and Frank Ikard of Texas, Richard Bolling of Missouri, John McCormack of Massachusetts and some Republican leaders, swapped stories, sipped bourbon, and discussed affairs of state.

MacNeil asserts:

These private sessions were one of the most useful tools of the Speaker's leadership in the House. . . . Other influential men of the House were invited to these sessions, particularly when their expert knowledge of specific problems was needed, and they, too, would participate in developing the Speaker's strategy (1963, pp. 83–84).

Interviews with House members in the 95th Congress indicate that, although no woman has been granted access to a group comparable to the Board of Education, a good many have become members of structured informal caucuses. There are many more of these groups today than when Gehlen studied women in the 88th Congress. But even after taking such a change into account, membership in informal groups by congresswomen seems to have increased out of all proportion to the number of opportunities made available to them in recent years. One congresswoman explained why:

A conscientious effort has been made to make congresswomen an integral part of the process. This has happened for two reasons. One, the woman's movement has raised men's consciousness about past discrimination against women. Two, women members have been assertive, so assertive that we will simply not stand for being excluded.

Two all-Republican groups, the "Wednesday Group" and the "Good Guys" included female members, even though the second of the two did not see fit to change its name when it admitted women. The Black Caucus, formed in the late 1960s, contained both men and women in its membership, as did the more recently established "Steel Caucus," which included a woman on its Executive Committee. One other group mentioned as admitting women is made up of about a dozen Democrats and meets for coffee regularly in the office of a southern member. It differs from the Wednesday Group and most other structured groups in that, as of the start of the Second Session of the 95th Congress, it did not have a title. Usually it was referred to by the name of the Representative in whose office meetings were regularly held. Otherwise it possessed several of the characteristics shared by "structured" groups—a constant membership, regular meetings, a pre-determined agenda, and reports by members.

House informants did not make a distinction between "structured" and "unstructured" informal groups, but there are compelling empirical and analytical reasons for emphasizing their differences. More than two-thirds of the women serving in the 95th Congress belonged to one or more of the former, even when affiliations with "class" groups, the Democratic Study Group, state delegations and, of course, the Congresswoman's Caucus are excluded.[3] Many of

the congresswomen who were interviewed attached importance to their
membership in these groups and several congressmen referred approvingly to
contributions women had made to them. One Republican congressman praised
the leadership of a woman who had chaired the Republican Study Committee
and another stated:

> I belong to the Wednesday Group, which is made up of moderate and
> progressive Republicans. There are two women members in the Club at the
> present time and they participate aggressively and are listened to. They are
> most welcome and attractive members and they are treated as 'one of the
> boys.'

Another male, a Democrat, felt the same way:

> I meet with a group once a week, sometimes twice a month. It was formed
> several years ago and is made up of about ten moderate Democrats. We are
> spread out on a number of different House committees and I like to think we
> have a little influence. One of the charter members of the group is a woman
> and she is a capable, imaginative member of our little caucus.

Finally, one female member commented in general terms about the access
women had to House groups:

> With few exceptions, members are not excluded from groups if they want to
> be in them. The cliques and groups around here are as old as the House
> itself . . . and from my experience I would say that women are not so much
> excluded because of their sex as they are included because they have a shared
> interest with the other members that make up the group.

Female presence in informal groups has not diminished since these
interviews were conducted. Mary Rose Oakar and Claudine Schneider, for
example, were among the earliest Representatives to affiliate with the
Congressional Space Caucus when it was launched in the 97th Congress, and
Lynn Martin was a member of three such groups when the 98th Congress
convened.[4] It would seem, then, that changes have occurred since Gehlen
conducted her inquiry, perhaps partly because of the increase in the number of
informal groups. Based on the comments offered by both male and female
informants, there is less male resistence to women becoming a part of such
groups than was the case in the past.

The same cannot be said of female membership in "unstructured" groups,
however. In fact, it is abundantly clear that women are systematically denied
access to them. The men who make up the membership of unstructured groups
are drawn together, often in late afternoon or in evening sessions, because they
want to discuss and attach meaning to the business that transpired during that

day. Some hold or aspire to hold leadership positions within the party and are looking for ways to augment and exert their influence. Others want to affect the course of future legislation. Unstructured groups are also formed because members have a common interest in using the House gymnasium, or because many of them find that they are frequently invited to attend the same parties and social events, or because they accept invitations to the same lobbyist-sponsored golfing or hunting excursions. Regardless of the origin, purpose, or setting of these groups, congresswomen are excluded from their membership.

The Representatives who interact in these groupings are not always the same, the opportunities they have to get together are intermittent and often spontaneous, and the duration of any regularized pattern of interaction may be extraordinarily brief. Whatever the group's characteristics, congressmen exploit the private, informal setting of group meetings to discuss their priorities and the business of the House, to organize their thoughts about matters that are important to them, and to talk about ways and means of affecting the flow of legislative events. Of course conversation touches on many other subjects, but a common interest in these other matters reinforces the political rapport members have already established and provides further occasion for exchanging ideas, frames of reference, and political support.

Most of the congresswomen who were interviewed acknowledge their exclusion from groups of this sort. One said:

> There is one problem area insofar as exclusion is concerned. When males get together in a group and drink together and talk together informally, women are never present. And you can't do that with female members. You don't have the 'buddy-buddy' system among women. When the day's business is over, we don't have the time to stay around. We have to rush and take care of the other things we have to do because we have no 'wives' to help us.

Most congressmen agreed with this observation. One described the setting for such a group and explained why he thought women were excluded.

> This room right here [an office in one of the House Office Buildings] is a meeting place. Different members come by and we sit and drink and rap and talk about how things are going. I have great difficulty imagining a woman coming in and joining the group. She would alter the entire atmosphere. Congressmen _____, _____, and _____ [a committee chairman, a subcommittee chairman, and an aspiring floor leader] and a few others come by and we rap. These men don't have the political rapport with women in the same way that they have it with one another. It would be awkward with women present. The men would feel constrained to straighten their ties, to watch their manners, and to stop themselves from saying 'go fuck yourself' when the kidding touched a sensitive nerve.

Several respondents referred to other settings in which male members established the bonds that defined the group with which they were affiliated. Some talked about the "gym fellowship" that is so important to many male members. Users of the gym make up not one group but a congeries of groups with shifting memberships and attendance. They have in common the all-male environment, the locker-room language and banter, and the opportunity to exchange ideas of mutual interest in an atmosphere which emphasizes the kind of physical activities which they see as natural extensions of their male identities. Many relationships established in the gymnasium are continued in other settings.

Some members mentioned the after-hours parties, thrown principally by lobbyists who themselves are trying to improve their rapport with influential congressmen. The nature of the entertainment provided on those occasions, along with the stag-party ambience that prevails on hunting trips, golfing weekends or cocktail parties, presupposes that no congresswomen or wives will be present and that these women would not want to be present even if invited. Several members also mentioned the discriminatory orientation of the Gridiron Club, an organization made of members of Washington's working press and a "lobby" in the broader sense of that term. It excludes women from membership and, until recently, tended to ignore congresswomen when extending dinner invitations to Representatives and Senators. When, in 1972, the Club altered that practice and invited nineteen women to its annual ball, among those asked was Shirley Chisholm, presidential candidate and congresswoman. But the Brooklyn Democrat used the occasion to record her disapproval of the Club's history of discrimination. She replied: "Gentlemen of the Gridiron Club: Guess who's not coming to dinner?"[5] Ten other women sent regrets.

House informants gave a number of reasons for the barring of congress-women from these settings, reasons which are by no means mutually exclusive. Many suggested, for example, that the presence of women within these informal groupings would force male members to alter their behavior. The men, they noted, would have to do and say things which were inappropriate to the circumstances which prompted the gathering (and, perhaps, the formation of the group) in the first place. They would have to give excessive concern to their appearance, their demeanor and language, and many believed that the nature of the conversations would be affected, as well.

Several male informants stated that women were excluded because they were "different." They were not the same as men in the sense that they had not been around Capitol Hill as long as most men; that they had not as yet established a rapport with male members which permitted or encouraged candid, trusting exchanges of confidence; and that, even if women were accepted by the male "fraternity," there were many men who would never be at ease with women. These men found affiliation with unstructured groups worthwhile precisely because they were able to cast aside the inhibitions that "mixed company" normally required them to sustain.

Some congressmen noted that whether these gatherings were in someone's office, a House dining room, or a downtown hotel, they were social, as well as political occasions. And they found that socializing with women colleagues when husbands were not present was awkward. The absence of spouses in these circumstances risked the accusation that a male and a female Representatives were more friendly than was good for the reputation of either. One congressman said that he was very careful about preserving a formal, businesslike relationship with women colleagues, even when meeting with them socially—which, he said, "was not very often."

THE CHOWDER AND MARCHING SOCIETY

Among the many structured groups which shape and are shaped by the informal behavior of House members today, The Chowder and Marching Society is one of the oldest and most prestigious. The origin of its name is uncertain, but it appears to have been chosen whimsically, in the absence of a more apt title. The group was begun in 1949 by Congressmen Glenn R. Davis of Wisconsin and Donald Jackson of California. The two conservative Republicans were disturbed because a costly veteran's pension bill had been rammed through committee, and they were determined to block its passage on the floor. They summoned thirteen, mostly young, Republicans to meet with them one Wednesday afternoon to consider how to defeat the measure, and the group's members have been meeting weekly ever since. The Society is dedicated to cutting federal spending and reducing the extent to which the national government tries directly to affect the lives of Americans in both their individual and corporate incarnations. Among the thirteen charter members were such notables as Richard Nixon, Gerald Ford, and Melvin Laird.

The group was one of several formed in the late 1940s and early 1950s. These caucuses reflected dissatisfaction with Republican leadership, specifically the party's Policy Committee, among younger, more energetic GOP congressmen. Others included "The Response Group," also known as "the Committee of 15," which sought to conduct research on enacted and proposed public programs, and "SOS" and "the Acorns," which like Chowder and Marching, were interested in filling members' social, as well as their political needs. The SOS group was formed in the 83rd Congress, the Acorns in the 85th (Jones 1964, p. 28).

Membership in Chowder and Marching grew to between thirty and forty, with one or more members inducted in each Congress, depending upon the number of Society members who did not return from the last Congress.

Republican floor leaders and ranking party members on influential standing committees have, with few exceptions been members of the group. In the 95th Congress, Minority Leader and Minority Whip, John Rhodes and Robert Michel, were among Society stalwarts. Top Republicans in the 98th Congress, including Whip Trent Lott and Conference Chairman Jack Kemp, as well as Floor Leader Michel, were also part of the group. Membership is for life and, even if Representatives go to the Senate, Cabinet posts, the White House, or back to private life, they are still eligible to attend Society meetings. Presidents Nixon and Ford both hosted White House parties given especially for Society members.

The group has no staff and members pay no dues. Weekly meetings are held in the offices of members and the meeting site rotates among them. The sessions are chaired by the person in whose office the meeting happens to be taking place. Only members are permitted to be present and staff personnel are barred from attending under any circumstances—a rule more stringent than the one followed on the House floor itself. Members may discuss pending legislation, legislative strategy, or other congressional or political matters. Someone who feels strongly about an issue, for example, is free to speak to it and try to influence others to adopt a like point of view.

The political importance of the group is disputed. According to one member, its role in shaping policy is limited. He conceived of it as a social, rather than a political, association, something akin to a Rotary or Kiwanis club. He acknowledged that members do, indeed, discuss what is going on in their committees, but claimed that no one tried to gather support for a bill or, like the Wednesday Group, relied upon prepared studies and recommendations as a basis for building a consensus. Nevertheless, he volunteered that his affiliation with Chowder and Marching was the most valued of all his associations with Washington groups.

Another Republican had a different view. For him, Society meetings were an important opportunity for influencing colleagues and for establishing frames of reference and impressions which give meaning and weight to future events. The things that are said and done at these meetings are often reflected in the behavior of Society members, as well as in the decisions of other Republicans and in the actions of the House itself. Group proceedings are considered to be confidential, however, and are not discussed with persons who are not members of the Society.

What makes this account relevant here is that no congresswoman is currently a member of the Chowder and Marching Society, nor has any woman ever been a member.[6] It represents, therefore, an important exception to the generalization offered earlier that "structured" informal groups in the House tend to admit both male and female members, although the Society possesses some of the attributes of an "unstructured" group, as well. Perhaps even more startling than the historic absence of women in so weighty a group is the fact that two of the Republican women who were interviewed, and a much larger number of female Democrats had either never heard of the Society or simply recognized the name without being able to attach substantive content to its title. It is almost as if congressmen who are members of the group and female members serve in two different institutions.

The last observation is partly based on the comment made by one Chowder and Marching Society member who said that it was probably among the most influential groups, if not *The* most influential group in the House. This was especially so, he said, since it began to hold breakfast meetings with SOS, a group whose membership in the past overlapped with the Society's. A Republican congresswoman, on the other hand, agitatedly added, after noting that she had never heard of the group, "And what's more I don't care about the Chowder and March on Society [sic], or whatever it's called. Groups like that have nothing to do with what's really going on here and it gives me a headache to think that you people [social scientists] are even interested in it."

Another Republican woman, one who said that she knew that no woman was a member at the time, was nonetheless astonished to learn that no woman had ever even been asked to join. She allowed that given the talent of some of the Republican women who served in the past, the exclusion of all of them certainly suggested that they were discriminated against because of their gender. Society members may have been reacting to charges of discrimination when they recently arranged for formation of a Chowder and Marching Auxiliary. Membership is limited to Representative's wives (*New York Times* March 15, 1982).

THE SIGNIFICANCE OF EXCLUSION FROM INFORMAL GROUPS

While both male and female House members acknowledge the systematic exclusion of women from "unstructured" groups and recognize, as well, their absence from the more visible Chowder and Marching Society, they did not agree among themselves about whether, as a result, congresswomen were less effective than they could be. A majority of male members said that women Representatives were not unduly handicapped by their absence from such groups, and that they had just as much of an opportunity as male members to help their constituents and to affect legislation. One congressman pointed out that, in the first place, women were, in fact, members of informal groups, such as the "Good Guys" and the "Black Caucus," and, therefore, had all the opportunities of which they could conceivably take advantage to make behind-the-scenes contributions. "In the second place," he said, "the number of groups of the 'after hours' kind, the frequency with which they meet and their importance have all diminished." Another congressman agreed, noting:

The days of Sam Rayburn's Board of Education are over. That was when a small group of men could dictate congressional decisions and the fate of the country. Now things are too decentralized. And the influence of groups that exclude women is minimal. Things are wide open now and there are many people in the House who influence policy.... The fact that women are excluded from some groups varies in signficance from the trivial to the inconsequential.

Female respondents were divided about equally among those who felt that exclusion limited the usefulness of their House service and those who did not. One Democratic woman maintained that the meetings of these groups were little more than "bull sessions," and she would decline to attend even if invited. Another Democrat was indifferent, she said that membership made little difference to her because she and other female members have learned how to achieve their goals without being part of such groups. "And besides," she added, "the Congresswomen's Caucus gives us our own group now. We get together and do our own thing. And some of the men have become suspicious of us because we often come on the floor together after a meeting and they wonder what we've been up to." Other women noted that they wouldn't have the time to participate even if they were granted access to such groups inasmuch as they had too many other things to do and, as a result, their service could not possibly be affected.

Some congresswomen, on the other hand, agreed with former Representative Edith Green who asserted in 1972 that women do not play an important role in Congress. She added:

In the days of Sam Rayburn, the most powerful group here was something called the "Kitchen Cabinet [sic]." They were Rayburn's male buddies who got together evenings . . . drank bourbon, talked, and decided the course of the nation. John McCormack was the same way. I guess his clique didn't drink bourbon, but over card games the males chose to make the big decisions that counted (Dreifus 1972).

Other female Representatives felt that they were unable to be as effective as they might be because they did not have the sounding boards and communication networks that these unstructured groups provided for male members. Two women in the 95th Congress pointed out important but relatively subtle handicaps under which they labored because of their exclusion from such groups. One recalled having reached an agreement with two male members about a language change they would jointly offer in legislation being considered by their subcommittee. When the proposal was introduced by one of the two men the following morning, it varied somewhat from the language upon which they had initially agreed. She recalled the incident this way:

I supported the new language, but after the subcommittee meeting I went up to Congressman _____ and asked him what had happened to the original language of the proposal. He said that he and the other fellow had thought up the second version while working out in the gym and, he kiddingly said, that I ought to take up paddle ball before I miss out on anything else. Now that happened just last week and if you had asked me about the importance of these groups before then I would probably have said that they were unimportant. But I can see now that they matter, not so much in terms of whether major legislation passes or does not pass, but in terms of what's in the bill and what's not in the bill.

The other congresswoman said that members miss out on something when they cannot participate in groups of this kind, something which is difficult to define. She put it this way:

Members who don't or can't participate in them are like the kid in college who has no one to study with; no one to exchange ideas with to get a broader idea of what's going on in the class; no one to work with to get the right kind of 'vibes' about the course and the teacher. It takes longer for that kid to understand what is going on and often that student is never as good as he or she could be.

The absence of a consensus about whether congresswomen are seriously handicapped by their exclusion from groups of this kind suggests that members differ not only with respect to what they hope to contribute to the legislative process but also with respect to what they hope to derive from their experience in Congress. They differ, as well, in their perceptions of what phases of the decision-making process happen to be important. It is also possible that the tendency to minimize the influence of these groups is, as Gehlen suggested, due to the fact that members who are not a part of them are disinclined to attribute much significance to them (Gehlen 1969, p. 39).

But perhaps the most crucial points to be made here are that these groups are indispensable for certain purposes and that systematic exclusion from them closes off opportunities some women might wish to exploit. Barring Republican women from The Chowder and Marching Society and from unstructured groups peopled by men who control (or aspire to control) leadership positions is bound to place women at a disadvantage with respect to these positions and to stategically useful information. As is made clear in the next chapter, the top of the leadership hierarchy is likely to be peopled by House members who were able to capitalize on relationships that informal group memberships institutionalize.

Exclusion of women also tends to delay, if not prevent altogether, placement of women's issues on the legislative agenda. Such issues have only recently surfaced as matters possibly within the direct reach of Washington, but male Representatives must first be convinced of their legitimacy before Congress can be expected to act on them. Exchange of views in a small group setting is frequently the most effective way of alerting members to the aptness and implications of these issues. Given the informality, intimacy, and exchange of trust obtaining in small group settings, they provide ideal arenas in which to begin to alter basic preconceptions of what the country's goals ought to be and which of our often conflicting values ought to prevail.

Consequently, to the extent that congresswomen, especially those with a feminist orientation, are denied the opportunity to alter the mind sets of their colleagues, such issues as aid to displaced homemakers do not rise to the top of the list of national and congressional priorities, if, indeed Representatives in sufficient number place them on the list at all. These programs would have more visibility if congresswomen supporting them occupied positions of leadership. But, as will be demonstrated in the next chapter, female Representatives have failed to gain access to the highest party posts, and they only recently began to secure more than a handful of positions at the middle levels of the leadership hierarchy.

NOTES

1. The official title of these groups is "legislative service organizations," although there is more variation in the structure, goals, funding, staffing, and degree of formal recognition among them than one would expect of agencies all falling under the same rubric. Late in 1981, the House Administration Committee ordered those LSOs accepting funds from extracongressional sources either to stop the practice or give up publicly supported staffs, office space, and other facilities. The ruling also required regular reporting procedures and stricter accountability in the use of office staffs and public funds. See *Congressional Quarterly Weekly Report*, Vol. 39, October 24, 1981, p. 2074. The new guidelines also had an important impact on the Congresswomen's Caucus, as is made clear in Chapter 11.

2. An exact count of caucuses is difficult to come by, but the figure of fifty is certainly a conservative estimate if partisan and bipartisan state delegations are included. Twenty-six such groups were officially registered with the House in 1981, but there existed at least the same number of caucuses which did not use House space, and which did not rely on designated staff personnel supported by clerk-hire or outside funding.

3. The Congresswomen's Caucus was formed in 1977, and it observed a prohibition on male membership until late in 1981. When men joined the group, it changed its name to the Congressional Caucus for Women's Issues. The former title is used when referring to group activities through 1981, the latter when alluding to events after that year.

4. One of the difficulties of documenting group membership is that information of this sort either does not appear in easily accessible sources or it is not published at all. The Space Caucus membership of Oakar and Schroeder is mentioned in the *Congressional Record*, Vol. 129, February 2, 1982, p. H 244. Martin's affiliations also appear in the *Record*—Vol. 129, February 23, 1983, p. E 581—reported in an inserted article about the Illinois Republican.

5. This was not the first time the Club had asked women to its annual dinner, but the nineteen invitations represented the largest number extended for any single event. In 1917, Club members,

curious about what the first woman elected to Congress was like, asked Jeannette Rankin to attend (*Washington Post* April 6, 1972).

6. A Chowder and Marching Society membership list was not obtained, and members do not readily volunteer the names of other members. The group's failure ever to admit a congresswoman was learned in interviews with two Society members in the 95th Congress and in follow-up inquiries made during the 97th Congress.

6 / Access to Leadership Positions

Selecting a woman for a country's highest government position is so uncommon around the world that when such a choice is made, it occasions a response otherwise reserved for landing a man on the moon. The anemic ranks of 20th century female leaders that included Indira Gandhi of India, Sirmavo Bandarnaike of Sri Lanka, and Israel's Golda Meir were augmented in 1979 by British, Portugese, and Bolivian leaders. Since then, voters and legislators in Norway, Iceland, the diminutive Caribbean island of Dominica, and Yugoslavia have followed suit.[1] But the isolated occurrences of these events have served to punctuate the limited progress women have made to date. Writing in 1955, the esteemed political scientist Maurice Duverger observed that however much women in government received the support and respect of male colleagues equality deteriorated when keen competition for legislative leadership developed between them. The French scholar added that he saw no signs to suggest change in these conditions (Duverger 1955, pp. 123–125).

NO ROOM AT THE TOP

Duverger may well have been describing the predicament of women in the House of Representatives. For, unlike their sisters in American state legislatures, congresswomen have been unable to penetrate the highest ranks of their party's hierarchy.[2] It seems almost unnecessary to note that no woman has ever served as House Speaker, floor leader, or Chief Whip. Moreover, no female Representative has presided over her party's Caucus, or chaired her party's Steering, Campaign, or Patronage Committees. None has directed the proceedings of a Committee on Committees, and few have served on, let alone headed, any of the four most coveted standing House committees—Appropriations, Budget, Rules, and Ways and Means.

If, then, we are to describe and analyze the progress congresswomen have made in securing leadership positions, our focus must be on secondary party posts—those to which their parties assign either limited or token responsibilities. Although not as influential as, say, the floor leader or party Whip, they are important because top leaders have recently delegated more power to them and because they frequently serve as springboards to higher party positions.

SECONDARY AGENCIES OF PARTY LEADERSHIP

Most of the secondary leadership positions appearing in Table 6.1 are of middling importance. Those who occupy them carry out a narrow range of responsibilities. Their opportunities to exercise influence are shared with more than a few colleagues, and differences between them and the party's top leaders with respect to perquisites and deference received are significant. Nevertheless, they affect selected decisions more markedly than do representatives who hold no party position at all.

Many secondary positions are of token importance. Most Representatives on the two parties' Campaign Committees, for example, do little to contribute to party fortunes. Rank and file members of the Republican Committee on Committees are similarly ineffectual (Jones 1965, p. 98). All three are made up of Representatives from each state sending at least one member of the party to the House. Each establishes an executive subcommittee, however, and these smaller agencies monopolize the decision-making process. Other members do little more than rubber stamp agreements hammered out in executive sessions— sessions often dominated by the committee chairman and by party leaders who are committee members *ex officio* (Jones 1965, p. 97; Peabody 1976, p. 271; Bone 1956, p. 118).

Republicans, particularly, stack the deck against rank and file representatives serving on these committees by giving each a weighted vote equivalent to the number of Republicans from his or her state, and by reserving most seats on the executive subcommittee for members representing the handful of states sending the largest GOP delegations to the House. Thus, committee members whose states send no more than two or three fellow partisans to Congress are unlikely to find themselves on the executive subcommittee, and their voting strength is insignificant even when they are accorded such recognition.

The number of secondary party positions has increased substantially in recent years as Democratic and Republican leadership structures have become more institutionalized. According to Table 6.2, Democratic positions have grown by thirty-six percent from 1949 to 1981. Marked changes have taken place

Table 6.1. Secondary Agencies of Party Leadership, 97th Congress

Democratic Agencies

Caucus Officers[1]	Whip Officials	Steering and Policy Committee[2]
Secretary	1 Chief Deputy Whip 4 Deputy Whips 23 Assistant Whips 15 At-Large Whips	12 Members Elected by Zones 8 Members Chosen by Speaker

National Congressional (Campaign) Committee[3]	Personnel Committee[4]	Rules Committee[4]
41 Members	4 Members	10 Members

Republican Agencies

Conference Officers[4]	Whip Officials	Policy Committee[5]	Committee on Committees[6]
Vice Chairman Secretary	1 Chief Deputy Whip 2 Deputy Whips 4 Divisional Whips 16 Assistant Whips	21 Members	14 Executive Subcommittee Members 35 Members

National Congressional (Campaign) Committee[7]	Personnel Committee[4]	Rules Committee	Research Committee[8]
11 Vice Chairmen 5 Executive Subcommittee Members 34 Members	7 Members	5 Members	18 Members

1. Other Caucus positions include the Caucus Chairman, a House member who is generally considered to be a part of the top Democratic Leadership, and an Assistant Secretary, a position that brings little influence with it and which has not been filled officially in recent years.

2. Other members of the Steering and Policy Committee include the Speaker, Floor Leader and Caucus Chairman, Representatives who serve respectively as Chairman, Vice Chairman and 2nd Vice Chairman of the Committee, and 6 *ex officio* Representatives: Party Whip, Caucus Secretary, and Chairmen of the Appropriations, Budget, Rules, and Ways and Means Committees.

3. The Chairman and Vice Chairman are excluded, as are four *ex officio* members: the Speaker, Floor Leader, Party Whip and Caucus Chairman. The Executive Subcommittee had not been selected when this Table was prepared.

4. The Chairman is excluded.

5. The Chairman and ten *ex officio* members are excluded: Floor Leader, Party Whip, Chairman, Vice Chairman and Secretary of the Conference, Chairman of the Campaign Committee,

Table 6.2. Change in Number of Democratic and Republican Secondary Leadership Positions from 1949 to 1981

Position*	Democratic		Republican	
	1949	1981	1949	1981
Deputy, Regional and Assistant Whips	16	43	12	23
Policy Committee Members[1]	14	20	17	21
Campaign Committee Members[2]	34	41	30	50
Committee on Committee Members[3]	14	—	30	49
Personnel Committee Members	2	4	—	7
Research Committee Members[4]	—	—	—	18
Rules Committee Members	7	10	4	5
Total	87	118	93	173
% Increase		36		86

*Committee Chairmen, Vice Chairmen, and Secretaries are omitted from the count, as are *ex officio* members.

1. Until 1973, the Democrats called this agency a "Steering" Committee. Since then it has been referred to as the "Steering and Policy" Committee. It assumed committee assignment responsibilities in 1975.

2. Delegates from the District of Columbia, Guam, American Samoa, and Puerto Rico are excluded.

3. Democratic members of the Ways and Means Committee performed Committee on Committees responsibilities until 1975, when they were given to the Steering and Policy Committee.

4. Established in 1965 as the Research and Planning Committee. Its persent name dates from 1967.

Sources: Figures for the 81st Congress, 1949–50, were obtained from several sources including the 1949 *Congressional Quarterly* Almanac, pp. 35–36; the 1949 *Congressional Record*, p. 1438; "Minutes of the Republican Conference of the Members of the U.S. House of Representatives," 81st Congress, December 31, 1948 and January 27, 1949. Figures for the 97th Congress, 1981, were obtained from the *Congressional Quarterly Weekly Reports*, Supplement to Vol. 39, No. 13, March 28, 1981.

and ranking members of the House Appropriations, Budget, Rules, and Ways and Means Committees.

6. The Floor Leader serves as Chairman and is excluded.

7. The Chairman and five *ex officio* members are excluded: Floor Leader, Chairman, Vice Chairman and Secretary of the Conference, and the Chairman of the Research Committee.

8. The Chairman and the Floor Leader, who is an *ex officio* member, are excluded.

Sources: Congressional Quarterly Weekly Report, Supplement to Volume 39, No. 13, pp. 43–46, March 28, 1981; and Charles E. Brownson (ed.), *The Congressional Staff Directory*, Volume 23, 97th Congress, 1st Session.

within the Democratic whip network, as well as in the size of that party's Campaign Committee—changes that more than offset the Democrats elimination of their Committee on Committees and the absorption of that panel's functions by a reorganized Steering and Policy Committee.

Proliferation in Republican positions has been even more dramatic, with increases in the size of the Republican whip system, its Campaign Committee, and its Committee on Committees most marked.[3] The addition of a Research Committee, together with growth in the size of the Republican Personnel Committee contributed appreciably to the overall increase. These new positions have augmented the opportunities available to representatives willing to serve on secondary party agencies. At the same time, the more sharply etched division of labor within the leadership structure and the *ex officio* additions of leaders to party panels have probably permitted these agencies to exercise more influence than they once did.

Modest though the responsibilities of these secondary party agencies have been, the importance of serving on them should not be underestimated. Party conferences and policy committees have been revitalized within the last twenty years, and leadership of the former and service on the latter have become more desirable (Peabody 1976, pp. 294–295). Former Speaker John McCormack began regular meetings of the Democratic Caucus in 1969, a practice continued and strengthened by his successors. Speakers Carl Albert and Thomas (Tip) O'Neill and Republican Floor Leaders Halleck and Ford all fostered more vital Policy Committees (Jones 1964, p. 104; Dodd 1979, p. 29).

Congressional Campaign Committees, too, have become more important, perhaps because public financing of presidential elections has had the effect of funneling larger private sums into House campaigns. Contributions of "in-kind" assistance by these panels, particularly by the Republican Campaign Committee, have become more important (Jacobson 1983, pp. 55–56). The increased costs of running for office and the more specialized skills needed to contest House seats have given these Committees unusual opportunities to contribute to the political futures of those who run under their labels.

The greater size and significance of the whip organizations is also worth noting. The addition of Deputy Whips and, for the Democrats, at-large whips, have made these networks more hierarchical. At the same time, recorded votes on floor amendments and electronic voting have required assistant whips to stay in closer touch with rank-and-file members and to attend more strategy sessions with party leaders (Dodd 1979, pp. 29–40).

Affiliation with these party agencies is important because conscientious service on them has frequently led to a top leadership position (Peabody 1976, p. 12). Massachusetts Congressman Joseph Martin was an assistant whip when named Republican floor leader in 1938,[4] and, one year later, John McCormack was promoted from Caucus Chairman to majority leader when Sam Rayburn became Speaker (Peabody 1976, p. 280). In 1961, four ambitious Republicans,

California's Bob Wilson, Michigan's Gerry Ford, Wisconsin's Melvin Laird, and Arizona's John Rhodes sought the chairmanship of their party's Campaign Committee. Wilson's victory did not deter the other three from later securing other intermediate party posts, positions from which Ford and Rhodes later vaulted to floor leader. More recently, Democrat Tom Foley was named party whip following two terms as Caucus Chairman.

Another reason for focusing on these secondary agencies is that accepting an appointment to them signals at least a modest desire to assume party responsibilities. The service itself, in turn, provides opportunities to demonstrate leadership qualities, to establish friendships and rapport with colleagues whose support may later be called upon, and to acquire knowledge about people and issues which may subsequently be employed to persuade other party members of one's personal and political prowess.

Of course, not all House members want a leadership position, and many of those who serve on party instrumentalities do not intend to use them as stepping stones to more important posts (Peabody 1976, p. 4). But experience on one or more of these agencies has come to be an all but necessary condition for selection as party whip, floor leader, and Speaker, and it seems appropriate therefore to note the changing frequencies with which female representatives have served on them.

CONGRESSWOMEN IN SECONDARY LEADERSHIP POSITIONS

In her analysis of the 88th Congress, Frieda Gehlen found that few female Representatives were members of their party's leadership hierarchy. Furthermore, the male House members with whom she spoke gave women no chance of being elected to senior party positions. The most common reason for this view was that women were unable to establish the informal relationships upon which would-be leaders must rely. Some congressmen thought that their female colleagues were too emotional or too idealistic; others that they were too subjective or too rigid. Accordingly, they saw little chance of a woman receiving enough votes from male members of her party, and some believed that leadership roles should, as a matter of course, be reserved for men (Gehlen 1969, pp. 39–40).

Had Gehlen made a systematic count of the women holding secondary leadership positions from the end of World War II to the 88th Congress, her findings would have corresponded to those appearing in Table 6.3. She would have almost certainly noted that, based upon available documentary evidence, a Democratic woman had yet to be appointed to her party's whip network or the House Rules Committee and that none had served on the Democratic Patronage Committee. On the other hand, she would have been able to point out that women had regularly served as Secretary to the Democratic Caucus, that a

Table 6.3. Congresswomen in Secondary Leadership Positions, 1947–1964

Congress (Years)	Caucus Officers	Whip Officials	Democratic Agencies				
			Steering Committee	Campaign Committee	Committee on Committees	Rules Committee	Patronage Committee
80th (1947–48)	NA	NA	NA	NA	None	None	NA
81st (1949–1950)	Woodhouse[1]	NA	Woodhouse[2]	None	None	None	None
82nd (1951–52)	NA	NA	NA	NA	None	None	NA
83rd (1953–54)	Kelly[1] Sullivan[3]	NA	None	NA	None	None	NA
84th (1955–56)	Kelly[1] Sullivan[3]	NA	None	NA	None	None	NA
85th (1957–58)	NA	NA	—	Green	None	None	NA
86th (1959–60)	Sullivan[1]	NA	—	Green Pfost	None	None	None
87th (1961–62)	Sullivan[1] Kee[3]	None	Sullivan[2]	Green Griffiths[4]	None	None	None
88th (1963–64)	Sullivan (1st)[1] Kelly (2nd)[1]	None	NA	Green Griffiths[4] Hansen	Griffiths	None	None

Republican Agencies

Congress (years)	Conference Officers	Whip Officials	Policy Committee[5]	Campaign Committee	Committee on Committees	Rules Committee	Patronage Committee
80th (1947–48)	None	NA	None	None	None	None	NA
81st (1949–50)	None	None	Bolton	None	None	None	None
82nd (1951–52)	None	St. George[6]	NA	None	None	None	NA
83rd (1953–54)	None	NA	NA	None	None	None	NA
84th (1955–56)	None	NA	None	None	None	None	NA
85th (1957–58)	None	NA	None	None	None	None	NA
86th (1959–60)	None	NA	Bolton	None	St. George[4]	None	None
87th (1961–62)	None	May[6] St. George[6]	Bolton Church St. George[2] Weis[7]	None	St. George[4]	St. George	None
88th (1963–64)	None	May[6] St. George[6]	Bolton St. George[2]	None	St. George[4]	St. George	None

"NA": Information Not Available

1. Caucus Secretary
2. Member Ex Officio
3. Caucus Assistant Secretary
4. Executive Subcommittee Member
5. Known as "Steering" Committee from 1947 to 1949
6. Regional Whip
7. Nonvoting Member

Sources: Congressional Record, Congressional Quarterly Almanac, Congressional Staff Directory, "Minutes of the Republican Conference of the Members of the U.S. House of Representatives."

99

woman had recently been appointed to the Democratic Committee on Committees, that a few, notably Edith Green, had served on her party's Campaign Committee, and that one, Martha Griffiths, had secured a position on that panel's executive subcommittee. Occasional *ex officio* service by the Caucus Secretary on the Steering Committee would also have deserved mention.

Republican congresswomen had fared at least as well as their Democratic counterparts. To be sure, none had been tapped for Conference Secretary, a niche that seems to have been more important to Republicans than to Democrats,[5] and none had served on the Congressional Campaign Committee. But several had been members of their party's Policy Committee, a more significant body than the Democratic Steering Committee (Jones 1964, pp. 104–105), and Katharine St. George had been appointed to both the executive subcommittee of the Committee on Committees, and the House Rules Committee. The influential New Yorker also served as one of three Regional Whips, a distinction shared by Washington state's Catherine May.

Differences between the parties increased significantly during the years that followed Gehlen's observations, however. Data in Table 6.4 indicate that Democratic women began to serve regularly on a renewed Steering Committee, with appointments increasingly awarded to women members who were not the Caucus Secretary. They began making regular appearances in the party's whip network and female Democrats continued to receive assignments to the Campaign Committee—with Yvonne Burke and Lindy Boggs following Griffiths on the executive subcommittee. Before committee assignment tasks were transferred to the Steering and Policy Committee, a congresswoman had become a fixture on the Committee on Committees, and, in 1977, a Democratic congresswoman joined the House Rules Committee for the first time in history.

While the collective fortunes of Democratic women rose, those of Republican women fell. After Katharine St. George's departure from the House in 1964, no GOP female member served on the Rules Committee or in her party's whip system until 1983. Five were appointed to the increasingly important Policy Committee, but none has thus far served for more than a single Congress. Catherine May, briefly, Millicent Fenwick, and Marge Roukema were members of the relatively new Research Committee, and a growing number of Republican women found their way on to panels responsible for filling committee vacancies and helping the electoral prospects of GOP House candidates. One notable achievement for Republican women during this period was the selection of Bobbi Fiedler and, later, Barbara Vucanovich for the Personnel Committee.

The data in Tables 6.3 and 6.4 have two important deficiencies, however. First, they do not distinguish between more important and less important leadership positions. Second, they do not take into account the number of congresswomen serving during each of the stipulated time periods, a factor which

Table 6.4. Congresswomen in Secondary Leadership Positions, 1965–1983

Congress (years)	Caucus Officers[1]	Whip Officials	Steering and Policy Committee[2]	Democratic Agencies			
				Campaign Committee	Committee on Committees	Rules Committee	Personnel Committee[3]
89th (1965–66)	Sullivan	NA	Sullivan[4]	Green Griffiths[5] Hansen	Griffiths	None	None
90th (1967–68)	Sullivan	None	Sullivan[4]	Green Griffiths[5] Hansen	Griffiths	None	None
91st (1969–70)	Sullivan	Green Sullivan	Hansen Sullivan[4]	Green Griffiths[5] Hansen	Griffiths	None	None
92nd (1971–72)	Sullivan	Green Sullivan	Hansen Sullivan[4]	Green Griffiths[5] Hansen	Griffiths	None	None
93rd (1973–74)	Sullivan	Green	Hansen[6]	Green Griffiths[5] Hansen	Griffiths	None	None
94th (1975–76)	Mink	Abzug[7] Collins[7]	Jordan[6]	Keys	—	None	None
95th (1977–78)	Chisholm	Collins[7] Schroeder Spellman	Jordan[6]	Burke[5] Keys	—	Chisholm	None
96th (1979–80)	Chisholm	None	Spellman[6] Ferraro[4]	Boggs[5]	—	Chisholm	None
97th (1981–82)	Ferraro	Oakar[7] Schroeder[7]	Schroeder[6]	Boggs[5] Schroeder	—	Chisholm	None
98th (1983–)	Ferraro	Oakar[7] Schroeder[7]	Ferraro[4] Schroeder[6]	NA	—	None	None

(continued on next page)

Table 6.4. (continued)

	Republican Agencies							
Congress (years)	Conference Officers	Whip Officials	Policy Committee	Campaign Committee	Committee on Committees	Rules Committee	Personnel Committee	Research Committee
89th (1965–66)	None	NA	Reid	None	May	None	None	May
90th (1967–68)	None	None	None	None	May	None	None	May
91st (1969–70)	None	None	None	None	May	None	None	May
92nd (1971–72)	None	None	None	None	None	None	None	None
93rd (1973–74)	None	None	None	None	Heckler	None	None	None
94th (1975–76)	None	None	Holt	Holt	Heckler	None	None	Fenwick
95th (1977–78)	None	None	Smith	Heckler	Holt Smith Snowe	None	None	None
96th (1979–80)	None	None	None	Heckler Holt	Holt	None	None	None
97th (1981–82)	None	None	None	Heckler Holt[8] Schneider	Holt Schneider Snowe	None	Fiedler	None

| 98th (1983–) | None | Martin Snowe[9] | Johnson Martin | Holt Johnson[8] Schneider Vucanovich[8] | Fiedler[10] Holt Schneider Smith Snowe Vucanovich | None | Vucanovich | Roukema |

"NA": Information Not Available

1. All were Caucus Secretary
2. Knows as "Steering" Committee until 1973
3. Known as "Patronage" Committee until 1977
4. Member *Ex Officio*
5. Executive Subcommittee Member
6. Selected by Speaker
7. Selected by leadership as "at large" whip
8. Committee Vice Chairwoman
9. Deputy Whip
10. Appointed late in 1st session as representative of the 97th Class

Sources: Congressional Record, Congressional Quarterly Almanac, Congressional Directory, Congressional Staff Directory, "Minutes of the Republican Conference of the Members of the U.S. House of Representatives."

would obviously affect how many could have possibly been elevated to secondary roles. The first of these limitations was approached by separating leadership positions into categories reflecting the nature of the responsibilities each is expected to fulfill. A category of "strategic" positions includes both parties' Regional and Assistant Whips, Rules Committee appointees, and executive subcommittee members of the Campaign Committees. These positions are defined as "strategic" because Representatives holding them normally help to shape and implement their party's legislative or campaign strategies. Decisions that affect schedules of committee and floor deliberations, the framework of debate, mobilization of party strength, and distributions of campaign contributions all have the character of partisan combat. They reflect efforts to gain legislative, political, and electoral leverage for partisan purposes.

Leadership positions defined as "integrative" are found most prominently on the Policy Committees, the Personnel Committees, the Democratic Committee on Committees, the executive subcommittee of the Republican Committee on Committees, and the Republican Research Committee. Caucus officers also play integrative roles. The functions of these positions are to reconcile individual aspirations with organization goals, and to promote cooperation and unity among party members. Representatives filling them distribute rewards in ways calculated to satisfy members' needs and to encourage them to seek consensus.[6] Integrative leaders facilitate intraparty discussion, invite expression of all points of view, award patronage plums, promote policy-oriented research, and formulate long-term policy goals. Distribution of committee assignments is among the most important integrative task performed within each party.

The third type of secondary leadership category is defined here as "token." It refers to positions which carry little responsibility, and which reflect a recognition for their occupants which is more apparent than real. Selection to either of the two Campaign Committees or to the Republican Committee on Committees, but not the executive subcommittees of these three panels, means that House members will make little more than token contributions to their parties' electoral, legislative, or organizational goals.

Of course, some party instrumentalities undertake both strategic and integrative tasks. Whip networks, for example, distribute information which could lead to consensus, just as they try to mobilize party members to do combat with the opposition. Policy Committees, particularly the minority party panel, seek to formulate legislative options which are both acceptable to their members and subversive of opposition party unity. And Rules Committee Republicans are *ex officio* members of their party's Policy Committee (Jones 1964, p. 55). Accordingly, the categories are not mutually exclusive and, for purposes of analysis, Democrats serving on the Steering and Policy Committee since 1975, when that panel began to determine committee assignments, are considered as exercising both strategic and integrative leadership roles. The distinctions made here are useful in spite of their limitations, however. They help shed light on the nature of the responsibilities parties have assigned to congresswomen, as well as the frequency with which each type of responsibility has been distributed.

This analysis of the progress congresswomen have made in obtaining secondary leadership posts has been aided by the application of a statistical measure which takes into account the number of secondary positions to be filled and the number of women serving in the House. Infrequent appointments may be as much a reflection of the small number of women elected to the House as it is an indication of leadership reluctance to elevate women to reasonably weighty party positions.

An "Index of Success" has been calculated for each of the three categories of positions.[7] A score of 1.00 indicates that women hold leadership positions equal in proportion to that which they would have been entitled if these positions were awarded randomly. If, for example, a total of ten Democratic congresswomen were eligible for 100 leadership positions also available to 190 Democratic males, the Index of Success would be 1.00 if five of the ten filled leadership positions. If, on the other hand, only two positions were assigned to women, the Index of Success would be 0.40, indicating that they held two-fifths of the positions that their number alone (as a proportion of the total number of Democrats serving in the House) suggests they should hold. An Index of 2.0 means that twice as many positions were filled by women than they would have if the vacancies were distributed randomly.

The figures appearing in Table 6.5 are Indexes of Success recorded by Democratic and Republican women from 1947 to 1983. This period has been divided to permit comparison of female success rates over time, as well as between the two parties. Thus, from 1947 to 1964, Democratic congresswomen were only one-half as likely (0.53%) as one would expect to serve in strategic positions, while just about holding their own in integrative leadership positions. They were almost four times more likely to be found on token party agencies than their numbers and chance would suggest. In subsequent years they improved substantially their rate of success in the first two categories, while the success rate for token party instrumentalities declined significantly.

By contrast, Republican women serving from 1965 to 1983 found themselves in strategic and integrative roles comparatively less often than they had in earlier years. During the more recent period, only two GOP congresswomen were selected to serve as a Deputy, Regional, or Assistant Whip, or as a Rules Committee member, and the selection of Holt, Johnson, and Vucanovich as Campaign Committee Vice Chairwomen in the 97th and 98th Congresses (See Table 6.4) raised the strategic Index to a relatively feeble 0.41. Republican women went from a slight overrepresentation to a slight underrepresentation on integrative positions. Whether they took consolation in the fact that they were doing a good deal better than holding their own in appointments to token positions, after securing none at all from 1947 to 1964, is doubtful.

Table 6.5. Congresswomen's Index of Success in Securing Strategic, Integrative, and Token Leadership Positions, 1947–1983

| Congresses (years) | Type of Position | | | | | | Average Number of Women Serving per Term | |
| | Strategic[1] | | Integrative[2] | | Token[3] | | | |
	Dem.	Rep.	Dem.	Rep.	Dem.	Rep.	Dem.	Rep.
80th–88th (1947–64)	0.53	1.09	0.95	1.18	3.94	0.00	6.9	5.9
89th–97th (1965–83)	1.35	0.41	1.80	0.80	1.55	1.56	10.3	5.1

1. Includes Democratic positions in the whip network and on the Rules Committee, the Steering Committee (later the Steering and Policy Committee), and the executive subcommittee of the Campaign Committee; Republican positions in the whip network and on the Rules Committee and the executive subcommittee of the Campaign Committee.

2. Includes Democratic positions on the Committee on Committees, the Steering and Policy Committee from 1975 to 1983, and the Personnel (Patronage) Committee, and Caucus officers who were *ex officio* members of the Steering (or Steering and Policy) Committee; Republican positions on the Policy, Research, and Personnel (Patronage) Committees, and the executive subcommittees of the Committee on Committees. Republican Caucus officers are also included.

3. Includes Democratic and Republican Campaign Committee members and Republican Committee on Committees members who did not serve on these panels' executive subcommittees.

The figures in Table 6.5 suggest first of all that party leaders have been more inclined to select women for integrative than for strategic positions. They also indicate that female Democrats have been increasingly successful in securing both kinds of positions, while the success rate of their Republican counterparts has declined.

Just why these patterns have emerged is not entirely clear. It is possible that most female House members did not have either the will or the seniority to capture strategic vacancies. Other explanations are more complex. To begin with, Representatives in strategic roles more than those in integrative ones work closely with the Speaker and floor leaders. They take their cues from these people and are expected to demonstrate party loyalty, reliability, and pragmatism in generous measure. Rules Committee members, for example, can normally be counted upon to subordinate ideological, constituency, and pressure-group concerns to the tactical and strategic necessities of their political party. It is conceivable, then, that few women in either party were appointed to strategic committees because few have been perceived as possessing these predispositions. Even when slightly overrepresented on strategic agencies, as Republicans were from 1947 to 1964, only two, Katharine St. George and Catherine May, occupied positions on them.

A related explanation inheres in the gender orientation of the leaders who filled party vacancies. If these people embraced traditional beliefs about the roles of women or if they were uneasy about consulting them, reasons for avoiding interactions with female Representatives were readily seized. Only one Democratic woman, Martha Griffiths, held a strategically important position while Sam Rayburn led House Democrats. And St. George's appointment as Regional Whip was made not by floor leader Joseph Martin, but by Chief Whip Leslie Arends—although consultation with Martin must certainly have taken place. Her assignment to the Rules Committee did not occur until after Martin was deposed by Charles Halleck and only after she was elected for an eighth term. The three Republican men newly appointed to that Committee at the time of her selection had served an average of three terms, and St. George had seen twice as much House service as the most senior of the three.

Martin and Rayburn were public men whose House careers enveloped their private lives. The first was a bachelor, and Rayburn's marriage in 1927, at age 45, ended in divorce after three months (Mooney 1964, p. 141). Both were reportedly uneasy in the company of female peers and they treated women as courtly gentlemen should. Thus the role orientations of both may have contributed to the infrequency with which congresswomen were selected for tasks requiring intimate contact with top leaders. This does not explain why Republican women were markedly underrepresented on strategic committees during the leadership of a more urbane trio of minority leaders, Ford, Rhodes and Michel, however. A decline in the average seniority of Republican women may explain some of the neglect.

The propensity to favor women for integrative rather than strategic positions has not meant that the former have always been readily accessible. Until 1981, both parties systematically excluded congresswomen from service on their Personnel Committees and the sharp decrease in the number of Republican women appearing in similar posts since 1965 is hardly encouraging. The early presence of a single woman on the Republican Policy Committee had its roots in a proposal offered during a meeting of the Republican Conference at the start of the 81st Congress. The meeting had been called to replace the Steering Committee with a Policy Committee. During debate, Representative Reid Murray of Wisconsin moved, and Edith Rogers of Massachusetts seconded, that a woman be included among the new Committee's membership. According to Conference minutes, Martin was presiding and he assured the body that the Committee on Committees would take note of the suggestion. Later, Frances Bolton was among the initial group of Republicans named to the panel. But, as Tables 6.3 and 6.4 make plain, the unwritten rule has not always been observed.

The Democrats, by contrast, have been much more receptive to placing and keeping women in integrative positions. Even Rayburn was prepared to select Chase Going Woodhouse as Secretary of the Caucus, although the position's title probably made the appointment a natural one for him. He also permitted her to serve as an *ex officio* member of the Steering Committee. However, the infrequency with which he convened that body and his action in 1956 to abolish the Committee signal the importance he attached to it. Recent Democratic leaders have made it a point to select at least one woman for service on the Steering and Policy Committee. Each congresswoman tapped for that panel was chosen directly by the Speaker, rather than elected by colleagues from geographic zones, a pattern which, while assuring the representation of women members, nonetheless lends support to Duverger's observation that equality deteriorates when men and women compete with one another for the votes of their peers.[8]

Democratic leaders were unusually stingy with positions on their Committee on Committees before the functions of that body were absorbed by a reorganized Steering and Policy Committee. The male monopoly on that panel prior to 1963 was probably related to the fact that, until 1975, committee assignments were determined by Democrats serving on the House Ways and Means Committee. This standing committee presides over such monumentally important subjects as taxation, social security, national health care, and tax expenditures, including mineral depletion allowances. Its substantive and committee assignment tasks, together with its relatively small membership, made it among the most prized committees in the House, and competition for a place on it was surely more spirited than if it had been responsible for committee assignments alone. Consequently, appointments to it were rarely conferred on the hesitant, on trouble makers, and on members considered marginal to the chamber's sociopolitical process.

Changes in the frequency with which congresswomen have been selected for token positions are the most obvious and, in some respects, the most puzzling. Who would have thought that no Republican woman filled a token position from 1947 to 1964, in spite of the fact that almost all state delegations were required to select two tokens. Far more mystifying is the fact that once Margaret Heckler, Virginia Smith, and Marjorie Holt began to accept routine appointments to both the campaign and committee assignment committees, women began to see less service on party instrumentalities that were valued by the House.

It would probably be an error to infer too much from the patterns revealed by these findings. We don't know the extent to which congresswomen actively sought secondary leadership positions and were rebuffed, although the ambitious may have been discouraged by low expectations of success. Furthermore, the inferences are made problematical by the small number of congresswomen with which the analysis deals, a factor which limits the usefulness of the Index of Success. It is possible, too, that a more rigorous control for seniority would have suggested other inferences. What does seem clear is that leaders of the two parties singled out two or three congresswomen in whom they were prepared to invest considerable confidence, and they loaded disproportionately large burdens on their shoulders while all but ignoring other congresswomen. The anointed were usually bright, politically savvy Representatives, women who displayed little emotion and who were electorally secure. They were prepared to compromise for the good of the party, and they possessed ideological predilections that were neither immutable nor outside their party's main-stream.

For Republicans, the chosen few were St. George and May. For Democrats, past favorites seem to have been Griffiths, Hansen, and Sullivan. Contemporary work horses include Schroeder and Ferraro. There is reason to believe that Barbara Jordan, too, would have been tapped for party service more often if she had remained in the House beyond three terms.

Finally, it is possible to explain variation in the success rates of the congresswomen as a consequence of their party's majority or minority status. Peabody believes that this status significantly influences the process by which leadership positions are filled. He points out, for example, that majority party leaders work within a climate of expanding rather than contracting credit. "Majority status promotes a search for compromise, accommodation, and the acceptance of established succession." The minority party, on the other hand, "operates in an environment of continuing frustration and increasing discord" (Peabody 1976, p. 302). Perhaps the frustrations of minority status make leadership positions within that party more attractive and, when keen competition develops, members perceived as marginal tend to be excluded. This would not explain the edge Republican women held over Democratic women from 1947 to 1964, when the former's party enjoyed majority status for only four years. Perhaps Speaker Rayburn's predispositions were more telling factors.

Thus, reliance on the formal record alone—the simple presence on, or absence from, party instrumentalities—has its limitations. Just because female Republicans have not served on secondary leadership positions as often as expected does not necessarily mean that they have been systematically discriminated against. And even though recent Democratic women seem to have held their own statistically, they might well have been frequent victims of bias based upon gender. Discussed below are perceptions and attitudes of twenty-four House members revealed in interviews conducted during the 95th Congress. Representatives were asked whether they believed a woman could be selected for a top leadership position in the near future. They were also asked about the circumstances under which such an event might take place, and the obstacles that might limit the choice of a woman, among other questions. (See Appendix C.) The responses provide an additional dimension to this study of female access to leadership positions in the House.

PERCEPTIONS OF LEADERSHIP OPPORTUNITIES
FOR CONGRESSWOMEN

Attaining a leadership position in the House is a product of many factors, some of which defy precise definition.[9] First, members must aspire to leadership responsibility and purposively work to obtain it. They know that these positions are neither awarded by default nor conferred on the timid. Normally, a person becomes a leader only after privately testing the waters, requesting support from the party colleagues most likely to give it, publicly announcing an intention to seek the post, and then working to muster the votes needed. But few House members actively seek these positions. Most are content to " . . . cultivate their constituencies" and "make their contributions through participation in committee and floor activity" (Peabody 1976, p. 4).

A member's ability to penetrate the leadership hierarchy is also related to his or her qualifications. Legislative and political skills, a knowledge and understanding of the House, and personality characteristics which are either appealing or which do not repel a large number of colleagues are of considerable importance. Other telling factors are length of House service (floor leaders in recent years served an average of eighteen years before their elevation to that post); the type of district and the state represented; policy orientations (although one study suggests that "moderateness" and party loyalty have not been particularly important criteria affecting leadership selection, Sullivan 1975, pp. 33 and 41); the extent to which an aspirant has supported successful contestants in previous leadership battles; and the particular "mix" of members who happen to make up the bulk of the leadership when a Representative attempts to be inducted into its ranks.

A good many House members are winnowed out of the leadership pool because they do not possess " . . . a set of more or less intangible traits labeled 'leadership potential'." They are unlikely to succeed unless they believe that they have that potential and unless they act on their belief "in characteristic ways" (Peabody 1976, p. 472). Finally, a leadership candidate's gender is an attribute of which House members are likely to be aware (even if they discount it) when deciding which colleague warrants their support.

Most of these factors were mentioned or referred to indirectly by 95th Congress informants who were asked about the degree to which the last of these considerations, gender, affected leadership choices rendered by House members. Although a few male and female Representatives said that they had once or twice voted for a woman because she *was* a woman, it should come as no surprise that most respondents pointed out the difficulty of explaining selection decisions in terms of a single, isolated variable. All informants were nonetheless prepared to comment on the importance of gender in the calculus of leadership choice, and these responses make it possible to draw inferences not only about the willingness of contemporary House members to select congresswomen to lead them, but also about the attitudes that contribute to the handicaps women suffer in this regard.[10]

Male Perceptions

Most congressmen interviewed were disinclined to choose a congress-woman for a top leadership position. Selection of a woman for a secondary party role was one thing—elevation to a major leadership role quite another. Some respondents said that they themselves might vote for a woman, but each added that their male colleagues were not ready to do the same. Several mentioned specific female Representatives whose future leadership prospects were bright. But more alluded to women who they believed would never attain a position of party responsibility, citing personal liabilities for the most part. They concluded that, given the attitudes of current colleagues, the emergence of a female floor leader or Whip or Caucus Chairman was many years away.

One congressman expressed directly the view only hinted at by others when he observed that it is unrealistic to expect a woman leader to be chosen before women become a larger proportion of the House membership. Only then, he asserted, are the chances of a woman being chosen significantly increased. He added:

> When you're dealing with a population that is so predominantly male, selection of a female leader would be inconsistent with the laws of probability. The leadership is likely to be representative of its constituency, and the overwhelming percentage of its constituents is not female.

Some informants speculated that if a woman were extraordinarily able, better qualified than her male competitors, she could conceivably be elected. But she would have to have demonstrated in unambiguous fashion that she was hard working, reliable, and flexible, and that she possessed both sound judgment and the interests of her party (and not only of her constituents and her ideological following) at heart. One Democratic congressman echoed the views of many other respondents when he said that "no woman is likely to be elected to a leadership position in the near future." What could happen, he continued, is that a female might be selected Democratic Whip since that is an appointive rather than an elected position. Her performance as Whip might then permit her to develop the coalition she would need to be elected floor leader and, perhaps, one day, Speaker. But, he added, "there is just no way a woman could make it today."

Congressmen varied in the reasons they gave for reaching this conclusion. Some attributed it to the attitudes of those making the selection, others suggested that it had to do with the qualities of specific female members and women in general, and some offered both kinds of explanations. A few noted that many of their colleagues believed it was "in the nature of things" for men to have authority over women, not the other way around. Some added that House members were unaccustomed to working with or for a woman before they came to Congress. They saw themselves as the principal authority figure in their own households, and they were not prepared to accept a sharp departure from such arrangements in Congress. Informants also suggested that some congressmen never even entertained the idea that they were the equals of the women with whom they were serving, and the possibility of their looking to a congresswoman for leadership was, for them, unthinkable.

Several of these same respondents said that many congressmen would find dealing with a woman leader awkward. These members, informants intimated, would not know how to adjust to conflicting role prescriptions. Their role as "males" who are supposed to demonstrate "masculine" respect for and deference toward a member of the "weaker" sex would clash with their role as "subordinates" who are expected to exhibit "political" respect for and deference toward a "powerful" House member who happened to be a woman. "There are some men in the House," noted one Congressman, "who simply cannot handle that kind of situation, and they would try to avoid it."

But about one-half of the male respondents suggested that the reasons women are unlikely to be selected for a leadership position in the near future inhere in the attributes of women generally and in qualifications of specific women serving in the 95th Congress. Several male informants said that most women do not want the kind of responsibility that goes with leadership. Women, they said, are accustomed to leaving management to men and they are happy to do that in the House. According to these members, women lack the drive and ambition needed to "position" themselves and win a battle for a leadership post. They are much less concerned about "getting ahead."

A few respondents maintained that the vast majority of women do not have the qualifications to perform successfully in a leadership position. They implied, for example, that floor leaders must be calm, rational, and firm, and often had to act aggressively and ruthlessly. They felt that most women were too emotional and too "soft" to manage the problems that develop in the House and that many would either go off "half-cocked" or passively permit the actions of others to shape political and legislative strategies and outcomes.

Almost all respondents were ready and even eager to discuss the shortcomings of specific female colleagues, after their anonymity was reaffirmed. Some women were described as "third" or "fourth" rate, others as "not smart enough." One congresswoman would never make it because she was so "threatening" that she was "hated," and another would never get anywhere because she was a "maverick" and always needling the leadership. Some women who succeeded their husbands were dismissed as not experienced or competent enough to warrant service in the House, let alone a leadership position. And two women were ruled out because they talked too much and said too little.

A few female members were singled out because they were "unrealistic" in their understanding of how a member achieved a leadership post. One informant said:

> There are some congresswomen who have strange ideas about how leadership positions are gained around here. They think that top jobs are handed out like badges. If you are here long enough, and if you are a good girl, one will be given to you. They think that a position should be given to a woman because there ought to be at least one woman on the leadership roster. . . . Maybe that's true for some things, but for positions that really count around here they would have to have much more going for them than a desire to be the 'token' woman.

Interviews with congresswomen revealed that most did not take so simplistic a view of how leadership positions are obtained. Almost all believed that hard work, intelligence, and ability are, and ought to be, more important than gender in securing the rewards distributed in the House.

Female Perceptions

Some contemporary congresswomen were more optimistic about leadership possibilities for women than were either female members serving sixteen years earlier or males interviewed during the 95th Congress. Among the thirteen congresswomen volunteering their views, four thought that a woman could be selected for a major leadership position in the foreseeable future. But two of the four, and almost all of the others who speculated about this hypothetical prospect, agreed that a woman candidate for a leadership post would have to be "twice as good" as any male even to be considered seriously for the position.

The most optimistic view came from a Democrat who had experienced some measure of party recognition and was almost euphoric in her expectations about women assuming leadership roles. This congresswoman recalled that when she first came to the House she never thought she would be as successful as she had been. In response to a question about discrimination based upon gender, she remarked:

> I personally don't experience obstruction. I have the complete acceptance of the men in my party. I have had my share of successes and who is to say where I can go from now on. . . . I have gained the respect of my colleagues, but when I first came to the House I wouldn't have dreamed that such things could happen.

The buoyantly positive tone of this response was not widely shared. Most congresswomen believed either that women would continue to be barred from leadership positions or that they would avoid leadership opportunities in order to give more attention to constituency and policy concerns—concerns which they were convinced had a more legitimate claim on their energies.

Republicans tended to be less sanguine than Democrats, and, given the absence of notable success among female Republicans who may have coveted secondary party positions, their gloom is understandable. One said simply that "Women will never get anywhere in the Republican party because the men in the House in my party cannot conceive of the prospect of sharing power with a woman or of taking directions from her." Another allowed that perhaps an "extraordinarily exceptional woman might get somewhere in Congress, but the rest of us are shut out."

Several women in both parties explained that their goals in the House were not entirely compatible with the tasks one performs when either seeking or exercising party leadership. They said that they came to Washington to represent the people who voted for them and that they would just as soon leave partisan concerns and political advantage to others. These women would not accept the charge that their goals were more modest than those who sought leadership positions. They argued that their goals were "different," and that by giving undivided attention to the legislative programs that mattered to them, by reaching out and "helping people," they were engaging their intellect and emotion in those activities from which they derived the most satisfaction.

For some women it was not so much a lack of interest in gaining the kind of influence leaders normally exert, as much as it was a distaste for the kind of behavior in which they would have to engage if they decided to make leadership responsibility one of their House goals. One highly regarded Democratic congresswoman, a member who believed that women could be selected for major leadership positions, said:

> Putting up with the process of cultivating colleagues, of getting them to like you and place their trust in you—which is what you have to do if you're going to seek a leadership position—is absolutely abhorrent to me. I can't imagine ever doing that. I become ill just thinking about it and I think a lot of other people, men and women, do also.

This woman's response refers to a process that was either explicitly articulated or implicitly alluded to by a majority of the congresswomen who were interviewed. One called it a process of "cultivating people," of getting them to "like you and trust you." These women agreed that people who groom themselves or who are groomed for leadership roles must establish close personal and professional relationships among Representatives upon whom they depend for political support. Developing such relationships took time, they pointed out, and required would-be leaders to invest enormous amounts of energy and emotion. To be successful, they had to exploit all available channels, formal as well as informal, by which to interact with party colleagues. Those who found such activities distasteful and who sought a leadership role were significantly handicapped.

Several women also discussed the need to be aggressive in order to make party leaders sit up and take notice, a style which some women were unwilling to adopt. Those who actively sought recognition, the informants continued, risked the enmity of men who believed that women should not behave in so castrating a fashion. Said one congresswoman:

> But you have to be that way in order to survive in the House. If you come on like Caspar Milquetoast, they'll trample all over you. On the other hand if you push aggressively for your goals, you are seen as a "pushy" woman, and they'll react with hostility.

A majority of women who were pessimistic about the future of would-be female leaders attributed their gloomy assessment less to female proclivities and personalities, factors congressmen thought were important, and more to established patterns of interaction in the House. They noted that women were systematically denied opportunities to deal with male colleagues in informal, unstructured settings. They had many fewer occasions, therefore, to demonstrate legislative and political skills, salutary personal qualities, "good fellowship," and those human frailties which party members could decide to overlook because sometimes these were virtues. As a result, the males with whom they would have to compete for leadership positions were likely to be better known, even if not necessarily more able supplicants for their colleagues' support.

One other handicap mentioned by several congresswomen when asked about the chances of one of their number obtaining a major leadership post was that none of the female members in the 95th Congress had been around long enough to make a legitimate claim to a top leadership position. Republican Margaret Heckler, the senior congresswoman, was in her sixth term at the time. The senior Democrat, Shirley Chisholm, was serving her fifth term. And almost all female respondents agreed that no House member could realistically expect to achieve top leadership status until he or she had been in Washington for fifteen years or more. They acknowledged that would-be leaders had to spend many years "paying their dues" before they could hope to obtain the recognition they sought.

A few congresswomen pointed out factors affecting leadership selection over which members had little control. Luck and happenstance, they noted, often separated the successful from the unsuccessful. One Republican speculated that these were the kinds of considerations that induced Barbara Jordan to retire from the House at the end of the 95th Congress. In July, 1978, just months before her retirement, Jordan was asked in a television interview whether the reasons she decided to leave Congress resided in the House or in herself. She replied:

> . . . it's a little bit of both. Now, if the Congress had offered me, let us say, an opportunity to work through the politics of Congress to a leadership role, I suppose that I could have been induced to forgo this tug of conscience [to leave Congress and do something else] for a little longer. But House politics did not seem to make it possible that I would be able to do that. There is also a sense—a sense that I have—of a diminution of my personal efficacy in the House. Now stated another way, I did not feel that I could further impact, dramatically or moderately, on the course of events personally as they moved through the Congress and the United States, that legislative process.[11]

Thus, institutional and personal considerations contributed to her decision. Among the former were the fact that Jordan had served in the House for a relatively short period of time and that her opportunities to exert substantial influence were several years away. But she could not have been oblivious of the fact that Jim Wright of Texas already had the number two position within the leadership hierarchy and was all but certain to succeed House Speaker O'Neill. Other Texans were, therefore, unlikely to move into one of the five or six major leadership positions very soon. But even if through sheer force of personality Jordan could have overcome this obstacle, a prospect entirely within the realm of the possible, she would have had to "jump over" Democrat Shirley Chisholm, a Rules Committee member and the Secretary of the Democratic Caucus. Another congresswoman who also happened to be black would have had to have displayed coalition-building skills more impressive than perhaps even those at the command of the redoubtable Barbara Jordan to have penetrated to topmost ranks of the leadership hierarchy.[12]

The dilemma faced by Jordan is experienced by male, as well as female Representatives. But from the vantage point of many congresswomen, this difficulty is a transitory one for men—one which is not likely to be accompanied, as it is for women, by gender-related bias. For about one-third of the female respondents however, lack of sufficient seniority represented the most important obstacle standing between a qualified, able, and ambitious woman on the one hand, and a major leadership post on the other.

DISCRIMINATION ON THE BASIS OF GENDER: TWO ALLEGATIONS

The problem of disentangling and weighing the factors contributing to the distribution of leadership positions has already been noted. A member's qualifications, goals, and seniority, along with many concrete and symbolic characteristics of incumbency all affect leadership prospects. That so few Republican women have penetrated the secondary leadership structure, and that none of either party has served in one of the top half-dozen positions, provides circumstantial evidence of discrimination based upon gender. Statements offered by informants in the 95th Congress are reason to take that evidence seriously. House members and their staffs alluded to several instances in which congresswomen making a claim to leadership role had been rebuffed because they were women. Frustrations experienced by two of them, one a former Representative, the other a member of the 95th Congress were recalled repeatedly.

The first instance involved Edith Green of Oregon and it was mentioned by both male and female informants, as well as by Green herself in a published interview (Dreifus, 1972). The Oregon Democrat was serving as Assistant Whip for the western zone when she received a call from Congressman Wayne Aspinall, Chairman of the Caucus of Western Democrats. Aspinall regularly attended meetings of the Democratic Steering Committee, but, since he would be unable to attend the next scheduled meeting, he asked Green if she would attend in his place. He had decided that since she was the Whip for the Western Region, she was the appropriate person to substitute for him. She agreed to attend.

Before the meeting, however, Green received a telephone call from Steering Committee Chairman Ray Madden of Indiana. Madden told her that he would not allow her to participate and that if she appeared he would cancel it. In recounting the incident, Green added:

> It was disgusting, really disgusting. No male member got up and said Madden's behavior was ridiculous, that I was representing the western region as a Democrat and had the right to attend. No one said that Ray Madden had no right to bar me (Dreifus 1972).

Few women served in Congress longer than Edith Green and fewer still were able to play so influential a role on their committees. During her years as Chair of Education and Labor's subcommittee on Higher Education, Green served as sponsor and floor manager of many important measures which later became law. Neither these successes nor her selection for secondary leadership roles, however, gave her reason to believe that leadership opportunities for women were equal to the opportunities available to men. When in 1972 she was asked whether she would consider running for a top leadership post, she replied:

> You know the saying: 'Negroes are fine so long as they know their place.' The same goes for women in Congress. A woman is fine as long as she knows her place. If a woman were to announce she was running for a party position, she would be considered an 'uppity female' (Dreifus 1972).

Green's bitterness was partly a product of the running battles she had had with other Democrats on the Labor and Education Committee and the unusually hostile comments regularly articulated by other members of her party—particularly John Brademas and Frank Thompson (Gladieux and Wolanin 1976, pp. 118–152). Her critics believed that she sought to dominate committee decisions affecting higher education while, at the same time, undermining proposals championed by other liberal Democrats with whom she worked. One congresswoman who observed Green's behavior and treatment in the committee setting remarked:

> When Green presided during markup sessions of the full committee and led the discussion, two things happened. First, the men, some of them, demonstrated their awe of her. They were in awe of her intellect and ability. She was so good at clarifying the issues—she was a real teacher, which is what she was before she came to the House. . . . And this intellect and ability really threatened some of the men—which leads to the second thing that happened. I saw hostility toward her. It was expressed in the inane and ridiculous remarks they made. And sometimes they were so exaggeratedly condescending it was disgusting.

In 1973, Green gave up eighteen years of seniority on the Education and Labor Committee and accepted a position on the Appropriations Committee. She explained the move by noting that national attention was then on the House "money" committees because of President Nixon's increasing impoundment of funds, his veto of appropriation measures, and his efforts to terminate important programs. That she had few allies left on the Education and Labor Committee must surely have made her decision easier.

The frustration of Congresswoman Marjorie Holt's bid for a leadership position at the start of the 95th Congress may be more to the point. After Republican Louis Frey of Florida announced he was giving up the chair of his party's Research Committee to become a candidate to head the Republican Policy Committee, Holt, who is perceived as being strongly conservative, announced her candidacy for the vacancy left by Frey. She was opposed in that contest by Congressman William Frenzel of Minnesota, a member of the moderate wing of his party.

When Republicans caucused to choose their leaders for the 95th Congress, the names of Holt and Frenzel were introduced for consideration, with nominating and seconding speeches presented on behalf of each. Just before the vote, however, the second ranking Republican, Minority Whip Robert Michel of Illinois, asked for the floor and urged his party colleagues to support Frenzel. He argued that since three of the top four leaders already chosen (floor leader John Rhodes, himself, and newly elected Policy Committee Chairman Del Clawson) were conservative and only one (Conference Chairman John Anderson) was a moderate, another moderate would give the party the ideological balance needed to make Republicans more effective in the new House. The vote was then called for and Frenzel won, 77–53.

Reactions of Republican respondents to Michel's action were mixed. Some felt that following Clawson's victory over Frey, the concern for ideological balance was a genuine one, even though Frey was no less a conservative. Some of these same informants noted that Frenzel was a capable, hard-working House member and deserved all the support he received, a sentiment they said was shared by many who did not vote for him. But several Republican members considered Michel's behavior unusual at the very least and outrageous at worst. Some said that they could not recall a leader ever intruding just before a vote to try openly to influence the outcome of this kind of contest. Naturally, leaders worked behind the scenes to try to affect the election result, but these members had never seen behavior similar to that engaged in by the Republican Whip. One Republican said:

> Michel's behavior was unforgivable. Marjorie had the votes all locked up until he spoke out. He probably turned around the votes of a dozen freshmen—many of whom Marjorie had gotten commitments from—because he spoke up. After all, Michel's the party whip. That's what he's supposed to do, round up votes for the leadership position. He certainly seemed to succeed this time.

A Republican congresswoman voiced similar sentiments, and added:

> I remember when it happened. A lot of people were stunned that he would do such a thing. . . . I voted for Marjorie and felt at the time that it was inappropriate for him to have spoken as he did.

Several respondents observed that Holt's unsuccessful effort to secure a leadership position foundered because she was a woman, although they mentioned other factors that may have been controlling. They alluded to her "inflexibly" conservative outlook, to Frenzel's longer House service and, without denigrating Holt, to the enormous respect in which the Minnesotan was held. But the belief by some that a party leader would not have gone to these lengths to defeat a male candidate with Holt's record suggests that some House members perceived the act as one which reflected bias based upon gender. Said one female informant:

> Those fellows just couldn't have been as relaxed with Holt as they were with one another. Frenzel is good, but I think that the leadership would have supported Ivan the Terrible rather than be saddled with a woman in that position.

Those who deny that Holt had been discriminated against and who accept explanations based on Frenzel's seniority and the party's quest for ideological balance could be given more credence were it not for the outcome of subsequent leadership contests. There is no evidence, for example, that Republican leaders applied the seniority rule or the principle of ideological balance when one of the most conservative House members, Pennsylvania's Bud Shuster, defeated the more senior Frenzel 90–55 for the GOP Policy Committee chair in the 96th Congress; or when, at the same time, Mississippi Republican Trent Lott won the Research Committee chair in a contest with the more senior and more moderate Lawrence Coughlin of Pennsylvania. The resulting line-up of Republican leaders, save for Anderson, was more conservative than ever. And Holt was defeated again before the 97th Congress convened when she challenged Richard Cheney, a former Ford White House aide who was about to begin his second term, for the GOP Policy Committee chair. She secured 68 of the 167 votes cast.

Disclaimers of bias are also made questionable by observations offered in the most comprehensive study of congressional leadership selection now available.

> The Republican . . . rather monolithic voting structure is skewed heavily in the conservative direction. Little attempt seems to be made by conservatives, who outnumber liberals by six, or seven, to one, to tolerate dissent or elect liberals to the party leadership. . . . Republican leaders are almost universally selected from the conservative mainstream of their party (Peabody 1976, pp. 307, 470).

The party made an exception in 1976 when it chose Frenzel over Holt. Had it not been the only time in recent Congresses that a vacancy was denied a conservative and filled by a moderate, the disclaimers could be given more weight.

*   *   *

Allegations of gender-based discrimination against congresswomen aspiring to leadership positions are difficult to confirm. The problem of disentangling gender bias from other possible explanations for denial of a leadership post, and the absence of hard, documentary evidence are just two factors contributing to that difficulty. Respondents in the 95th Congress, especially staff members, reported several instances of discrimination, but investigations more exhaustive than the ones described here are necessary if reasonable doubts are to be allayed. Nevertheless, the treatment of Green and Holt are consistent with circumstantial and attitudinal patterns revealed elsewhere in this chapter, and it suggests that, in spite of some progress, female Representatives must survive all of the trials their male colleagues face when seeking a major leadership post in the House—plus the one to which they are subjected by virtue of their being female.

WOMEN AND HOUSE LEADERSHIP

The pace at which women have gained access to leadership positions has been incremental at best. None has secured one of the major posts in her party. On the other hand, some advances have been made at the lower and middle party echelons, with Democrats particularly mindful of the growing number of women among their ranks. Sullivan, Kelly, Chisholm, and Ferraro have made the Caucus Secretary a female preserve and their selection often meant something more than simply choosing a token woman to do what women are alleged to do best—keep minutes of meetings. Of course much has depended upon how skillfully the Secretary exploits the opportunities the position affords her—her *ex officio* memberships and the regular access to top leaders these memberships make possible. Chisholm's elevation to the Rules Committee, together with the advancement of Griffiths, Jordan, Spellman, Boggs, and Schroeder constitute concrete gains made since Gehlen's study of the 88th Congress. Frequent selection of Democratic women to serve in the party's whip network reflects the same trend.

Members' perceptions about the status of women in the House have also undergone change. Whereas almost all male and female representatives interviewed in 1962 ruled out the possibility of a woman floor leader or whip in the foreseeable future, among those interviewed in 1978, about one-fifth of the males, one-third of the females, and about one in five Capitol Hill staff members were able to conceive of such a prospect. Some respondents went so far as to name specific women who they believed would make excellent leaders. None volunteered the name of a Republican woman, however, more because of the "unreconstructed" orientations of that party's leaders than because of the qualities and ambitions of Republican congresswomen. Their smaller number through the 95th Congress has been an important obstacle, as well.

But small numbers are not a problem for Republican women alone. Many explanations for the treatment women receive in the House can eventually be traced to the anemic size of the total female contingent, and this insuperable condition overwhelms the more subtle factors detailed above. A larger number of congresswomen, on the other hand, is only the most prominent of five important circumstances that would facilitate their selection to leadership positions. An increase in the number of congresswomen would force party leaders to choose more of them for middle level positions, if for no other reason than that there are a large number of such positions to be filled. And, as has been noted, a secondary leadership role has become a necessary condition for elevation to a major party post.

Almost as important as numbers and apprenticeship is length of service. No floor leader since World War II served as few terms as the most senior woman in the 95th Congress and it would be unreasonable to have expected a woman to have occupied a major party post in 1978. Lengthy service is a precondition for leadership not only because time is required to learn the trade, but because seniority itself is valued by some and it permeates decision rules. Time is also needed to build a coalition large enough to elect would-be leaders and to compete with ambitious male members who have both long service and the other valued qualities that accompany realistic aspirations.

A fourth and related condition facilitating a member's selection to a leadership position is access to the House's informal influence structure. As was noted in Chapter 5, more women have gained entry into this network and many have been accepted as equals by those with whom they interact. On the other hand, women have not yet penetrated the less visible, relatively unstructured groups in the House. Consequently, women who aspire to a major party post cannot rely upon the exchanges of trust and support that affiliation with such groups encourages. Perhaps only with the admission of a woman to the Chowder and Marching Society will a Republican woman find a springboard to a major leadership position.

Service on a significant standing committee of the House is neither a necessary nor a sufficient condition for advancement within one's party, but it, too, facilitates achievement of such a goal. Increased expertise in important policy areas, opportunities to help other members, and occasions for demonstrating political skills are three of the more important by-products of service on these committees. It should come as no surprise that an unusually large proportion of leaders saw prior service on the Appropriations, Rules, or Ways and Means Committees before they rose to a high party office.

In sum, the prospects of would-be female House leaders are linked to an increase in the number of women colleagues within their own party; to service in secondary leadership positions; to youth, good health, constituency appeal, and stable district boundaries sufficient to permit a return to the House often enough to acquire considerable seniority; to entry into informal groups and communications networks which give them opportunities to establish a camaraderie and rapport with those over whom they will exercise leadership; and to performance on a major House committee which calls attention to their mastery of the legislative process, and the personal and political skills that House members expect leaders to possess. It is possible that even if all five of these conditions materialize, no woman will soon emerge as, say, floor leader. But it is reasonably certain that if none of them materializes in abundant measure, men will continue to monopolize those party positions which the House values most.

NOTES

1. In 1979, Conservative Party leader Margaret Thatcher was made Great Britain's Prime Minister, Maria de Lourdes Pintassilgo became (for a short time) Portugal's first woman Premier, and Bolivian leaders temporarily conferred the Presidency upon Lydia Gueiler Tejada (only to force her resignation in a military coup a year later). The same year also saw appointment of France's Simone Veil as President of the 410-member European Parliament.

2. Githens and Prestage (1978, p. 267) found that fourteen percent of women state legislators responding to questionnaires held leadership positions. When they took seniority into account, however, they concluded that women were underrepresented. Kirkpatrick notes that female legislators have been successful in securing leadership positions partly because they have been willing to fight for them (Kirkpatrick 1974, p. 127).

3. During this period, Republican leaders began to select more than one member from some states, appointing representatives of congressional "classes" to the Committee on Committees, for example.

4. Martin's position was more important than its title in contemporary usage suggests. He was one of two Assistant Whips and ranked immediately below the floor leader.

5. The Republican Conference Secretary is a more sought-after position than is the same post among Democrats inasmuch as it has sometimes been a springboard to Conference Vice Chairman, an office Democrats never created.

6. According to Jones (1964, pp. 72–73), this is one of the central tasks of the Republican Policy Committee.

7. The equation employed to determine the Index of Success for women in each party was derived as follows:

$$x = x_m + x_w$$

$$n = n_m + n_w$$

Where x equals the number of leadership positions available within the party; n equals the number of Representatives in the party; and where m signifies men and w signifies women. Thus, if $x_w/x = n_w/n$, then the Index of Success = 1.00.

8. In the 98th Congress, eight committee members were chosen by the Speaker, eleven elected from geographic zones. Some observers maintain that the Speaker's choices are likely to be more influential than zone representatives because the former's selection is both a consequence and a reflection of their loyalty to him. Zone representatives may have the confidence of House members in neighboring districts, but they are likely to be more independent of the Speaker and, therefore, less trustworthy in his eyes, because he played a smaller role in their elevation to the Committee.

9. The best treatment of this subject appears in Peabody 1976, Chapters 10 and 16. Part of the discussion that follows draws generously on this work.

10. See Appendix C for questions employed to obtain these responses.

11. See transcript of "The Macneil/Lehrer Report: Barbara Jordan Interview," July 4, 1978, Educational Broadcasting Corporation and Greater Washington Educational Telecommunications Association, Inc., 1978.

12. In a letter to the author written on November 17, 1978, Congresswoman Jordan stated, in response to a request to explain her retirement from the House: " . . . in House politics, you get in at the bottom and await your turn to move up. The line is long." She also noted that her statement on the "Macneil/Lehrer Report" had nothing to do with race, sex, or state of origin.

Part IV
Behavior

7 / Changing Legislative Opportunities

Most women legislators around the world have specialized, willingly or otherwise, in those substantive issues believed to be peculiarly within the interest and competence of their gender. They have been especially active in such policy domains as education, health, welfare, local government, and domestic relations, and many have sought avenues to promote peace and international harmony as well. Few, on the other hand, have seized (or been permitted to seize) opportunities to shape tax laws, hammer out appropriation's measures, or fashion rules to govern commercial and financial practices. They have also had little to do with writing civil and criminal codes or with creating military and defense policies.

This pattern has been reasonably well documented for West European parliaments. In 1955, when Maurice Duverger expressed doubts about women's leadership opportunities in European governments, he also noted that these same women were usually limited to subsidiary policy matters. He pointed out that women in the German Bundestag, for example, occupied as many as one-half of the positions on committees dealing with public health, welfare, and juveniles, and one-quarter of the seats on panels devoted to labor and social welfare. Few women sat on committees dealing with the nation's budget and taxes, however, and none was a member of an economic policy committee. Moreover, one-half of the motions, reports, and speeches offered by female members of that body related to social issues—welfare for mothers, equal pay for women civil servants, and the relationship between parents and children. Similar findings emerged when Duverger examined the subject matter of speeches given by women in the French National Assembly (1955, pp. 95–97).

Matters were much the same on the other side of the Channel. In the 1920s, it was unusual for female M.P.s to speak out on economic issues during debate in the House of Commons (Brookes 1967, p. 53), and even in the years following World War II, they were inclined to limit their attention to legislative measures touching on health, education, matrimony, pensions, widows, and orphans (Mann 1962, p. 34). When asked if he would like to see more women in politics, Conservative Party leader Edward Heath replied: "Yes, ... *so long as they are providing what women can do and not just duplicating what men can do*, which would lead to them not making a woman's contribution ... " (Brookes 1967, p. 267. The emphasis is Brookes's).

One explanation for this pattern holds that women are by nature, experience, and interest better able to deal with some issues and less adroit when addressing others. Accordingly, they gravitate (or are escorted) toward the former. A second maintains that questions of taxation, government spending, national security, the administration of justice, and business and commerce are the most consequential matters with which a polity must come to grips and, since men, after all, determine the national agenda and apportion substantive responsibilities among lawmakers, they are in a position to relegate female colleagues to policy areas of secondary importance. In his analysis of European legislatures, Duverger embraces the latter explanation. He concludes that the findings are less a product of men and women possessing different interests and competencies than they are a function of male unwillingness to permit women to serve on legislative instrumentalities that shape their countries' fundamental policies.

THE SPECIALTIES OF EARLY CONGRESSWOMEN

The legislative experience of congresswomen serving between the World Wars was not fundamentally different from that of their European counterparts. Moreover, many Americans who otherwise bristled at discrimination against women saw nothing wrong with female lawmakers concentrating energies on subjects with which by nature and training they were believed to be most familiar. Even those who took vehement exception to the limited political opportunities available to women believed that politics had a natural division of labor. Sophonisba Breckinridge, for example, argued that women should enter legislatures to fashion governmental policies that are domestic in character—to transfer to the public arena those skills and services which women normally exhibited in the home (1933, p. 295).

These views were shared by even the most liberated of the early congresswomen. When asked why a woman should serve in Congress, Jeannette Rankin replied:

> There are hundreds of men to care for the nation's tariff and foreign policy and irrigation projects. But there isn't a single woman to look after the nation's greatest asset: its children. (Quoted in Chamberlin 1973, p. 5.)

And Ruth Bryan Owen maintained:

> Through thinking, training, experience, the woman in politics has a most
> definite original contribution to make in such fields as child welfare,
> education, the removal of inequalities of women before the law, and
> international relations. More women assisting in the delicate contacts between
> country and country would mean, I firmly believe, more surety of world peace
> (Owen 1933, p. 30).

It should come as no surprise, then, that most congresswomen who served
between the wars were assigned to standing committees that dealt with issues
deemed appropriate to their gender. The pattern began to change in the 1940s,
however, particularly after passage of the 1946 Legislative Reorganization Act.
At the same time, female Representatives gradually began to gain positions on
the House's most valued committees and subcommittees at a pace similar to that
of their male colleagues. As will be demonstrated in the pages that follow,
women today are as likely to shape policy in nontraditional domains as they are in
domains customarily considered to be female preserves.

EXPANDING COMMITTEE AND SUBCOMMITTEE OPTIONS

To demonstrate the extent to which congresswomen have achieved access
to nontraditional policy domains, subjects dealt with by Congress were first
categorized as being either more or less amenable to female treatment.
Congresswomen's committee assignments were then aggregated by time
periods—1917 to 1946, 1947 to 1964, and 1965 to 1983. Deciding which policies
(and the committees responsible for them) were more compatible and which less
compatible with women's interests strains the imagination. The observations of
those who perceived such distinctions (Breckinridge, Owen, and Gehlen [1969,
p. 36], among them), are useful, however, and, for the purposes of the discussion
that follows, "women's" committee and subcommittees are those which consider
health, education, welfare, and family matters. Subsumed under the same rubric
are issues affecting members of disadvantaged groups (Indians, women), local
government (the District of Columbia, territories), and veterans' and civil service
benefits. Housekeeping details, concern for foreign (but not defense) policy, and
the efficient and ethical running of government are also matters in which women
have been reputed to possess unusual interest and competence. (For a list of
committees and subcommittees considering issues typically regarded as being of
interest to women, see Appendix D.)

Committees dealing with issues which are not traditionally thought of as
women's concerns focus upon defense policy, internal security, manufacturing
and trade, business and finance, agriculture, taxation, public works (and other

matters that encourage horse trading for palpably parochial benefits), civil, criminal and constitutional law, and the appropriations process. The artificial nature of distinctions between traditional and nontraditional areas of alleged female interest becomes clear when politics are interpreted within a perspective broader than is customarily brought to bear. Matters of war and peace, the sufficiency and quality of agricultural products, street crime, the size and source of tax revenues, the distribution of these revenues among the poor and the ill, and the allocation of resources generally can be construed as "health" and "welfare" issues. Political and social conventions in both Congress and the country have discouraged this broader view, however.

If, then, we accept the more narrowly conceived differences among issues, the information in Table 7.1 is revealing. It indicates first of all that almost two-thirds (64%) of the initial assignments distributed among congresswomen serving between 1917 and 1946 were to committees concerned with matters to which women were understood to bring unusual facility. Among them were those dealing with Indian affairs, women's suffrage, education, pensions and other benefits for veterans, civil service, and the manner in which executive agencies are organized to expend appropriated funds, a subject which should not be confused with the appropriations process itself.

A few congresswomen were awarded seats on Banking and Currency, Rivers and Harbors (a major pork-barrel committee), and Military or Naval Affairs, but they were among the little more than one-third who were assigned to panels dealing with issues not traditionally defined as female. The Table does not show that no woman was placed on such weighty House committees as Ways and Means, Agriculture, Interstate and Foreign Commerce, Appropriations, and Judiciary.

With the implementation of the 1946 Reorganization Act, the pattern changed, abruptly at first, and then gradually. The proportion of assignments to committees whose subject matter was not normally considered food for female thought increased significantly. Between the 80th and 88th Congresses, first-term congresswomen were appointed to such previously all-male preserves as the Judiciary, Merchant Marine and Fisheries, and Agriculture Committees, and a few found their way to the new panel on Science and Astronautics. Change since 1965 may have been more important than is indicated by the six percentage point shift recorded in Table 7.1, inasmuch as congresswomen, were assigned seats on virtually all remaining nontraditional committees. Neophyte Barbara Mikulski, for example, penetrated the previously all male Interstate and Foreign Commerce Committee in 1977.

The shift over time seems equally compelling when we consider committee choices made by women after they completed their first terms. As Table 7.2 makes clear, more than two-thirds of the relatively few transfers and additional assignments undertaken by congresswomen prior to 1947 sent them to panels whose subject matter was stereotypically suitable for them. The figure decreased

Table 7.1. Initial Assignments to Committees and Subcommittees Whose Subject Matter is of Traditional Interest to Women, 1917–1983

Time Period (Congresses)	Percent (and Number) of Assignments to Traditional Committees and Subcommittees	Total Initial Assignments of Congresswomen
1917–1946	64	
(65th–79th)	(47)	73
1947–1964	56	
(80th–88th)	(33)	59
1965–1983	50	
(89th–98th)	(64)	129

Note: When women were assigned to two or more committees, each was categorized separately.

Sources: Barbara L. Schwemle, "Women in the United States Congress," Congressional Research Service, Library of Congress, March 9, 1982; Congressional Quarterly, Inc., *Congressional Quarterly* Almanac, 1955–1981; *Congressional Quarterly Special Report*, Vol. 41, No. 13, April 2, 1983.

significantly during the post-World War II period, however, and the point has been reached today where no House committee or subcommittee is beyond the reach of a congresswoman interested in serving on it. Subcommittees devoted to advanced technology, the latest developments in weapons systems, tortuous commercial regulations, and intricate tax and banking arrangements are now routinely made up of at least one congresswoman.

At the same time, female House members continue to serve on committees devoted to subjects of traditional interest—veterans, hospitals, health care, education, and the environment. In fact, they occasionally appear to be grossly overrepresented on one or more of the committees dealing with these issues. Bella Abzug suspected ulterior motives when she called attention to the fact that five of the twelve women in the 92nd Congress served on the Education and Labor Committee. "Maybe they figure if they get us all in one place we'll cause less trouble," she said (Abzug 1970, p. 26). But the precongressional experience of the five, along with their policy and political orientations surely must have contributed to the skewed distribution to which Abzug alluded.[1] As recently as 1982, however, Shirley Chisholm remarked: "When you talk about . . . the different kinds of programs that deal with human beings, it's women who will have to be leaders on those issues because the gentlemen find other issues more exciting" (Payne 1982, p. 132).

Another committee to which contemporary congresswomen have flocked is the Select Committee on Aging. Although it is not a permanent standing

Table 7.2. Post-First Term Transfers and Additional Assignments to Committees and Subcommittees Whose Subject Matter is of Traditional Interest to Women, 1917–1983

Time Period (Congresses)	Percent (and Number) of Assignments to Traditional Committees and Subcommittees	Total Transfers and Additional Assignments of Congresswomen
1917–1946	71	
(65th–79th)	(12)	17
1947–1964	51	
(80th–88th)	(30)	59
1965–1983	51	
(89th–98th)	(97)	191

Note: When women were transfered or subsequently assigned to two or more committees, each was categorized separately.

Sources: Barbara L. Schwemle, "Women in the United States Congress," Congressional Research Service, Library of Congress, March 9, 1982; Congressional Quarterly, Inc., Congressional Quarterly Almanac, 1955–1981; Congressional Quarterly Special Report, Vol. 41, No. 13, April 2, 1983.

committee, and is excluded, therefore, from the tabulated findings, the issues with which it comes to grips have become extraordinarily salient in recent years. Its membership ballooned to sixty in the 98th Congress, thus becoming the largest in the House. Six of the twenty-one women seated in January, 1983, choose to retain positions they had already secured on the panel.

But the continued attraction congresswomen have for committees treating issues that are conventionally "female" does not alter the fact that many are addressing nontraditional subjects with a frequency which is considerably higher than was true in the past. Apparently neither they nor their male colleagues have been as apt as their predecessors to permit stereotypical views of women's interests to color decisions affecting committee assignments.

A compelling explanation for this development is the changing attitudes about female interests and skills within society in general. The House may simply be recording changes already reflected in the private choices made by women throughout the country. Contemporary congresswomen may also be more aggressive than past women House members, more insistent in their demands for a committee assignment compatible with their nontraditional interests and more determined to be where important policy decisions are being made. Although they have not achieved notable gains in penetrating the House leadership structure, as is maintained in the preceding chapter, they do not seem to be deterred from securing access to the policy domains they prefer to influence.

ACCESS TO EXCLUSIVE COMMITTEES AND CHAIRS

Recent congresswomen have begun not only to specialize in subjects formally regarded as less suitable for females, but also, as we shall see, they have begun to gain seats on the most prestigious House committees. Access to these critical policy-making arenas supply participants with uncommon tactical advantages. For one thing, colleagues who do not serve on them seek committee members' support more often than would otherwise be the case and, when help is proffered, the gratitude generated in return can only redound to the donor's benefit. For another, the reciprocity exchanged among members of these coveted committees is likely to aid the political and electoral fortunes of them all.[2]

Congresswomen have not been nearly as successful in securing committee chairs as they have been in receiving assignments to valued committees, but, since the 1950s, they have held their own with male Representatives in the frequency with which they have been named subcommittee chairs and ranking minority members. As will be made clear below, however, their overall success in this connection has not been particularly evident on the House's most prized committees.

Assignments to Exclusive Committees

There is overlap between committees dealing with subjects previously deemed unsuitable to female talents and those considered most prestigious by the House. But the two categories are not identical and there is no reason to believe that the rates at which congresswomen have been awarded the two types of assignments should be the same. And they are not.

The figures in Tables 7.1 and 7.2 indicate that no more than about one-third of the congresswomen serving between 1917 and 1946 filled vacancies on committees whose subject matter was perceived to be less appropriate for female consideration. Table 7.3, on the other hand, makes clear that a significantly larger proportion of these early congresswomen sooner or later found themselves on exclusive House committees.[3] Six different women, including Ruth Bryan Owen, Effiegene Wingo, Edith Nourse Rogers, Frances Bolton, Emily Douglas Taft, and Helen Gahagan Douglas, served on the Foreign Affairs committee, and Margaret Chase Smith saw initial service on Post Office and Post Roads, both of which were defined as "exclusive" at the time.[4]

Nonetheless, the earliest congresswomen as a group did not do as well as their male contemporaries. Whereas little more than one-quarter (27%) received exclusive assignments in their first terms, one-third of the freshmen congressmen were just as successful. Furthermore, the women seem never to have caught up with (although they approached) the rate of exclusive committee assignments

Table 7.3. Male and Female Representatives Serving on Exclusive Standing Committees during Their First Five Terms, 1917–1983

Time Period in which First elected	Gender	1st Term	2nd Term	3rd Term	4th Term	5th Term
1917–1946	Male	33%	55%	66%	69%	70%
(65th–79th)	Female	27%	43%	50%	57%	67%
1947–1964	Male	3%	11%	16%	22%	28%
(80th–88th)	Female	0%	5%	12%	14%	23%
1965–1983	Male	5%	14%	28%	30%	30%
(89th–98th)	Female	8%	24%	30%	31%	33%

Note: Exclusive Committees during the 1917 to 1946 period include: Agriculture, Appropriations, Banking and Currency, Foreign Affairs, Interstate and Foreign Commerce, Judiciary, Military Affairs, Naval Affairs, Post Office and Post Roads, ·Rules, and Ways and Means. See George Galloway, *The Legislative Process in Congress* (New York: Thomas Y. Crowell, 1953), p. 281. Exclusive committees during the latter two periods include Appropriations, Rules, Ways and Means, and, beginning in 1975, Budget.

Source: *U.S. Congressional Directory*, 1917–1983.

males with comparable service received during their first five terms. For example, two of three male Representatives (66%) in their third term during this period were assigned to exclusive committees, compared with only one of every two congresswomen. The three percentage point difference between men and women in their fifth terms seems to be of little importance, except that the delay congresswomen experienced almost certainly diluted the effect their House seniority could have on (the more important) committee seniority, inasmuch as influence on committees depended upon the latter rather than the former.

The House career of California's Florence Kahn reflects the difficulties some congresswomen experienced in the years before World War II. Kahn sought to replace her husband on Military Affairs, a committee which he had chaired before his death, but she received, instead, three minor committees, one of which was Indian Affairs. The San Francisco Republican refused to accept this last assignment, noting that the only Indians in her district were in front of cigar stores and beyond any assistance she could provide. The Republican leadership then awarded her a vacancy on the more appealing Education Committee (Gilfond 1929, p. 159). But Kahn had to wait until her third term before securing a Military Affairs seat and two more terms before being given a vacancy on the Appropriations Committee.

These early cases may not be strictly comparable with assignments distributed following committee reorganization in 1946, but the disadvantages congresswomen suffered relative to their male colleagues did not abate between the 1940s and the 1960s. Not a single female Representative was initially assigned to an exclusive committee—then defined as including only Appropriations, Rules, and Ways and Means—as compared with three of every 100 fledgling congressmen. The difference may not be a significant one, but it seems formidable if only because the percentage for women simply could not have been lower. And their failure ever to equal the success rate of males with comparable service underscores the handicap imposed upon them during their first few terms.

Contemporary congresswomen have reversed the pattern, however. A larger proportion of first-term women than men have been appointed to exclusive committees (expanded since 1975 to include the Budget Committee), and, as their terms of service progressed, they maintained an important, even if eventually diminishing, advantage. The small size of the female universe makes one hesitant about placing too much confidence in the comparison, but the fact remains that Martha Keys (Ways and Means) and Lynn Martin and Bobbi Fiedler (Budget) received prestigious committee assignments as soon as they arrived on Capitol Hill. And other females elected since 1964 transferred to exclusive committees at a slightly more rapid rate than males with equal years of service.

It would appear, then, that women elected to the House since the mid-1960s have been more successful than their female predecessors in securing prestigious assignments, and that they have fared better as a group than the males whose House careers began when theirs did.

Committee and Subcommittee Chairs

Before the 1946 Reorganization Act was passed, five women had headed standing House committees. Mae Nolan led the Committee on Expenditures in the Post Office Department and Caroline O'Day chaired the Committee on the Election of the President, Vice President, and Representatives in Congress. Leadership of so inconsequential a pair of committees was unlikely to confer an important policy role on either woman, however. When Mary Norton chaired first the District of Columbia Committee and then the Labor Committee, on the other hand, she gained national recognition, even if not always the leverage needed to exercise significant influence within the House. The chair of the first earned her the designation "Mayor of Washington" and the position on the second gave her the opportunity to sponsor and manage important legislation—notably the Wages and Hours Act of 1938. But when the Labor Committee was combined with the Education Committee in 1947, Norton moved to the nonexclusive House Administration Committee, where her considerable seniority soon elevated her to the chair of that less prestigious House panel.[5]

After passage of the 1946 Act, Edith Nourse Rogers chaired the nonexclusive Veterans Affairs Committee, and in the 93rd and 94th Congresses, Leonor Sullivan led the similarly nonexclusive Merchant Marine and Fisheries

Committee, a post with some opportunities for leadership, but one whose subject-matter jurisdiction made it of limited importance, nonetheless.

No congresswoman is even close to chairing a House committee in the 98th Congress, but two relatively recent developments portend a change in policy leadership opportunities for female Representatives. The first is the proliferation and growing importance of subcommittees. The second is the Democrats' decision to limit the number of subcommittees each member may chair. The former has increased the number of opportunities for policy leadership available to all House members. The latter seems to have had a slight chilling effect thus far on such opportunities for women inasmuch as a number of senior congresswomen headed, until recently, two or more subcommittees that were components of the same full committee.

Support for this conclusion emerges from a systematic examination of the frequency with which congresswomen have served as either subcommittee chairs or ranking minority members, relative to both their numbers and the frequency with which they could conceivably have been chosen for such posts. A count was made of just how many women have been elevated to top subcommittee positions beginning in 1955—a time when most, even if not all, standing committees had established subcommittees.[6] Their number was analyzed in terms of how many subcommittee chairs existed on the full committees to which they were assigned and the number of male Representatives with whom they were competing for such positions.

The figures in Table 7.4 reflect the level of success congresswomen achieved collectively, with an index of 1.00 denoting a level one would normally expect to occur by chance, a figure of 2.00 indicating that the women were twice as successful as their numbers and opportunities would permit on average, and anything less than 1.00 implying that women were underrepresented in subcommittee leadership positions.[7]

The Table suggests that the success rate of female House members has fluctuated over time, but that generally they have held their own. Democratic women have been more consistently successful in securing subcommittee chairs, although their index has been declining. Between 1955 and 1974, they were slightly more than 1.5 times as likely as male Democrats to be elevated to a subcommittee chair. Their rate of success during the most recent period is little more than one would expect if chairs were distributed randomly. The frequency with which Republican women have been chosen ranking members of subcommittees has been erratic, with their success rate during the middle period especially noteworthy. In recent years, however, they have been underrepresented as ranking members of subcommittees.

A closer look at the House service of selected congresswomen helps to refine the findings and explain some of the variations. The high index of success among Democratic women during the first two periods is largely a product of the seniority of first Congresswomen Edna Kelly, Elizabeth Kee and Gracie Pfost

Table 7.4. Index of Success* in Securing Subcommittee Chairs and Ranking Minority Positions, 1955–1983

Time Period (Congresses)	Democratic Congresswomen	Republican Congresswomen	Total Congresswomen**
1955–1964 (84th–88th)	1.54	.90	1.24
1965–1974 (89th–93rd)	1.51	1.94	1.73
1975–1983 (94th–98th)	1.16	.80	1.02

*See Chapter 6, note 7 for a description of how the Index was derived.

**Women serving on committees that did not have subcommittees are excluded.

and, later, Edith Green, Leonor Sullivan, and Julia Hansen.[8] Several of these women chaired more than one subcommittee. The index recorded by Republican women during the middle period rests on the ranking positions and multi–subcommittee memberships of Representatives Frances Bolton, Florence Dwyer, and Catherine May.

The recent decline among Democratic women and the underrepresentation of Republicans is partly a product of the limit placed on the number of subcommittee chairs a member may hold and party a result of retirement and election defeat among more senior women. Elections to the 93rd, 94th, and 95th Congresses brought in thirteen more Democratic women, but they also accompanied the retirement of such Democratic stalwarts as Green, Hansen, and Sullivan. Among Republicans, May and Dwyer left the House in the early 1970s, and it wasn't until the 97th Congress—when four new Republican women joined the House—that their party's ranks were restored. Obviously, the low seniority of these women has limited their leadership opportunities on subcommittees. As Geraldine Ferraro noted: " . . . women's lack of seniority, not gender differences . . . " is today's principal obstacle to such opportunities (Ferraro 1979, p. 22).

The depressed rate for contemporary Republicans was also due, in part, to Congresswoman Fenwick's difficulties in securing a seat on the Foreign Affairs Committee. When elected to her first term, she believed that her cosmopolitan background, her fluency in French, Spanish, and Italian, and the service of her New Jersey predecessor, Peter Frelinghuysen, on Foreign Affairs made her a natural choice for the Committee. She was mistaken, and later concluded that her early failures in this regard were possibly the result of her liberal political orientation (Lamson 1979, p. 30). Fenwick recalled her first term frustrations in a 1981 interview.

> I at once wrote to the leadership of the party, because somebody told me that's what you did, and said that I hoped very much to be a member of the Foreign Affairs Committee. . . . I was put on Small Business and Banking and

on the Ethics Committee. . . . The only reason I got on Ethics was that nobody wanted to serve on it. I knew nothing about banking. It was an agonizing learning experience. Required great self-discipline. But I thought, maybe next year. . . . Nothing happened. If I'd been a better politician, I don't think that would have happened. . . . I'm on Foreign Affairs finally. Last year I got Foreign Affairs and the District of Columbia, which is not the most desirable committee to serve on. But I did. I served faithfully. Now this year I have Foreign Affairs and Labor and Education and I couldn't be more satisfied. But here I am in my seventh year (*Washington Star*, May 27, 1981).

During her four terms, Fenwick spent no more than two on any one committee. As a result, she did not gain ranking status on any of the five subcommittees of which she was a member.

An additional, more important, reason for the decrease in the frequency with which women have secured subcommittee leadership positions is linked to an increase in their appointments to prestigious committees. As has been noted, recent congresswomen have gained seats on exclusive committees at a slightly greater pace than that of men. But selection to subcommittee leadership positions on exclusive committees requires more seniority than does elevation to a subcommittee chair on a lesser committee. Thus, the relatively low seniority of contemporary congresswomen has put them at a disadvantage for the time being. Democrats Yvonne Burke, Elizabeth Holtzman, Martha Keys, Shirley Chisholm, Lindy Boggs, and Pasty Mink (in her sixth term) won appointments to the Appropriations, Budget, Rules, and Ways and Means Committees. But the route to subcommittee responsibility on these panels is normally longer and, with the exception of Holtzman, none secured a subcommittee chair. Republicans fared a bit better, with Smith and Martin (while still in her first term) filling key subcommittee slots on the House's most prestigious committees.

Differences in leadership opportunities on exclusive and less exclusive committees is illustrated by the distribution of subcommittee chairs among Democratic women between 1975 and 1983. Of the twenty-one subcommittees these women headed during five Congresses, ten were Post Office and Civil Service panels, five were components of Government Operations, and one a subcommittee of the Committee on Interior and Insular Affairs—three of the least coveted among House standing committees.

In sum, congresswomen have expanded the range of issues to which they give their attention and, as a result, they have augmented their ability to lead the House in selected policy domains. Since the 1960s, they have served on subcommittees that dealt with such matters as nuclear energy and nuclear weaponry, telecommunications and transportation, international law and criminal justice, to mention only a few subjects largely inaccessible to female Representatives in years past. They have also gained seats on those committees that most influence fiscal decisions, with almost all Congresses convened in the last decade having at least one women on each of the money committees—Appropriations, Budget, and Ways and Means. Female membership on the powerful Rules Committee has been more intermittent.

Over the years, few women have been chairs of standing House committees, and the handful who have, headed relatively unimportant panels. On the other hand, the frequency with which they have claimed top positions on subcommittees has been slightly greater than chance alone would dictate. Democrats, particularly, have been successful in securing subcommittee chairs, although the recent increase in the number of young, energetic GOP women suggests that Republicans, too, will soon begin to hold their own with male cohorts.

Failure of congresswomen to rise to subcommittee leadership positions on highly prized committees has thus far limited their opportunities to shape policies on issues which attract greatest congressional interest. Since the pace at which they have been assigned to these prestigious panels has been greater than that of men in recent years, however, congresswomen now serving on them have a better chance through the seniority rule of capturing a chair or ranking membership than either their predecessors or their male contemporaries.

*   *   *

Women's service on a relatively narrow range of committees before the 1960s does not mean that they did not shape national policy. It means only that they were limited with respect to the policy domains to which they could confidently apply their talents. The achievements of Mary Norton in the governance of the District of Columbia and in labor policy, and of Edith Rogers in veteran's legislation, for example, are undisputed. Until the 1960s, however, no women were identified as principal proponents of laws in such fields as taxation, social security, business and banking practices, and budgetary policy.

With adoption of a less restrictive committee assignment process, however, an increasing number of them turned their talents to these issues. At about the same time, female Representatives, sensitized to the growing demands expressed by leaders of the feminist movement, began to champion measures directly impinging on women. Before long, some of them began to combine their interests in the two groups of policies and they came to the astonishingly fundamental realization that all important issues were women's issues; that all basic government decisions influencing the distribution of financial and other resources had a different impact on most females, as compared with most males, and that, the great majority of these decisions had placed women at a disadvantage.

As the next chapters make clear, congresswomen began to help redefine the nature of women's issues, to alter their own representational role orientations, and to effect significantly the disposition of legislative measures affecting contemporary women. They concluded that American women needed champions in Washington who were prepared to determine and speak for their collective needs.

NOTES

1. Two of the five, Edith Green and Shirley Chisholm, shared an interest in education which predated by many years their election to the House. Louise Day Hicks had built a political reputation on her opposition to school busing for purposes of racial integration and had served on the Boston School Board before coming to Washington. Ella Grasso, whose husband was a school superintendent, had established a record of achievement in the field of education while holding public office in Connecticut, especially through programs to help the retarded and blind. And Patsy Mink's close ties to organized labor made her assignment to the Committee a reasonable one. If those controlling the distribution of assignments meant to isolate the influence of these women by putting them on the same committee, as Abzug suggested, they were assisted by the relatively narrow range of vocational pursuits from which society expected women to choose.

2. Democrats serving on the Ways and Means Committee before 1975 were in a particularly advantageous position inasmuch as they constituted their party's Committee on Committees (Manley 1967, pp. 76–78). They continue to exercise influence on minor tax provisions of special interest to colleagues whose constituencies are likely to be directly affected in ways which the rest of the country will not be. Unusual opportunities to help another Representative's standing with constituents are similarly available to Appropriations Committee members (Fenno 1966, pp. 87–88).

3. The following committees were defined as "exclusive" between 1917 and 1946 (Galloway 1953, p. 281): Agriculture, Appropriations, Banking and Currency, Foreign Affairs, Interstate and Foreign Commerce, Judiciary, Military Affairs, Naval Affairs, Post Office and Post Roads, Rules, Ways and Means. After 1946, the term applied only to Appropriations, Rules, and Ways and Means. For purposes of the analysis that follows, the Budget Committee, established in the mid-1970s, has also been included in that category.

4. Smith was not satisfied with her assignments, preferring a seat on Naval Affairs to one on the once important but by then overrated Post Office and Post Roads Committee (Lamson 1968, p. 11). On the other hand, the House increased the size of the Foreign Affairs Committee in the 71st Congress to accommodate Owen (Paxton 1945, p. 6).

5. Norton's decision to move from a more to a less prestigious committee was apparently voluntary, prompted mainly by Republican success in the 1946 elections, the shift in House control from Democratic to Republican, and the elevation to the chairmanship of the Education and Labor Committee of New Jersey Republican Fred Hartley, Jr. At first Norton explained her shift to the House Administration Committee as motivated by the Democrat's loss of a New Jersey Senate seat and her need to " . . . take over a great amount of work for my state . . . somewhere I can be most useful" (*New York Times*, January 4, 1947). But during House debate over what later came to be called the Taft-Hartley Act, Norton was asked to explain her departure from the Labor Committee. She replied:

Frankly, in one sense I regret that the gentleman has asked me that question because I have never knowingly hurt a member of Congress on either side of the aisle. I have a very great respect and affection for the members I have served with, but I regret to say I have no respect for the present chairman of the Labor Committee. And I could not serve with a chairman for whom I hold no respect. My reason for that is that during the ten years I was chairman of the Labor Committee, the gentleman from New Jersey, who is now the chairman of the Labor Committee and who comes here before you and talks about labor as if he knew something about it, attended exactly six meetings in ten years. That was my reason for leaving the Committee on Labor (*Congressional Record*, 80th Congress, 1st Session, Vol. 93, Part 3, April 15, 1947, p. 3432).

6. Standing committees that had established subcommittees by the 84th Congress (1955) included Agriculture, Appropriations, Armed Services, District of Columbia, Foreign Affairs, Government Operations, House Administration, Interior and Insular Affairs, Interstate and Foreign Commerce, Judiciary, Public Works, and Veterans' Affairs. Banking and Currency, Education and Labor, Merchant Marine and Fisheries, and Post Office and Civil Service adopted formal subcommittee systems in the 85th Congress; Ways and Means in the 93rd; Small Business (as a permanent committee) in the 94th; and Rules in the 96th. The Budget Committee created "Task Forces" in the 95th Congress and they are treated here as if they were subcommittees. Congresswomen assigned to committees having no subcommittees were excluded from the analysis. Information about assignments was gathered from *The Congressional Quarterly Almanac*, 1955–1981, and *Congressional Quarterly Special Report*, Vol. 41, No. 13, April 2, 1983.

7. See Chapter 6, footnote 7 for a description of how the index was derived.

8. Hansen's leadership of a subcommittee of the prestigious Appropriations Committee was celebrated with the effusive praise that members often lavish upon one another. While acting as floor manager of her first appropriations measure, Hansen was interrupted by Speaker John McCormack.

Mr. McCormack: Mr. Chairman, I want to call to the attention of my colleagues the fact that history is being made today. Another event in the great history of this body is taking place today, because the distinguished gentlewoman from Washington is the first lady to be chairman of a subcommittee of the Committee on Appropriations and the first gentlewoman of the House to handle on the floor of the House a bill coming out first from the subcommittee on Appropriations of which she is chairman. . . .

Mr. Chairman, I sincerely feel that all of us should pause to recognize and realize what this wonderful legislator has contributed today and shall continue to contribute to the history of this great body. . . .

Mrs. Hansen: . . . Mr. Chairman, I thank the distinguished gentleman from Massachusetts, the distinguished Speaker of the House of Representatives, for those remarks.

Further, Mr. Chairman, I would like to say that it gives me great pride, under the magnificent leadership of the distinguished gentleman from Massachusetts, the Speaker of the House of Representatives, . . . to express my personal gratitude for this opportunity. . . .

Mrs. Kelly: Mr. Chairman, I wish to associate myself with the remarks which have just been made by our beloved and distinguished Speaker. I, too, want to say that not alone is the chairman of this subcommittee most capable and most able and well liked, but I further wish to say that the distinguished Speaker . . . has played no small part in seeing that the rights of women in this House of Representatives have had equal jurisdiction and recognition.

Mrs. Hansen: . . . I wish to thank the distinguished gentlewoman from New York for her remarks, and to again reiterate that it has truly been a demonstration of equal opportunity for me to serve in this great deliberative body . . . under the distinguished leadership of our very beloved Speaker (U.S. Congress, *Congressional Record*, 90th Congress, 1st Session, April 26, 1967, pp. 10781–782).

8 / Women's Issues:
Changing Legislative Priorities

Before World War II, most bills introduced by congresswomen either ignored women as a class or spoke to a narrow range of their problems.[1] Reasons for this lukewarm approach included a lack of interest in women's issues, a determination that a public display of interest would be politically damaging, a conviction that the problems women faced should be resolved at the state level or without benefit of governmental intervention, and a belief that a congresswoman associating herself with such issues would weaken her effectiveness among House colleagues. In fact, most legislative proposals directly affecting women were introduced by male lawmakers.

It was during the mid-1960s that the balance shifted, and today, female Representatives are much more likely than were their predecessors to sponsor legislation designed to help members of their gender. This change in representational role orientations, however, cannot be divorced from the transformation that has taken place in the character of women's issues. Increased readiness of congresswomen to stake out positions on matters of concern to women has been accompanied by changes in the nature of these issues. Accordingly, variations in the character of women's issues must be traced before coming to grips in the remaining chapters with changing priorities female Representatives have fashioned with respect to these issues. What follows, then, is a description of how the definition of women's issues has been broadened, with some reference to the contributions congresswomen have made to the change.

THE CHANGING CHARACTER OF WOMEN'S ISSUES

Over the years, proposed legislation directly affecting women has generally fallen into one of three categories. Legislative measures, first of all, reinforce *traditional* role performance. Such bills address women's needs in terms of their roles as mothers, wives, homemakers, and dependents. Other measures are *equalitarian* in intent, seeking to elevate women to positions of equality with men in the marketplace, government, and the academy, as well as in the public consciousness.

A third category of bills is *affirmative* in character. Affirmative measures facilitate women's claims to the resources and recognition normally offered men as a matter of course and tend to free them from the social, economic, and cultural constraints under which they have customarily labored. Affirmative measures are those which asservate the importance of women's role in history and society, which support and reinforce women's claims to economic independence, and which assist them in overcoming the social and cultural constraints imposed upon them by a male-dominated society. This broad range of measures may be classified further into three subtypes: *symbolically* affirmative, *economically* affirmative, *socially* affirmative. Examples of traditional, equalitarian, and affirmative legislation are presented in Table 8.1.

Not all legislative initiatives fall under one of the three headings, and some satisfy criteria for at least two of the three. But the typology is useful for classifying most of the bills affecting women directly during the last sixty-five years, and it helps provide a conceptual framework within which to describe and interpret the changing character of women's issues. Moreover, the behavior of congresswomen is better appreciated when it is understood as an expression of shifting legislative priorities. During the years between the World Wars, for example, a significant majority of the bills they introduced reinforced the roles women traditionally performed. Under the provisions of these measures, women were defined in terms of their relationships to men.

Following the conclusion of World War II, congresswomen turned their attention to legislative measures designed to make women the equals of men. These bills sought to eliminate barriers to women's vocational, financial, and academic achievement. Since the early 1970s, congresswomen have increasingly championed proposals affirming the historic, economic, and social initiatives of women pursuing goals which were either reserved in the past to males or which, although traditional in nature, were deemed by males to be unworthy of support by the federal government.

Proposals in all three categories were offered by House members during all three periods, but, as will be demonstrated, the trend from *traditional* to *equalitarian* to *affirmative* has been a clearly observable one.[2]

Reinforcing Traditional Role Performance

Between the World Wars, the overwhelming majority of House proposals designed to assist women were submitted by men and were traditional in nature.

Table 8.1. Types of Women's Issues

Issue Type	Legislative Examples
Traditional	Pensions for widows of military veterans
	Social Security benefits pegged to husband's earnings
Equalitarian	Equal Pay Act of 1963
	Title IX of the 1972 Education Act Amendments
Affirmative	
1. Symbolic	Establishing a "Working Mother's" Day
	Creating a Susan B. Anthony Silver Dollar
2. Economic	Federally-funded day-care centers
	Support for displaced homemakers
3. Social	Aid to victims of domestic violence
	Prevention of unnecessary mastectomies

Many congresswomen elected during the period, particularly those who succeeded their husbands (Mae Nolan, Pearl Oldfield, and Effigene Wingo, for example), and who served for a short time (Ruth Pratt, Isabella Greenway, and Ruth McCormick, for example) introduced no measures directly affecting women. Most of the remaining female Representatives confined their attention to bills whose treatment of women was linked to their status as spouses and mothers. Thus, Alice Robertson urged that pensions be paid to retired U.S. deputy marshalls (or their widows) assigned to the federal district court in Oklahoma. And Katherine Langley urged an increase in the pensions of widows whose husbands had served in the Mexican, Civil, and Spanish-American Wars.

In addition, dozens of bills were introduced allocating economic and symbolic rewards to World War I veterans and their surviving spouses, often extending benefits to wives of veterans whose disabilities and deaths were not service-connected. Other proposals provided assistance to widows of foreign service officers, to Gold Star Mothers, and to veterans' widows who, after remarrying, became single again. Of course, not all of these measures were enacted into law. But the aid provided female spouses and parents was pegged to the experience and status of the men with whom they bore an accepted, traditional relationship and of whom they were considered extensions.

Labor laws protecting women workers were also proposed during this period and they, too, were traditional in character. State and local governments, more than Congress, had to deal with protective proposals in the years between the Wars, but the House and Senate regularly received petitions to enact national labor legislation. Shorter hours, better working conditions, minimum wages, and restrictions on recruitment to dangerous occupations were among the work rules sought. As the principal funding and governing body for the District of

Columbia, Congress was also required to consider protective measures for women employed in the capital. Mary Norton considered many such bills while serving as chair of the District of Columbia Committee, but most congress-women gave the subject little attention.

Nonetheless, the issue was a controversial one and bitter battles were waged between representatives of most women's groups on the one hand, and employers groups (and the National Woman's Party) on the other. Management saw these laws as infringing on their right to hire employees under conditions of their own choosing, and as undermining the sanctity of contracts. The former were interested in humane work rules and saw them as harbingers of more enlightened employment arrangements for men. The courts, in turn, interpreted protective labor legislation as an unconstitutional violation of the free market in the case of men, but permissible for women. One Supreme Court justice noted that because of their delicate physical stature and maternal responsibilities, women workers required government protection from " . . . the greed as well as the passion of men" (quoted in Lemons 1973, p. 143). While protective legislation for women drew a wide range of positive and negative responses, the major premise of its judicial justification averred that women would be unable to perform their traditional roles without it.

Not all of the proposed women's measures rewarded women. Some of the bills introduced between the Wars penalized them because their behavior violated traditional role expectations. During the recession that followed World War I and in the depths of the depression, working married women were often threatened with diminution of pay or, worse, unemployment, in order to increase the number of jobs for men. Married women who were civil servants and whose husbands were also government employees were especially vulnerable. In 1932, Congress passed the Government Economy Act, a law designed, in part, to cut the size and cost of the bureaucracy. Section 213 of the Act provided that among those employees to be dismissed first were people whose spouses also worked for the federal government (*Congressional Record* June 23, 1932, pp. 13, 796–797). The language of the Act did not specify which spouse should be fired or furloughed, but, inasmuch as wives were almost always earning less than husbands, the former were more likely to give up their jobs. Moreover, civil servants whose husbands were in the armed forces were sometimes required to relinquish their positions even though they earned considerably more than spouses whose enlistments still had several years to run.

Although a small number of married couples were ultimately affected by the law (only about 2,000 federal employees were forced to leave their jobs under this provision of the Act), three-quarters of those terminated were married women. A large proportion of them were holding down low-paying jobs in the Treasury and Commerce Departments and in the Veterans' Administration (Becker 1981, p. 203). The hardship experienced by these women was considerable and no one knows how many affianced couples, both of whom were civil servants, delayed their marriages rather than risk a significant cut in their collective income.

Congress repealed Section 213 five years after its passage. Arguments in favor of repeal included the charge that, in practice, it discriminated against married women, even though either spouse could have been affected; that it resulted in dismissals based on marital status rather than on job performance, with negative consequences for morale; and that its implementation affected unskilled and semiskilled rather than high-salaried workers, reducing expected economies to a minimum. Whereas no female House member had spoken against Section 213 when the Act was passed (Edith Rogers and Mary Norton criticized other portions of the measure), and whereas all but Norton supported its final passage, each of the women serving in the House in 1937 spoke out strongly for its repeal (*Congressional Record* July 8, 1937, pp. 6925–953).

Their behavior in this regard constituted one of the several exceptions to the general rule followed by congresswomen between the Wars—that of confining their support for women's issues to measures reinforcing traditional gender roles. But by the late 1930s, congresswomen were beginning to speak out more often on behalf of women, and apparently the flagrant discrimination against married women in this case was too much for even the more circumspect female Representatives serving at the time.

The Drive for Equality: Early Years

Most of the other exceptions to this rule were recorded on a relatively narrow range of subjects. The congresswomen departing from the usual pattern were not as active or as bold as many male colleagues, but the few nontraditional initiatives they undertook were unmistakably equalitarian in conception and purpose.

Women serving their country in the military and related services were probably the class of females most often singled out for equal treatment. After World War I, attempts were made to confer belated military status (and, therefore, the benefits associated with such status) on women who had served overseas. Abortive efforts were made to award the Congressional Medal of Honor to some women, as well. When World War II began, the Women's Auxiliary Army Corps, the country's first female military unit, and other women's military and defense services were established. Later, permanent commissions were conferred on army and navy nurses, and a Medical Specialist Corps was created, giving officer status to dietitions, and physical and occupational therapists. Their recognition as professionals constituted an important departure in principle, even if not always in practice, from the statutory treatment women customarily received.

Women working in the civil and government-related service and female aliens were also intended beneficiaries of equalitarian measures during this early period. Several unsuccessful bills were offered to equalize the pay scales of men and women employed by the federal government, and others sought to do the same for private-sector workers engaged in war-related jobs. One measure made a modest effort to end discrimination based upon gender in awarding government contracts, and some proposals were designed to increase the number of government service opportunities for women. The latter, of course, were at cross purposes with such laws as the Government Economy Act—at least insofar as married women were concerned. Caroline O'Day sought unsuccessfully to confer equality on some alien women by sponsoring a bill to give female ministers and professors who emigrated to the United States under the nonquota provisions of the 1924 Immigration Act the same privileges available to alien men in the same vocations. Under the 1924 statute, the latter could bring dependents, the former could not.

But perhaps the most important immigration bill affecting women at the time was sponsored by Ruth Bryan Owen, among others. Before 1922, an American woman marrying a foreign subject lost her citizenship, even though the marriage was later dissolved through divorce or death and she returned to the United States for repatriation. Legislation passed in 1922 eliminated that problem for women marrying non-Americans *after* adoption of the Act, but provided no remedy for those who had done so before 1922. As someone who had married a British subject, lived abroad, and then returned to the United States to nurse an ailing spouse, Owen identified closely with women in the same predicament, and she vigorously supported a measure to give women not covered by the 1922 Act the same opportunities as those married after that date. The proposal had special significance to her because her unsuccessful opponent in the 1928 congressional election challenged her right to serve on the grounds that she was not a citizen. The House decided otherwise.

Other equalitarian, and some affirmative, measures introduced during this period included a proposal to extend suffrage to all American women (offered, of course, before the adoption of the 19th Amendment), and to women residents of U.S. territories; a bill to recognize women's interests in aviation; a proposal to establish a federal Department of Home and Child, an affirmative step to elevate the role of homemakers and recognize the special problems they faced; and legislation offering federal funds to states which provided instruction on the hygiene of maternity and infancy. This last proposal was enacted in 1921, but was permitted to lapse in 1929.[3] At the same time, scores of Resolutions were submitted calling for an Equal Rights Amendment to the Constitution. None was sponsored by a woman House member until 1945, however.

The equalitarian impulses of House members introducing these measures put them ahead of their time, although the few female Representatives contributing such proposals usually served on the committees which claimed jurisdiction over the bills' subject matter. Thus, many of the attempts to confer veteran's status on women were authored by Edith Rogers of the World War Veteran's Legislation Committee. Service on the Naval Affairs Committee doubtless gave Margaret Chase Smith the expertise and opportunity successfully to secure passage of her bills to permit Women Accepted for Volunteer Emergency Service (WAVES) to see overseas duty and to establish a permanent Nurse Corps. And Caroline O'Day's assignment to the Committee on Immigration and Naturalization added credibility to the measures she introduced extending equal benefits to male and female aliens.

In spite of these efforts, congresswomen demonstrated much less concern than male Representatives about women's issues, equalitarian or otherwise, even after taking into account their significantly smaller numbers.

The Drive for Equality: Post World War II

If most of the congresswomen serving through World War II were inclined either to say nothing about women's issues or to propose measures reinforcing their traditional roles, most serving in the postwar period made public commitments to end discrimination based upon gender. True, many proposed new or increased pensions for women whose spouses' past employment made them inheritors of such benefits. Rogers continued to introduce bills helpful to veterans' widows, particularly during the 83rd Congress when, because Republicans controlled the House, she chaired the Veterans' Affairs Committee. And Ohio's Frances Bolton reminded the country to honor Blue Star Mothers. But Rogers, Bolton, and especially the congresswomen who took their seats in the three or four Congresses following the War increasingly lent support to measures providing equality for women.

Among the most popular of their proposals was one calling for equal pay for equal work, an idea ultimately given expression in the Equal Pay Act of 1963. The legislation received early support from Helen Gahagan Douglas, Margaret Chase Smith, and Chase Going Woodhouse, and even the more cautious Bolton introduced a bill authorizing a study of discriminatory pay practices. By the late 1950s, almost one-half of the women House members had introduced measures requiring the federal government or private companies involved in interstate commerce to provide the same compensation to men and women employed in the same capacity.

Among the Representatives playing an important part in convincing the House to come to grips with the measure was Oregon's Edith Green. Green was a member of the Education and Labor Committee, the panel having jurisdiction over the equal pay bill, and for years she had unsuccessfully tried to persuade Labor Standards subcommittee chair Phil Landrum, an opponent of the measure, to clear it for committee and floor consideration. On one occasion she approached Landrum and asked the Georgia Democrat to introduce a "minor" bill which she wanted to sponsor but, for political reasons, could not. Landrum, happy to oblige, agreed before knowing what Green had in mind. He was appalled when she proposed reducing the salaries of congresswomen by $5,000. Green argued that the bill was a reasonable one because congressmen worked so much harder, put in longer hours, introduced so many more bills than did women lawmakers, and, therefore, deserved more pay. The Georgian demurred, insisting that women worked just as hard as men and withdrew his offer to sponsor the proposal. Whereupon the Oregon Democrat said that she was happy he felt that way because she had an "equal pay for equal work" bill in his subcommittee and she would be grateful if he would schedule hearings on it (Driefus 1972).

Landrum never did oblige. In 1960, Education and Labor Committee Chair Graham Barden of North Carolina retired and was replaced by New York City's Adam Clayton Powell—a Representative considerably more sympathetic to the Equal Pay bill. Landrum lost his subcommittee chair, and it was New Jersey Democrat Frank Thompson's Special Subcommittee on Labor that reported out the equal pay measure. He was supported in the debate by veterans Frances Bolton, Katharine St. George, Edna Kelly, and Green, among others.

One reason the bill passed was because it was tame by comparison with another proposal for which support had been growing—the Equal Right's Amendment. The ERA had long been a subject of political and legislative concern. It had been introduced in the House as early as 1923 by Nebraska Representative Daniel R. Anthony, a relative of Susan B. Anthony, and had attracted the support of an increasing number of male Representatives over the years. Many women's groups opposed it, believing that such an amendment would deprive women of some of the benefits they enjoyed by virtue of their gender.

The manner in which congresswomen coalesced to support the ERA had a logic all its own. In the pre-World War II period, no female House member publicly identified with the Amendment. Opposition to it by most major women's groups and support for the measure by the suspect National Woman's Party doubtless encouraged congresswomen to maintain a respectable distance from the proposal. A great majority of women leaders saw ERA as a mortal threat to protective labor legislation, laws in which they had a significant investment and which had been difficult to pass in a climate that was hostile to the labor movement (Lemons 1973, p. 142).[4] They believed the Amendment would force women workers to abide by the more forbidding work rules governing male employment.

Most labor organizations also opposed the ERA. Union leaders feared the amendment would provide an excuse for employers to reduce benefits received by male workers as soon as more generous emoluments had to be extended to women employees. They also believed that jobs held by men would be lost to women. Many employers, on the other hand, hailed the measure, construing it as a way of undermining the integrity of the unions and of ending protective legislation for women. Among the Equal Rights Amendment's earliest supporters was the National Association of Manufacturers (Lemons 1973, p. 191).

The first congresswomen to support the ERA, therefore, were not New Deal, prolabor Democrats who generally took the lead on issues of political and economic equality, but conservative, probusiness Republicans. In 1942, Jessie Sumner, perhaps the most conservative Republican in the House, male or female, expressed strong support for the ERA, although she did not go so far as to introduce a Resolution. Three years later, Republicans Margaret Chase Smith and Edith Nourse Rogers, broke the ice and became the first female House members to cosponsor the Amendment (*Congressional Record* January 31, 1945, p. 669). Soon thereafter, it was another Republican, conservative New Yorker Katharine St. George who led the ERA battle. For several years she had only male Representatives to keep her company, seventy-nine of whom joined her in signing a petition to discharge the Judiciary Committee, led by Brooklyn Democrat and ERA antagonist Emanuel Celler, from further consideration of the Resolution (Locket 1950). In the meantime, such progressive Democrats as Chase Going Woodhouse and Helen Gahagan Douglas worked actively to stall the Amendment. In 1953, two other conservative Republicans, Ruth Thompson of Michigan and Margaret Stitt Church of Illinois added their support and, two years later, additional Republicans and the first group of Democrats signed on as ERA cosponsors.[5]

As women's groups began to change their positions on the Amendment, leadership among congresswomen shifted to liberal Democrats. Martha Griffiths, Gracie Pfost, Coya Knutson, and Julia Butler Hansen, among others, began to champion the measure. In the end, it was Griffiths who, in August, 1970, forced a vote on a successful petition to discharge the Judiciary Committee from further consideration of the Amendment and force it to the floor for a vote. She also took the lead in mobilizing support for the Resolution when it passed in the next Congress. Democrat Leonor Sullivan was the lone woman among the twenty-four Representatives voting against the ERA (*Congressional Quarterly Almanac*, Vol. 24, 1971, p. 68-H).

The ERA, of course, was a comprehensive measure, one which was calculated to impose an equalitarian stamp on virtually all economic, social, and political relationships in which discrimination based upon gender had important consequences. Its adoption by the Senate in 1972 ended a decade of other, more modest efforts to pass legislation defining and legitimizing women's claims for equal rights under the law. Apart from the Equal Pay Act, Congress passed measures establishing task forces and commissions to study the legal status of women. It also approved Title VII of the 1964 Civil Rights Act prohibiting sex discrimination in employment; the Equal Employment Opportunity Act of 1972; and Title IX of the 1972 Amendments to the Education Act, which insisted upon equal treatment of women in higher education.

Congress later enacted the Equal Credit Opportunity Act of 1974; the equal opportunity provision of the Career Education Incentive Act of 1977 (to help overcome sex stereotyping in employment); the Women's Educational Opportunity Act of 1978; and the Defense Appropriation Act of 1976, one provision of which authorized the admission of women to the military service academies. In 1977 veterans' status was conferred on 850 surviving members of the World War II Woman Air Service Pilots and, one year later, the time period for passage of the ERA was extended. Unlike the pattern revealed between the Wars, the congresswomen who introduced and championed these equalitarian measures did not necessarily serve on the committees having jurisdiction over them—perhaps in part because the House began to permit joint sponsorship of bills during this period.

The drive for equal treatment almost always focused upon women as the victims of discrimination. From the outset, however, congresswomen were sensitive to the extent to which laws and practices discriminated against men. A number of bills were introduced to provide for the appointment of men as armed forces nurses, and Margaret Stitt Church of Illinois was among the first female Representatives to offer amendments to the Railroad Retirement Act, the Civil Service Retirement Act, and the Social Security Act to give husbands and widowers the same benefits that had been awarded to wives and widows. These proposals paved the way for similar bills, among them Millicent Fenwick's proposal to apply the Mann Act, prohibiting the transportation of women across state lines for immoral purposes, to males.

Not all of the measures offered by congresswomen during this period were traditional or equalitarian in their intent. As early as 1949, bills were introduced to provide a tax deduction for the costs of a housekeeper or a day-care center to look after dependents while taxpayers were at work. The measure would apply both to single or married parents and, while the law was designed to benefit both men and women, the latter were far more likely to be single parents. They were also likely to be the more dispensable wage earner when both wife and husband were employed. Thus began the post-War movement for affirmative legislation, a trend which burgeoned in the 1970s.

The Shift Toward Affirmative Legislation

Success in sponsoring equalitarian measures, along with the realization that equal opportunity under the law did not necessarily mean equal opportunity in fact, emboldened Representatives to introduce affirmative proposals. These measures were introduced by congresswomen in far greater proportion than their numbers suggest. Many of the bills did not even mention gender, and some applied explicitly to men, as well as to women. But all were expected to help the latter far more than the former in practice. Several were perceived as necessary *because* earlier equalitarian measures had been passed. Some women could take advantage of equal job opportunities and equal pay for equal work only if adequate day-care centers were available for their children, only if there were enough part time or "flextime" jobs accessible to permit them to fulfill domestic, as well as career, responsibilities.

The range of affirmative legislative measures is broad, with each proposal addressing at least one of three general goals— symbolic, economic, and social. Symbolic measures place a higher value on women's traditional role performance, reinterpret more positively contributions women made in the past, celebrate these contributions with appropriate ritual, and, in the process, sensitize public consciousness to their significance. Economically affirmative laws compensate women for socioeconomic constraints under which they have labored while fulfilling traditional role responsibilities, make them independent of such restraints, and provide both the material and moral support needed to achieve that independence. Bills falling into the socially affirmative category are more difficult to define. They lift from women the social and cultural limitations imposed upon them by men—husbands, lawyers, bureaucrats, local, state and national lawmakers, and physicians, among them—who are ignorant of, or insensitive to, women's needs and who reflect these shortcomings in the rules they create (or fail to create) and implement.

1) *Symbolically Affirmative Measures.* The easiest affirmative measures to trace are those which sought to commemorate the achievements of female leaders and to institutionalize rituals celebrating the courage and devotion of a liberated American womanhood. More than a half-dozen congresswomen sponsored measures to establish Eleanor Roosevelt and Mary McLeod Bethune historic sites; and Margaret Heckler took the lead in naming a hospital in Bedford, Massachusetts, for Edith Nourse Rogers. Mary Rose Oakar succeeded in passing a bill to put Susan B. Anthony's profile on the newly minted silver dollar, but only after beating back efforts to use the anonymous "Miss Liberty" on the coin. In a letter to the Treasury Department, a group of congresswomen opposed selection of a mythical female figure. They said, in part:

> Although we applaud your decision to place a woman's face on the coin, we don't think the choice of the mythical figure, "Miss Liberty," is particularly appropriate since there are many female American historical figures who could certainly qualify for the honor. Moreover, "Miss Liberty" has previously graced numerous coins—several Liberty dollars, the Liberty dime, and the winged Liberty head (Mercury) dime, among others.
>
> We can't recall an instance where a male mythical figure was placed on a general circulation coin solely to avoid controversy over which male should

garner the honor—Kennedy, Roosevelt, Jefferson, Washington, Lincoln, and Eisenhower made it over Father Time, Uncle Sam and Neptune.

There have been many women whose mark on American History is such that they could appropriately be placed on a general circulation coin: Susan B. Anthony, Betsy Ross, Eleanor Roosevelt, Helen Keller, Amelia Earhart, Harriet Tubman, Jane Addams, Alice Paul, Nellie Ross, and Molly Pitcher, to name a few.

Scores of Representatives and Senators joined forces to restore the Congressional Medal of Honor to the only woman ever to have received it but from whom it had been stripped fifty years after it had been conferred. Mary Edwards Walker had been a Civil War surgeon attending Union soldiers on Virginia and Tennessee battlefields. She was captured, spent four months in a southern prison, and was exchanged "man for man" for a confederate major. Generals William T. Sherman and George N. Thomas recommended that she be awarded the medal, President Lincoln agreed, and President Andrew Johnson performed the ceremony on November 11, 1865. In 1916, a military review board recommended that Walker's medal, along with similar awards to 911 servicemen, be revoked. Congress approved the recommendation, but Walker wore the decoration until her death in 1919.

Her descendants claimed that the revocation was based upon the physician's gender and her unorthodox life style and beliefs. Walker was an ardent suffragist. She wore men's trousers and frock coats, and gave feminist lectures attired in men's evening dress with the Medal of Honor on her lapel. On June 10, 1977, the medal was posthumously restored by Army Secretary Clifford Alexander, following a barrage of congressional demands that the 1916 revocation be overturned (*New York Times* June 4, 1977). Shortly thereafter Walker was the subject of a commemorative stamp issued by the U.S. Postal Service.

Among other affirmative measures of this type were bills acknowledging women's collective achievements and future promise. Proposals to establish a "Women's Equity Day," and a "Women's Rights Day" were introduced. Laws were passed designating an International Women's Year and establishing a Women's Rights National Park in Senaca Falls, New York, site of the 1848 Women's Rights Convention. A "Working Mother's Day" was approved, and Barbara Mikulski successfully spearheaded the drive to establish a "Women's History Week." Finally, some congresswomen proposed that the House impanel a select Committee on Women, lest women's problems and contributions be relegated once again to the darker recesses of the legislature's (and the public's) consciousness.

One purpose of these bills was to resurrect and burnish the reputations of women who had made significant contributions to society, but who were either forgotten or consigned to a footnote in history. Young Americans, particularly, were given female role models whom they could venerate and imitate. Many of these measures also sought to elevate the importance of the routine tasks that were part of women's traditional roles, but which were undervalued by society precisely because the work was done cheaply, often, without complaint, and by women. One goal was to make these activities valuable not because they were done to complement traditional male responsibilities, but because they were done so well by women. Some of the measures had important social and economic consequences, but their principal function was to attach new and renewed value to the uses to which women's efforts have customarily been put, and to increase the worth of all of their efforts, traditional and otherwise.

2) *Economically Affirmative Measures.* A second type of affirmative legislation sought to lift or ameliorate economic constraints on women, whether manifested in the law, in practice, or in public expectation. Equalitarian measures passed through the mid-1970s were intended to overcome barriers to independence and achievement, but many women were neither trained nor otherwise prepared to capitalize on the new statutes. Others were impeded by prior commitments to home, children, and spouse—commitments which could be broken or bent only at considerable emotional cost.

Thus, something more than legal equality was needed if women were to realize their potential. And, in the mid-1970s, congresswomen introduced scores of bills to relax the circumstantial tethers in which women found themselves. Mention has already been made of tax credits for child-care costs and day-care centers for children in whose households both parents worked. The mid-1970s saw the reintroduction of these ideas, many with important refinements. Proposals were offered to increase the number and quality of day-care centers for children of welfare recipients and low-income families, a considerable majority of which featured women as heads of households. And Shirley Chisholm sponsored bills to reimburse relatives, including grandparents, for child-care costs incurred at home (not just at a day-care center) while the childrens' parents were working.

These measures, like many others falling within the category of affirmative legislation, made little or no mention of women. When introduced, however, House debate made clear that they were expected to apply to women much more often than to men. Other bills calculated to help women take advantage of economic opportunities sought to establish part-time and flextime employment within the federal government and to provide incentives to employers interested in creating similar opportunities in the private sector. To preclude the already illegal discrimination on the basis of marital status, Bella Abzug led an effort to prohibit the use of prefixes "Miss" or "Mrs." before the names of persons applying for jobs.

An increased divorce rate, together with the continuing tendency of wives to outlive their husbands, stimulated concern House members gave to the predicament of "displaced homemakers." These were women who were cut off from economic opportunities because of a spouse's death or estrangement, but who had never had the occasion to acquire marketable skills, or had been too long out of the labor pool. When divorced, they were usually deprived of the pension and health benefits upon which they had once counted as spouses of gainfully employed males.

Economically affirmative legislation offered some remedies. Several bills called for a government-funded network of centers throughout the country to help displaced homemakers become economically self-sufficient. Related proposals held out incentives to employers who might hire these women. In 1978, Congress approved an amendment to the Comprehensive Education and Training Act directing the Secretary of Labor to develop and establish employment and training programs for middle-aged and older workers. The Secretary was also called upon to facilitate the transition of workers over fifty-five from one occupation to another and to help prepare those who had never worked for entry into the labor force.

In the meantime, innovative measures were introduced treating the homemaker as an independent wage earner, with the size of her social security payment determined not by her spouse's income, but by the number of years she was married. Just as controversial were bills which guaranteed a portion of a former husband's pension and health benefits to a divorced homemaker even when the ex-husband had remarried. Other proposals gave homemakers the opportunity to allocate household allowances to Independent Retirement Accounts, regardless of whether their spouses were eligible for such accounts.

But the most comprehensive effort to compensate women for the socioeconomic limitations imposed upon them was first introduced in the 97th Congress. Called the Economic Equity Act, it contained many of the affirmative measures to which allusion has already been made. The omnibus bill was sponsored by scores of Representatives. According to Margaret Heckler, it was an attempt to counter "policies in the public and private sector that are completely at odds with work patterns determined by the realities of women's dual wage-earning and parenting roles" (*New York Times* April 18, 1981).

The measure made it easier for women to secure the pensions and annuities of retired, deceased, or estranged husbands. It also allowed a homemaker with no earnings or lesser earnings than her husband to contribute to a spousal IRA as much as her husband might contribute, and gave tax credits to employers who hired displaced homemakers. Other provisions made dependent care financially more viable for women who work; barred discrimination on the basis of race, color, religion, and national origin, as well as gender, in the determination of insurance premiums; and encouraged bureaucrats to implement laws already on the books in a nondiscriminatory fashion. Some of the bills' provisions were enacted in 1982. Others were reintroduced in 1983.

3) *Socially Affirmative Measures.* The third form of affirmative legislation embraced proposals calculated to lift those restraints on women which were a

product of male insensitivity to women's noneconomic needs. The males in question were husbands, bureaucrats, lawmakers, and physicians, among others, who established public and private priorities and who shaped the national agenda.

In 1975, a provision of the Public Health Service Act established a National Center for the Prevention and Control of Rape. The law created an advisory committee (a majority of whose members were required to be women) to advise the Secretary of Health, Education and Welfare on such matters as the treatment and counseling of victims; development and maintenance of a clearinghouse of information on prevention, control, and treatment of victims; rehabilitation of offenders; and possible assistance to local mental health centers. Elizabeth Holtzman successfully sponsored an amendment to the Federal Rules of Evidence which made inadmissible, except under certain conditions, the introduction of evidence of past sexual behavior of an alleged rape victim. A related measure was introduced to eliminate spousal immunity to a charge of rape. In the meantime, almost all congresswomen cosponsored bills to deal with wife abuse and domestic violence and to treat humanely victims of such violence.

Often neglected medical needs were addressed in bills to preclude unnecessary mastectomies; to provide explicit social security, medicare, and medicaid coverage for diagnostic tests for uterine and breast cancer; and to authorize the Public Health Service to provide counseling and aid to pregnant women, especially teenagers. One measure made abortion a constitutional right. Another directed the Secretary of Health, Education and Welfare to alert women who used the drug DES while pregnant to the health hazards of the substance and to reimburse them and their daughters for one-half the costs of diagnosis and treatment.

＊　＊　＊

Affirmative proposals offered through the early 1980s represented a political response to the social, economic, legal, and cultural restraints that a male-dominated society had imposed on women—restraints which many women, as well as men, had accepted as natural and just. Whereas legislation offered before World War II sought to reinforce traditional role performance of women, treating them as extensions of men, later bills sought to free them of that dependence, to permit them to reject traditional tasks if they so chose, to make such rejection less costly, to give greater priority to problems they believed to be peculiarly their own, and to force policy makers to adopt a more universal perspective when framing the national agenda.

The categories of *traditional*, *equalitarian*, and *affirmative* measures are not mutually exclusive and introduction of each type was not confined to only one of the time periods defined here. All three types of measures were introduced in each of the three periods, although few affirmative proposals were broached before the 1940s. Moreover, recent years have witnessed sponsorship of bills that are throwbacks to an earlier era. Constitutional amendments to overturn the Supreme Court's 1973 abortion decision have been proposed by many House members, and other legislative efforts have been made to limit women's choices in this regard. Extension of the time for passage of the ERA was strenuously opposed by a number of male Representatives, and doubt remains as this is being written whether the 98th Congress will approve another ERA Resolution for state consideration. Finally, the Reagan administration's dismantling of the CETA Program and the economically affirmative provisions that were part of it was supported by most Republicans, female as well as male.

But these proposals have not significantly changed the dominant character of women's legislation considered by recent Congresses. They may have slowed the pace at which affirmative legislation has been accepted, but they have not fundamentally altered its course. And, as the 98th Congress got underway, presidential advisors, concerned about Mr. Reagan's unpopularity among women, began to consider ways of blunting charges that the President was insensitive to women's needs and that his economic policies had "feminized" poverty. Closing the gender gap, some reasoned, is likely to require more than appointment of women to a few key positions, more than stepped up presidential public relations.

CHANGING REPRESENTATIONAL ROLE ORIENTATIONS

Accompanying changes in the type of legislative proposals congresswomen were prepared to introduce were related changes in the way these women defined their role as representatives. Most who were elected to the House between 1917 and World War II were inclined to reject the claim that they were in Washington to represent American womanhood, and most who served through the 1960s did not go out of their way to make such a claim. Jeannette Rankin, of course, was an important exception, and several others maintained that they could make a contribution to legislative deliberations by injecting a woman's point of view into the proceedings. Few, however, were prepared to acknowledge that they were in Washington to represent the interests of women as a discrete group.

One of the more preceptive political activists of the earlier period, Emily Newell Blair, deplored the absence of a feminist orientation among the great majority of women who sought public office. Blair had been a leader in the suffrage movement and had expected women who gained positions of influence to provide instrumental support for women's causes. She tried to live up to that promise during her seven years as Vice Chairman of the Democratic National Committee, but was discouraged to find that she was part of a distinct minority.

"Women today," she asserted, "do not have the feminist point of view." Once they received the right to vote, she continued, they dropped their feminist orientation. A woman who runs for office makes " . . . no appeal to women to put a woman in office, no argument as to her right to hold office, but [there is] a minimizing always of her sex. And yet, thousands of votes were cast against her, for no other reason than that she was a woman" (Blair 1931, pp. 21–22).

Blair maintained, moreover, that once in office, women ignored other women. Those who serve on party committees " . . . give their proxies at committee meetings to men by whose influence they have been elected," and they "do what they are told by these men to do." She recognized that the heart of the problem was that rank-and-file women did not mobilize their resources behind women's candidacies. As a result, congresswomen " . . . owe their election far more to the support of men than to the backing of women, and . . . they must give recognition to men rather than women . . . if they expect to get reelected" (Blair 1931, pp. 21–22).

Another commentator of the period, diplomat-lawyer George Anderson, reached the same conclusion.

> A member of Congress, whether man or woman, is responsible for the legislative interests of the district he or she serves, representing men as well as women. . . . The result is that, in the practical work of legislation, a woman member of Congress finds herself associated with or pitted against men and women similarly representing group interests. . . . Accordingly, legislation for women becomes no more important to most women members of Congress than legislation for men. They become immersed, perforce, in the general problems of the country and of their respective districts (Anderson 1929, p. 533).

Anderson concluded that the most successful congresswomen were those who ignored their gender and who operated upon the same representational premises as male members of Congress. He may have had Ruth Baker Pratt in mind when he made this observation. Pratt had served two terms on the New York City Board of Alderman and was later elected to the House. The New York Republican sponsored no measure directly affecting women, but was, instead, a zealous partisan.

> As I see politics, it is a game—like any college football game. Once a man has selected his college and joined a football team, in the heat of the game, even though the opposing captain seems abler, cleverer, more apt to win, he doesn't slacken his efforts or do anything to help the other side win—he puts his back into the game harder than ever. It is just this sort of courageous, fighting spirit that is going to strengthen party machines and make them better (Pratt 1926, p. 23).

Other women serving in the early 1930s may not have been as ardent partisans, but most were no more likely than Pratt to champion women's causes. Florence Kahn, Katherine Langley, Virginia Jenckes, and Isabella Greenway scarcely mentioned the interests of their gender, with one of Kahn's few contributions coming in her first term when she submitted a bill authorizing a cloakroom attendant for women Representatives. Even Margaret Chase Smith, who left the House in 1948 to go to the Senate, eschewed a feminist orientation.

> In my service in the U.S. House of Representative, I was perhaps identified more with WAVES [Women Accepted for Voluntary Emergency Service] legislation than any other. It left the impression, I'm afraid, that I was a feminist concentrating on legislation for women. And if there is one thing I have attempted to avoid it is being a feminist. I definitely resent being called a feminist (Lewis 1972, p. 85).

By minimizing their identification with women's issues, these early congresswomen were doubtless following a prudent course. If they wanted to be taken seriously by constituents and colleagues, they were obliged to assign high priorities to the same matters that concerned constituents and colleagues. Some contemporary lawmakers operate under the same constraints. Kirkpatrick reports that female state legislators serving in the early 1970s did not emphasize women's issues when campaigning in the same way that " . . . a black might articulate group demands" of blacks (Kirkpatrick 1974, p. 100). Women who otherwise work harmoniously with male legislators are met with hostility by these same men when they become champions of women's issues (Kirkpatrick 1974, p. 124).

It is clear, however, that an increasing number of women elected to the House have been feminists. Bella Abzug, about whom more will be said below, was surely the most vocal and visible of these Representatives. Her bold positions probably made the relatively restrained feminism of other congresswomen more acceptable to male House members. But a half-dozen years before Abzug took her House seat, Patsy Mink made clear that she planned to represent women as a class. "With so few women in Congress, I feel an obligation to respond to the needs and problems of women in the nation" (Lamson 1968, p. 107).

Emulating Mink in the House later were such self-proclaimed feminists as Margaret Heckler, Shirley Chisholm, Elizabeth Holtzman, Patricia Schroeder, Yvonne Brathwaite Burke, Martha Keys, Gladys Spellman, Mary Rose Oakar, and Barbara Mikulski, among others. While campaigning for her first term, Mikulski told a group of garment workers that she would give special attention to women, adding, "If I don't, who will?" (*Washington Post*, November 1, 1976). More recently Geraldine Ferraro wrote:

> The Congresswomen carry a special responsibility, as do all 'minority' politicians. They are called upon to speak with a single voice for the cause of 'women's issues.' The women of America are a diverse population and the women in Congress reflect that diversity. . . . Nonetheless there are areas of mutual agreement which allow us to formulate a common legislative agenda (Ferraro 1979).

In the meantime, Schroeder gained the enmity of some male colleagues by conducting a campaign to end discriminatory treatment of women employees on Capitol Hill. She and Charles Rose of North Carolina unsuccessfully tried to establish grievance machinery for staff personnel who believed they had been discriminated against because of their gender. The Congresswoman from Denver was particularly effective in helping to secure restitution for a female aide of former Representative Otto Passman—after the Louisiana Democrat stated that he would not promote the woman to a high administrative post because he wanted a man for the job. Said one Representative who abhorred the Schroeder-Rose initiative, "No one's going to mess around with my slaves" (*Washington Post*, August 10, 1976). Schroeder also used her position on the Armed Services Committee to promote the admission of women to the service academies, to prohibit performance of topless go-go dancers in officers' clubs; and to establish day-care centers on military bases.

Several contemporary congresswomen have pointedly declined to adopt a feminist representational orientation—either because they are generally unsympathetic to feminist goals or because they have rejected its political efficacy. Congresswoman Barbara Vucanovich is among the former; Marilyn Lloyd is among the latter.[6] For some women, the political risks of such an orientation are substantial, and they may decide to give expression to feminist inclinations on only a few, carefully selected issues. Margaret Roukema's mixed feelings are evident in a statement she made soon after arriving in Washington.

> I do feel a special responsibility to women. But I wasn't sent here for women's issues. I was sent here for all the people in my district. I'm troubled by the isolation of women. Unless we mainstream, we're losing the opportunity to earn policy-making positions (*Washington Star*, May 27, 1981).

*   *   *

The rise in the number of congresswomen prepared to invest their resources in women's issues was a product of several factors, among the more obvious are an increase in the number of politically active women who sought House seats, and the emergence of an electorate prepared to put up with, if not actively support, a female candidate for whom women's issues are salient. But both of these circumstances probably would not have produced the torrent of affirmative women's legislation had it not been for an additional development in the House—the formation in 1977 of the Congresswomen's Caucus. The activities and goals of the Caucus did not necessarily encourage all of its members to adopt a feminist orientation. But they did serve as a magnet for female representatives interested in at least one women's issue, and as a source of positive reinforcement for those who were inclined to politicize incipient women's issues which had not yet become part of the national agenda. Thus, the ascendency of affirmative legislation and the tendency toward a feminist representational orientation were intimately linked with the activities of the Congresswomen's Caucus.

NOTES

1. The act of introducing a bill is not the only indication of a member's interest in a subject, and it is not necessarily the best evidence of such interest. Measures are often proposed or cosponsored simply to relieve constituency pressures or to support the initiative of a colleague. In some cases, sponsors would be dismayed if their bills actually became law. Nevertheless, introduction of a bill is a public act. It bears a reasonable relationship to a member's interests and priorities and, at the very least, it means that a Representative is prepared to have constituents and colleagues identify him or her with its substance and alleged consequences. Legislative proposals need not have become law to merit their inclusion in the discussion that follows.

2. Although there is some reason to believe that the same pattern has been reflected over time in the goals established outside of Congress—by women's groups or among organizations in the vanguard of reform—no such claim is made here. The pattern has not necessarily been given expression in either the policies of state and local governments or in the priorities of political parties and their nominees for President. This progression is a distillation of thousands of issues occupying Congress and made a part of the *Record*. The transition from traditional to equalitarian to affirmative proposals has been evident at the national level and in the legislative branch. Different patterns may have emerged out of ideas generated in other political arenas.

3. The so-called Sheppard-Towner bill occasioned much controversy but was nonetheless passed in 1921. It authorized $1.25 million to be distributed over a five-year period among those states creating programs to instruct residents in the hygiene of maternity and infancy. The states were eligible for the funds if they devised a plan for transmitting the health information, and if the plan received the approval of the Department of Labor's Children's Bureau. The legislation was allowed to lapse in 1929, but was reborn in the 1935 Social Security Act. A history of the Act appears in Lemons 1973, chapter 6.

4. The most prominent women's lobby of the period, the Women's Joint Congressional Committee, established a subcommittee to work for the defeat of the ERA (Breckinridge 1933, p. 270), and the National League of Women Voters, the National Women's Trade Union League, the YWCA, and the General Federation of Women's Clubs were among the more formidable organizations opposing the measure.

5. The names of the women claiming sponsorship of the ERA in the 84th Congress appear on page 2922 of the *Congressional Record*, 2nd Session. The Index to the *Record* for that year (1956), however, indicates that many of them failed to introduce ERA Resolutions of their own, perhaps a not unusual occurrence in a period during which the House prohibited joint sponsorship of bills. Five

years later, in the 87th Congress, as many as ten of the eighteen congresswomen individually introduced ERA Resolutions.

6. Lloyd was the only congresswoman expressing opposition to the August 1978 Resolution to extend the period of time during which states might approve the Equal Rights Amendment. She did not vote against extension (no congresswoman did) but she was absent when the Resolution was considered and was "paired against" it.

9 / The Congresswomen's Caucus: Preliminaries

When Congresswoman Patricia Schroeder came to the House in 1973, she assumed that the female members of Congress met regularly to discuss the status of women. Her expectation was a reasonable one, given the ease with which informal House groups have formed whenever a handful of Representatives believed that a point of view important to them was not being addressed effectively through established congressional channels (Stevens et al. 1981, p. 432).

But Schroeder was surprised and disappointed to find that there was no women's group (*Washington Post* April 25, 1978). Not that there had been an abence of attempts to create such a caucus. Republican Margaret Heckler and Democrat Bella Abzug had separately tried to organize one, but neither had achieved notable success. Abzug, particularly, had attempted to unify congresswomen behind feminist legislation, but, save for interest aroused among a handful of liberal colleagues with whom she served, her efforts proved fruitless. The New Yorker's success in helping to form the Capitol Hill Women's Political Caucus, a group offering membership to all women staffers, was no substitute for her more ambitious goal of fashioning a caucus to which all women Representatives would belong.

A beginning was made in 1975, the start of the 94th Congress, when Democratic congresswomen met to talk about committee preferences. The most senior member among them, Leonor Sullivan, agreed to channel committee requests to the Speaker, but she was opposed to calling the group a "caucus" and she was inclined to limit discussion among the women to committee choices. It was not until April, 1977, that the Congresswomen's Caucus became a formal House group.

The event took place after the feminist movement had gained momentum, several years after similar caucuses had been formed by women in state and local government (Margolis and Stanwick 1979), and well after such women's groups as the National Organization for Women and the National Women's Political Caucus had begun to establish avenues of access to Congress. It is reasonable to ask, therefore, what took congresswomen so long to create a specialized instrument to dramatize and respond to women's concerns?

The answer is not a simple one. Part of it resides in the anticaucus orientations of a few senior congresswomen whose support was crucial to formation of a women's group. Even though the House paid less obeisance to seniority in the 1970s than it did in earlier years, its members normally could do little that was innovative without at least the tacit support of veteran Representatives who had a stake in the venture. Personality differences between senior and junior women members did not make matters easier.

Delay in formation of the caucus can also be explained by the questionable legitimacy some felt such a group would have in the House. Would-be members were uncertain of its purposes and feared the ambiguity of its goals. Finally, no broad-based women's caucus was likely to be established as long as Bella Abzug was a member of the House. Each of these explanations is explored below.

OBSTACLES TO CAUCUS FORMATION

In the 1960s and 1970s, Leonor Sullivan was a formidable presence in the House. By the time of her 1976 retirement, she headed the Merchant Marine and Fisheries Committee, chaired the Banking, Currency, and Housing subcommittee on Consumer Affairs, and was a high-ranking member of the subcommittee on Housing. She had also acquired a national reputation for "truth-in-lending" and other consumer protection measures.

But Sullivan harbored traditional views about the role of women. Although she acknowledged that there was room for women in public life, she believed that their involvement in politics should come only after they fulfilled their responsibilities to husbands and children. She held further that women could make important contributions to public policy precisely because they brought to bear points of view different from those shared by males (Dudar 1967). She maintained, however, that these contributions would be jeopardized if women called attention to their gender by uniting with other women for policy-making purposes.

Furthermore, Sullivan was contemptuous of the feminist movement. She was the only woman in the House to vote against the Equal Rights Amendment; she insisted on being identified as "Mrs. John Sullivan"; and she urged that the House adopt a dress code that would prohibit women from wearing pants suits in the House chamber. Her opposition to forming a women's caucus, then, was a product of deeply rooted social orientations (Lamson 1979, p. 105).

The Missouri Democrat probably would have held these views even if she had not occupied leadership positions in her party and within the House. But, as Secretary of the Democratic Caucus and as a committee chair, she had iron allegiances to those mainstream Representatives who had helped her achieve her status and great confidence in those agencies through which she and they exercised their influence. A women's caucus would too easily be construed as divisive or marginal by male colleagues and affiliation might cause her to lose the support of congressional leaders and the members of her committees. Sullivan's reluctance to single out women for special treatment was reflected in her decision as chair of the Consumer Affairs subcommittee to extend provisions of the Equal Credit Opportunity bill to social groups other than women—to minority groups and the aged. Organized women's lobbies resisted, however, because such action would obscure the issue of gender discrimination and endanger passage of the measure. She eventually backed down (Gelb and Palley 1979, p. 370).

Sullivan also concluded that differences in district needs and in the partisan and ideological orientations among congresswomen would make an all-female coalition based on substantive issues unmanageable. This is why, when she met informally with other congresswomen at the start of the 94th Congress, she refused to call the gathering a "caucus" and limited its business to helping to secure useful committee assignments for its participants.

Sullivan was not the only veteran congresswoman responsible for delaying formation of a caucus. Neither Julia Butler Hansen, who served from 1960 to 1974, nor Edith Green, who retired in 1974 after twenty-two years in the House, saw participation in a caucus as a worthwhile expenditure of their energies. Hansen, considered by many as the most "professional" woman in the House, had served in the Washington state legislature for more than twenty years before coming to Congress. Said one male Representative with visible admiration, "Hansen was a pleasure to watch. She did her homework, had the respect of the members, and never gave a thought to the fact that she was a woman." Like Sullivan, the Washington Democrat was too intimately associated with the prevailing House power structure seriously to consider affiliating with a women's caucus, even though, unlike Sullivan, she was sympathetic to most of the goals of the women's movement.

Although Green believed that her House career suffered because of discrimination by male colleagues, she, too, rejected prospects of a congressional women's group. In fact, Green may have been the least enthusiastic of the three. Since her imprint on higher education legislation could never be rivaled by any success she might claim as a member of a women's caucus, there seemed little reason for joining, let along championing, such an organization. She had helped produce such ground-breaking measures as Title IX of the 1972 Amendments to the Higher Education Act, and had been instrumental in passage of the 1963 Equal Pay Act. Green had also helped Martha Griffiths pry the Equal Rights

Amendment out of the House Judiciary Committee, and no one could fairly accuse her of being unresponsive to inequalities women experience. Nevertheless, she believed that a women's group in the House would do more to call attention to social and political divisions within the country than it would do to ameliorate those divisions. Her distaste for the Congressional Black Caucus grew out of the same conviction.

The institutional and role orientations of these women contrasted sharply with those of younger congresswomen, and the differences prompted occasional clashes between members of the two generations. Interviews with women members of the 95th Congress revealed bristling exchanges between Sullivan and Schroeder, for example. "They were at each other all the time," said one House member. Another suggested that Sullivan and Abzug saw things so differently that their disagreements took on a personal dimension. Said one observer, " . . . each had a firm idea of what a woman should be and the gulf between these views simply couldn't be bridged." And, when a younger congresswoman who had served in the early 1970s was asked why birth of the Caucus took so long, she replied " . . . because Leonor Sullivan was against it and before her Julia Hansen and that woman from Oregon whose name I'm blocking because she made me so angry. That's why we couldn't get anything going."

Although the Caucus was not established until after these senior women left the House, their opposition to its formation was not the only factor contributing to the delay. A second is associated with disagreement among congresswomen about what functions a caucus could serve and whether concentration on women's issues was an appropriate investment of time for House members elected to represent men, as well as women. When the idea of a caucus was broached in the early 1970s, some women envisioned a group which would define important women's issues, fashion legislative language needed to address these issues, mobilize support for its initiatives inside and outside the House, create a united front to enact its proposals into law, and ensure that the new rules were vigorously enforced.

Many congresswomen were simply unwilling to submit to the discipline of such a group, however, not least because they anticipated fundamental disagreements with other women on what constituted a fit subject for caucus deliberation, and because they anticipated insoluble disputes on what position the caucus should take on some issues. Recalling these earlier days, one congresswoman said:

> Some of the younger women wanted to use the group as a real "caucus," but we couldn't do that given the different points of view among us. I was opposed to calling it a "caucus" because, given the disparities among our districts, we couldn't unite on issues or take action in concert. And I know that at least three or four other members felt that way, too.

But for some of these women, as well as for others who came after them, a caucus based upon their gender was unacceptable no matter how much consensus could be reached on issues. Most saw nothing wrong, and much that was right, with caucuses based upon economic, ideological, or district common-alities. But they were unwilling to conceive of or classify women's issues in the same way. Part of this predisposition inhered in the political realities they faced. Women's groups in their districts which would applaud association with a caucus were either weak or unlikely to offset a possible negative reaction that affiliation with a congressional women's group might trigger in men's circles and among traditional women. Furthermore, membership in such an organization would call attention to a feature of their biographies whose accentuation could increase their liabilities in the next election. In addition, some congresswomen believed that gender was an unacceptable basis upon which to forge a coalition, and a women's caucus would lack the legitimacy granted other groups by House colleagues.

But even some of these women may have been willing to affiliate with a limited, loosely structured, barely visible congresswomen's groups had it not been for an additional obstacle with which they had to contend—the presence in the House of Bella Abzug. Before her election in 1970, Abzug had gained national recognition as a champion of liberal causes. She had been an attorney for the American Civil Liberties Union, an organizer of the Women's Strike for Peace, a celebrated speaker on feminist issues, and among the most charismatic leaders of the civil rights and antiwar movements. She had been relentless in articulating her views, unyielding in the belief that they were right, impatient with delay in their adoption, and critical of whoever opposed them.

Abzug did not alter her behavior after she won her House seat, and she came to be one of the most controversial individuals ever to serve in Congress. Although the Manhattan Democrat spent only six years in the House, she was better known and occasioned more comment than colleagues whose service was three or four times as long. To understand fully why the presence of a single person was so important a factor in retarding the formation of the Congress-women's Caucus, elaboration of her orientations, her goals and her personal style is useful.

BELLA ABZUG'S WORLD

In the House, Bella Abzug was *sui generis*. She evoked strong responses from colleagues, reactions which varied from approbation and respect to ridicule and contempt. Those who agreed with her policy preferences nonetheless acknowledged that she was sometimes harder on her allies than on her enemies, and that she was a difficult person with whom to get along.

Some have argued that there were two Bella Abzugs: a "good Bella" who worked hard, fought for what she believed in, and forced the House to grapple with the most pressing issues facing the country; and a "bad Bella," who harrassed her colleagues, violated the norms of the House, and could not accept the fact that those with whom she disagreed were just as interested as she in representing constituents (Auletta 1975). But it seems evident that the same set of forces produced both the "good" and the "bad" Bella. For Representative Abzug was an unusually bright, energetic, and resourceful House member. She believed passionately in the justice of the causes she embraced and had little patience for human and procedural obstacles that got in the way. The intensity, righteousness, and imagination that fueled her behavior contributed to both the positive and the negative vibrations she transmitted.

It was impossible not to form an opinion about her. The unconventional way in which she defined her role as a congresswoman, the hostility she often displayed toward House leaders and toward Congress as an institution, and the distinctive style which spiced her personal relationships made her stand out from other members. These features of her House service combined to discourage other congresswomen from associating with an incipient group whose most visible member could make caucus affiliation a significant political liability.

The Nature of Her Constituency

Abzug never forgot that she represented a Manhattan district, but she insisted that she spoke for a national constituency, and she was inclined to infer national sentiment from district attitudes. She believed that the country's powerless people—women, the young, minorities, the poor, and those who opposed the war—looked to her to redress their grievances. Moments after she officially took her House seat she moved out to the Capitol steps and was sworn in again, this time by Brooklyn's black congresswoman, Shirley Chisholm. Inside the Capitol she had promised to defend the Constitution of the United States. Outside, in front of hundreds of women who had come to Washington to see her, she pledged to work to end the war and to redirect the country's resources toward peaceful purposes.

Once in office, she found it impossible to ignore the demands made by scores of national groups with whom she was sympathetic. When thousands of young people came to Washington in May, 1971, to protest the war, she was among a handful of Representatives to address them—and was understandably outraged by the haste with which they were being arrested even while she was still speaking to them. She was equally attentive to women's groups from states and districts other than her own, and when delegations from the Women's Strike for Peace, or the National Women's Political Caucus beckoned, she was unable to turn away. Overworked, overcommitteed, underorganized, she sometimes told those who came to her to contact their own representatives. But her inclination to serve as a champion of society's underprivileged was reinforced when they told her that other political leaders were not nearly as committed to their cause as she (Abzug 1972, p. 150).

Of course all House and Senate members occasionally claim to speak for the American people when they know full well that they are expressing sentiments peculiar to their districts. But, save for those members of Congress who were orchestrating presidential campaigns in the early 1970s, Bella Abzug, more than any other legislator, acted as if her constituency were continental. She genuinely believed that she was the country's first national congresswoman. Looking back at her record at the end of her first year she concluded:

> ... perhaps the biggest thing of all that I've done is establish myself as a representative of women, of young people, of minorities, and as an outspoken and uncompromising advocate of turning the nation's priorities around to benefit the poor, and lower-income people. I symbolize these new priorities because of my actions inside and outside of Congress (Abzug 1972, 301).

Inside the House she missed few opportunities to force members to take a position on the war; to compel administration spokesmen to explain why there were not more women in the bureaucracy; and to urge both representatives and administrators to appropriate more money for social services. She believed that an organization like the Democratic Study Group should relentlessly raise the issue of the war on the Floor until Congress finally acted (Abzug 1972, p. 53). And, when she was asked to summarize rather than read her complete statement on the Equal Rights Amendment before the House Judiciary Committee, she replied that she would either present it in its entirety or not read it at all (Abzug 1972, p. 79).

Outside the House she traveled around the country speaking before peace rallies, women's organizations, and minority groups, frequently moving them to tumultuous responses by her passion and eloquence. But Abzug was so consumed by her mission and by her vision of the country's goals that she seemed unable to establish and maintain close personal relationships. She acknowledged this void in her life soon after she took office.

> ... on the surface I appear to be very involved in a lot of social relationships. But that's just not the case, because inside I'm not relating to anybody. I find it all a strain and an interference. I feel detached in social situations. I'm always thinking about other things, about Congress, about the issues, about the political coalition I'm trying to organize. It never leaves me. I even have trouble relating to some of my closest friends, though God knows, I still love them, even if they don't know it (Abzug 1972, p. 103).

Later she lamented the fact that she had cut herself off from other people, but she concluded that there was no alternative. If she allowed her personal feelings and needs to claim her attention, she would be unable to look after the people she represented, the people who regarded her as their champion: young people, the poor, blacks, people opposed to the war, and women.

Relations with House Leaders

Abzug's distraction from those human relationships which ultimately fuel all institutions and her obsession with political and social goals produced a chasm between her and congressional leaders. In private, most Representatives are affable, undoctrinaire, accommodating people. They respect the views of their colleagues even when these views differ significantly from their own. But they expect partisan and ideological opponents to treat them similarly. Abzug appeared systematically to violate this practice, speaking out as if she were the only member who knew the truth and implying that those who disagreed with her were misinformed, stupid, or ill-intentioned. When her colleagues were reluctant to accommodate her, she made congressional leaders the targets of her frustration and the House the object of her scorn.

Abzug had the energy and zeal of a crusader and, like most crusaders, she was uncomfortable with the deliberate pace of the legislative process. As an ardent reformer, she was distressed, as well, by the gentlemen's agreements entered into by most veteran House members who believed that public policy should be changed incrementally or not all. She saw other members as pursuing careers, bargaining, negotiating, compromising to avoid today what might be embarrassing tomorrow. She saw herself as part of a people's movement, a movement that demanded change now, immediately, before more lives were lost or wasted and more injustice perpetrated.

Her criticism of the House hierarchy left few leaders untouched. She railed against those who permitted the Pentagon, big business, and war contractors to take over the power structure. She condemned Democratic leaders for not trying to get legislation passed, even though a majority of the party was behind it. They seemed to her more interested in building unconscionable coalitions with members of the right wing (Abzug 1972, p. 299). And she excoriated a Speaker of the House whose bipartisan foreign policy was crafted as if he were still fighting World War II (Abzug 1972, p. 299). Her answer was to try to figure out " ... how to beat the machine and knock the crap out of the political power structure ... " (Abzug 1972, p. 209).

Abzug defined the country's problems within an "us against them" perspective, and most Democratic celebrities were "them." Less than two months after taking her seat she openly berated House Speaker Carl Albert for preventing the Democratic Caucus from taking a position on the Vietnam War.

She accused him of being in league with President Nixon in wanting to prolong the war and, when he began to anger before her onslaught and to counterattack, she reminded him of the movement that had sent her to Washington to end the war. Even after tempers cooled she warned the Speaker that she would force a vote on continuation of the war (Abzug 1972, p. 64).

The following day, during a roll call vote on government financing of a supersonic transport plane (a project she opposed but which most party leaders supported), Democratic Whip Hale Boggs passed her on the Floor and said, "We're losing by ten votes." She responded:

> What do you mean *we're* losing by ten votes. *You're* losing, not *us*. And this is only the beginning, only the first defeat. From now on it's going to be one after another. Next we're going to beat you on the war. We're going to beat you because we're where the people are, and you and your guys might as well face it (Abzug 1972, p. 68; the emphasis is Abzug's).

In front of Government Operations Committee members, she vigorously denounced Chairman Chet Holifield for placing her on the Conservation subcommittee rather than on one dealing with military operations. "Had you had the guts to put new members, like myself, on committees which have something to do with our mandates . . . you might have helped the whole rotten Congress, if not the country. You, mister, have made a terrible error" (Abzug 1972, p. 59).

Her reputation for baiting the leadership prevailed throughout her six years in the House and, when she left in 1976, her staff remembered her pugnacity in verse, part of which read:

With hat firmly planted
She never recanted
On the stump, on the floor, in committee
Standing up for the weaker,
Standing up to the Speaker,
A symbol of people and city (*New York Times* December 11, 1976).

But Abzug had mellowed during the later years of her congressional service. She seemed to get along better with Tip O'Neill than she had with Carl Albert, and the Speaker from Massachusetts made her an "at-large" whip. He referred to her as " . . . one of the most knowledgeable legislators in the House . . . " and " . . . without a doubt the hardest working Member." As she was about to leave the House in 1976, O'Neill asserted:

> Bella Abzug has been a breath of fresh air. . . . While three years ago she probably held the title for maverick of this Chamber, she has now become an effective, hardworking and productive Member of the 'establishment' whip organization. . . . I appointed her to the whip organization because I respected

her abilities, talents, and real legislative acumen (*Congressional Record*, Vol. 122, September 30, 1976, p. H 12060).

But not all Democrats agreed with O'Neill, partly because they had been victims of her wrath and partly because her reputation as a maverick was unaltered.

Relations with Colleagues

Just as congressional leaders were assaulted by her acerbity, so, too, were the customs and practices of the institution itself. She was impatient with the deliberative process, with the establishmentarian views of House members, with the wheeling and dealing in which they engaged, and with the propensity of members to compromise their principles (Abzug 1972, p. 6). She condemned the unwritten rule which holds that "to get along you have to go along," and she did neither.

During debate to extend the draft she outraged her colleagues on the House floor by threatening members who planned to support the measure with retribution at the voting booths. The women of this country and their sons, she claimed, would never forgive those Representatives who sent young men to an illegal war. She said:

> I urge you to consider the full power of this combined group; seventy-three percent of the people [those opposed to the war] have been trying to get through to you, and these women and young people will lead them against you unless you vote against the draft bill which is before you today (*Congressional Record*, Vol. 117, April 1, 1971, p. 9022).

Fellow Democrats were appalled when she inserted in the *Congressional Record* a supposedly secret roll-call vote taken in the party caucus. The vote was on a Resolution to set a date for withdrawal of U.S. troops from Vietnam. In spite of the fact that the yeas and nays had already been printed in a Baltimore newspaper—it was this news items that she had inserted—many Democrats were furious with her for violating the secrecy of the Caucus and for creating a potential source of political embarrassment. They were upset, as well, by her unremitting effort to force the Caucus and the House to deal with the war—to call a halt to U.S. involvement in the war, to bring American forces home, to reduce military appropriations. Some thought her requests for time-consuming roll call votes were counterproductive because they produced lopsided majorities against whatever she proposed.

She also managed to annoy even hardened House veterans by finding the most inappropriate occasions to champion her causes. During time set aside to pay tribute to Emanuel Celler on his 84th birthday, for example, Abzug was among a dozen members to take the floor to recognize the House's longest serving Representative. But, after briefly lauding her fellow New Yorker, she praised groups of antiwar activists who had come to Washington and were then choking House galleries, and she asked Speaker Albert to tell the House what President Nixon had told him about the war in a White House meeting that day (*Congressional Record*, Vol. 118, May 9, 1972, p. 16, 292). There is no evidence that Albert complied with her request, but the galleries roared their approval. Celler may not have resented the indiscretion, but other House members must have deplored Abzug's judgement and her violation of two of the chamber's honored constraints—suspending political dialogue when celebrating a member's private achievement, and avoiding references to people seated in the galleries.

If her unorthodox methods did not gain adoption of her initiatives, they nonetheless attracted the notice of the Washington press corps. Frequent national exposure was a mixed blessing, however, because it irritated House members who resented the amount of attention she received and pleased her ideological adversaries because she was often portrayed as a person with whom responsible Representatives from conservative districts should have little to do. Furthermore, some liberal members felt that she should be spending more time doing her legislative homework and less time finding ways of making news. Abzug acknowledged the ease with which she received national exposure and attributed it not to conscious courting of headlines but to saying what was on her mind. During her first year in office she found it impossible to keep up with her appearances on television or radio (Abzug 1972, p. 131).

House members who were concerned about her attacks on the chamber in which they served, her willingness to reveal publicly what they considered to be private political acts, her resort to dilatory tactics, and her inclination to be what students of Congress call a "showhorse" (as distinct from a "workhorse")[1] must have been equally disturbed by Abzug's doubts about the responsiveness and the efficacy of Congress. Early in her House career she noted that she had

> . . . no desire to become a privileged member of 'the Club,' nor do I care to build a career for myself if it's going to be at the expense of the people who elected me. What that means, frankly, is that I don't give a damn about being reelected unless I am able to do what I want to do. I want to bring Congress back to the people. If that proves to be impossible to do working from within, then I'm prepared to go back outside again—to the streets—and do it from there (Abzug 1972, p. 7).

Personal Style

It is possible that many of Abzug's colleagues would have been prepared to accept her policy orientations, her unorthodox behavior and her low regard for their institution if her style were ingratiating. But that was not the case. She often personalized her attacks, making them all but impossible to ignore. During the draft debate, for example, she criticized the older members for sending young men to be killed in battle.

But her personalized criticism probably did the most damage in dealings with people who were natural allies—her own staff, members of the New York City delegation, liberals, and Democratic leaders of the Committees on which she served. Her relations with those she hired to serve her in Washington were often stormy. Capitol Hill observers reported frequent shouting matches between Abzug and her aides, with the latter publicly abused and often denied even a scintilla of self-respect. One assistant who left the Washington office stated:

> She's supposed to be a great humanist, and yet she's very cruel to people. At staff meetings, she'll say, 'Oh, shut up, you never had any sense. Stupid, why are you saying this?' Her face gets all tight and you see the rage (quoted in Winfrey 1977).

A staff member who called in sick was told, "I don't give a damn. As long as I'm paying your salary, you'll show up" (Brenner 1977).

Staff turnover, a relatively frequent occurrence in most congressional offices, was a way of life in Abzug's office. During her first four years in office, she went through five chiefs of staff (four administrative assistants and an executive assistant) and six personal secretaries—even more if a woman who was on and off the payroll on three different occasions is counted more than once (Auletta 1975). Said a former campaign manager: "The people who stay with her are either masochists or ideologues" (quoted in Brenner 1977). When trusted aides announced that they were leaving, she felt betrayed. Abzug named a major campaign advisor as her first Administrative Assistant, but when she quit, because the job was too difficult, Abzug was outraged. She condemned the assistant for not staying on while, at the same time, demeaning her performance as office manager (Abzug 1972, p. 158).

Democrats in the New York State delegation are hardly known for their unity, but Abzug proved to be a notably discordant force within a group plagued by personal animosities and petty political squabbling. During her first two weeks in office, she managed to insult and exasperate veteran Hugh Carey, New York's representative on the Democratic Committee on Committees. She told Carey that she wanted a seat on the Armed Services Committee, a panel whose legislative subject matter would give her a platform and some leverage to try to end U.S. involvement in the war. She was not optimistic about securing the seat, but she believed (rightly, as matters turned out) that even if she was unsuccessful, perhaps her campaign would make it possible for another liberal to gain the assignment (Abzug 1972, p. 21).

Carey later called Abzug while the Committee on Committees was meeting to tell her that she had not been placed on Armed Services. There were already four New Yorkers on that panel, he said, two Democrats and two Republicans, and the Committee had decided not to add any more Representatives from the state. Abzug was incensed.[2] When Carey asked what he should do about recommending her for another committee, inasmuch as she had listed no other choices, she replied: "I don't give a damn what you do. . . . If I were you I'd resign. You have no power" (Abzug 1972, p. 22). Carey was reported to have said later that "if the Second Coming were tomorrow, even He couldn't get Bella Abzug on the Armed Services Committee" (Abzug 1972, pp. 28–29).

Toward the end of her first year in the House she was accused of sabotaging a delegation luncheon by encouraging other New York Democrats to boycott it. The charge produced a strenuous denial from her, along with denounciations of Congressmen Ed Koch and Ben Rosenthal for leaking a story about the alleged boycott to the New York City newspapers. Abzug knew she had detractors among the delegation and that they had no compunctions about damaging her politically. But she was prepared to work without them.

Later she found that few New York Democrats would support her when she ran in the 1976 Senate primary. Congressman Jerome Ambro of Nassau County said that having Abzug at the top of the ticket in his district was like running with Mao Zedong. She was outraged by Ambro's comment, asserting that if he could not support her at least he should not criticize her. The Long Island Democrat apologized for the remark, but neither he nor any other Democrat, with the exceptions of Bronx Representatives Herman Badillo and Jonathan Bingham, endorsed her candidacy. And, when she lost the primary to Daniel Patrick Moynihan, she lashed out at fellow Democrats in characteristic fashion, calling Brooklyn Congressman Stephen Solarz a "coward," and Harlem's Charles Rangel "corrupt."

Abzug wore out her welcome among most liberals, just as she did among her neighbors. She was unrelenting in her efforts to force the Democratic Study Group to take a strong position on ending the war in Southeast Asia, believing that if she were unable to get her party's caucus to count the yeas and nays, at least she could force the issue within the House's most important liberal bastion. But she found that although they discussed the issues, they would take no action (Abzug 1972, p. 53). Even when cautioned that she was irritating some of the group's members by insisting on a vote to end the war, she rejected the warning (Abzug 1972, p. 119).

Later, when some of the most liberal members of the Democratic Study Group (including fellow New Yorker William Fitts Ryan) were considering the possibility of forming a smaller, ideologically purer House group, they were uncertain about including Abzug. Although they agreed with her on most issues, they felt that she was too aggressively compulsive about her own concerns and that she would affect deleteriously both the new group's effectiveness and the rapport of its members. According to one congressman, she was finally invited to join. But the group soon disbanded, partly because it had become too large, thereby making ideological unanimity all but impossible.

Abzug's relations with her committee chairmen were not uniformly poor. She got off to a bad start with Holifield on Government Operations, but Public Works Committee chairman John Blatnik of Minnesota was more sensitive to her skills and her political goals. Blatnik left the House when the 1974 session ended, however, and Robert Jones of Alabama succeeded him. Jones was not nearly as patient with Abzug as his predecessor had been and, according to one member of the Committee, he had little liking for her. Unfriendly exchanges punctuated panel discussions and Jones began to call her "Bella Donna," a term which sounded enough like "prima donna" to suggest part of Jones's meaning, but which, of course, is also the name of a poisonous herb.

In sum, Abzug left a trail of distrust, frustration, hostility, ridicule, and personal animosity in her dealings with people whose help she might normally have expected. She terrorized her staff, exasperated her New York colleagues, scared off fellow liberals, and alienated her committee chairmen often enough to strip herself of the few reliable allies upon whom she should have been able to count for political support. Said one former aide, "Half of working for Bella is repairing the damage" (quoted in Brenner 1977).

Abzug's Effectiveness

But, for all of her liabilities, many members of the House regarded her as an effective congresswoman. In the first place, she did not always behave irrepressibly. Most of the time she was a reasonable, diligent, intelligent House member. Second, her attendance on the Floor and in committee meetings was good; she did her homework before attending these sessions and her questions to witnesses were thoughtful and informed. Furthermore, her relations with other committee members were often friendly and cordial. One House member with whom she served on the Public Works Committee said, "Bella has been given a bum rap. Sure she came on strong. She could really dish it out. But she could take it, too. She could deal and compromise with the best of them and she was one of the ablest people in this place."

Three congresswomen with whom she served acknowledged that she had a problem in "human relations," but each concluded that her contribution to the House was considerable. "Bella Abzug was an abrasive person but, still, I think she was one of the most effective people we had here and her defeat [for the House seat given up by Ed Koch when he was elected Mayor in 1977] was a great shame." The second admiringly alluded to Abzug's skill and purposiveness in getting antisex discrimination provisions added to House bills. And, in defense of the "abrasiveness" label pinned on the New York Congresswoman, another member asserted: "Why should you have to be nice if you disagree so fundamentally with someone on matters that are as important as the ones Bella concerned herself with?"

Abzug's awareness of her reputation and her conscious effort to amplify some components of her image suggests that she exercised greater control over her behavior than her seeming irrepressibility might suggest. The journal she published after her first year in office reveals more guile and self-knowledge than critics are usually prepared to acknowledge. The floppy hat that became her trademark, the forceful, irreverent, antiestablishment speech, the persistent calls for change were features which she assiduously cultivated and which defined her persona. In a Los Angeles appearance before the California Democratic Councils she chose a dress only because it could be worn with a hat (". . . how could I deprive them!" she explains). Her introduction was followed by a tumultuous demonstration, after which, she reports with considerable detachment: ". . . I went into my song and dance and moved them to a five-minute standing ovation—very spirited crowd this one, I must say, though it happens everywhere I speak across the country" (Abzug 1972, p. 99).

She knew that she was a proselytizer and that she could lecture people for hours if they would let her; she knew that she was sometimes a "bully" and that the biggest bully in the House, Wayne Hays of Ohio, might not prevail if they started bullying each other; and she knew that she was often "pushy" and could sympathize with "pushiness" when she saw it in others. She knew, in short, that she was not an easy person to live with. Speaking at a Women's National Press Club dinner soon after taking her House seat she quoted a daughter's statement at an election night celebration: " 'Thank God we're getting her out of *our* house and into *their* House'." "After being in Washington for a week," Abzug continued, "I'm beginning to get the impression that a lot of fellows are feeling the same way as my daughter. . . . 'God, if we could only get her out of *our* House and back into *theirs*' " (Abzug 1972, p. 18; the emphasis is Abzug's).

But, most important, she believed that the liabilities accompanying her style constituted a price she had to pay to get what she wanted. For she was, above all, an activist. "I want action—not talk," she asserted.

> You can't just sit around and think or talk and expect to get anywhere. It's not that I don't *think*. Of course I do. But my thing is *doing*. I don't go around philosophizing. I go around *doing*. . . . I move instantly, prepared to take risks (Abzug 1972, pp. 166–67; the emphasis is Abzug's).

Reputation and Legacy

She took the risks and she paid the price. For those who believed in her causes she was a dynamic, courageous, oratorically gifted, and effective leader. For those who did not, she gained a reputation in Washington as an abrasive, uncompromising, irresponsible, unpleasant, and fanatical woman whose support could be the kiss of death, whose behavior was subversive, and whose image was a source of ridicule.

And, in Washington, reputation is everything. Hundreds of political and social calculations are made on the basis of startlingly imperfect knowledge, and decision-makers are forced to rely on the stereotypes of which they happen to be aware. Once an image is created, it is difficult to alter—and Abzug's image was indelibly burned into the minds of Washington opinion leaders.

After-dinner speakers, looking for a laugh from their audiences, needed only to mention her name to evoke the desired response. Her stout figure was a frequent target of men who were trying to be funny. Abzug quotes Vice President Spiro Agnew speaking at a fund-raising dinner as saying "Republicans should work for adoption of environmental programs, welfare, revenue sharing, and *most importantly, we have to keep Bella Abzug from showing up in Congress in hotpants*" (Abzug 1972, p. 49; the emphasis is Abzug's). When Governor Nelson Rockefeller testified before the Public Works Committee and his dollar figures were contradicted by the Manhattan congresswoman, he responded: "The distinguished Representative from New York has questioned my figures. My concern is that in challenging my figures, she has none to substitute, except a very beautiful figure of her own" (Abzug 1972, p. 285). And, when two vacancies simultaneously occurred on the Supreme Court and President Nixon was reported to be considering a woman for one of them, *Washington Post* columnist Morris Siegel urged Nixon to appoint Bella Abzug to both seats (Abzug 1972, p. 251). It is difficult to imagine Agnew, Rockefeller, and Siegel making the same remarks about a stout male Representative.

When Abzug left the House there remained a legacy impossible to ignore— even by those who did not serve in Congress until after she gave up her seat. One liberal Democrat who had never met her noted (in response to a question about the treatment of congresswomen by their male colleagues) that all congresswomen were treated as equals. "Perhaps things are this way," he added, "because there is among the women in the House no one like Bella Abzug." A conservative Republican, whose service overlapped Abzug's, commented on her loss to Republican William Green in the 1978 race to fill Koch's vacancy: "Abzug . . . was the most unpopular member of the House. She was so abrasive that even the Democrats were not unhappy when she lost last month." And, when President Carter created a National Advisory Committee for Women a year and one-half after Abzug left Congress and appointed her codirector, Kentucky Democrat Carroll Hubbard remonstrated on the House floor:

> I can assure President Carter that ninety-nine percent of the taxpayers in the Commonwealth of Kentucky are opposed to any new Federal agencies or committees, and 99.9 percent of Kentuckians are opposed to Federal tax dollars being spent by Bella Abzug . . . It is difficult to believe that President Carter interprets the taxpayer revolt in this country to indicate that what we

need now in Washington is Bella Abzug giving advice (*Congressional Record*, Vol. 124, June 13, 1978, p. H 5354).

It is no wonder, then, that the New Yorker's presence in the House retarded the development of a Congresswomen's Caucus. Other women members would have difficulty enough explaining affiliation with a group which called attention to their nontraditional roles and whose legitimacy was in doubt. To be associated, at the same time, with a woman who had a reputation for radical views, flamboyant behavior, and incendiary speeches was politically unacceptable.

Before she left the House, Abzug met occasionally with a small group of women liberals (Patsy Mink, Patricia Schroeder, Elizabeth Holtzman among them) to discuss common interests. The difficulties such a group would have had in expanding while Abzug remained a House member was underscored in 1978 when she was nominated to replace Koch. Prospects of her return sent waves of trepidation through not only conservative groups that had little use for her combative admonitions, but also among women Representatives who, following the establishment of the Congresswomen's Caucus, had come to believe that membership in it was politically useful. There was concern that she would "take over" the Caucus without even trying, and thereby destroy it. Some privately feared that Abzug's powerful personality would again command the attention of the press and that she would dominate the life of the Caucus, perhaps reversing the acceptance it had begun to receive in its early months.

These fears proved to be premature, of course, inasmuch as Abzug lost. But the loss was viewed with mixed feelings by several Democratic congresswomen whose legislative objectives differed little from those of the redoubtable New Yorker. They regretted the result because Abzug was so forceful a champion of causes in which they fervently believed. But they did not lament it as deeply as they might have because the viability of their fledgling organization was, for the time being, secure.

At the same time, they realized the profound effect that Abzug had on the House, on congressional consideration and treatment of women's issues, and on the propensity of other congresswomen to adopt feminist orientations. As we shall see, Abzug's forceful advocacy of women's rights and women's needs, and the frames of reference she imposed on them paved the way for House acceptance of the very same perspectives when offered in a manner that House members found less offensive.

NOTES

1. Donald R. Matthews employed these terms when discussing what he called the "folkways" of the Senate. Senators interested in generating publicity, in making the headlines, were "showhorses" and their behavior violated Senate norms. "Workhorses" were too busy mastering the

details of proposed legislation to attract the attention of the media. Thus, the latter gained the respect of their colleagues while the former were suspect (Matthews 1960, p. 94).

2. One reason Abzug was upset was that the Committee on Committees had decided to rescind its appointment of freshman Herman Badillo to the Agriculture Committee after the Bronx Democrat heatedly refused to accept it, and to recommend him for the Education and Labor Committee, instead. Two years before, the Committee had done the same thing for Shirley Chisholm, shifting her from the Agriculture Committee to the Veterans' Affairs Committee when the Brooklyn congresswoman strenuously objected to an assignment she believed had little relevance to her black constituents in Bedford-Stuyvesant. Abzug saw the Committee's failure to alter its decision in her case as a personal affront (Abzug 1972, p. 22).

10 / The Congresswomen's Caucus: Early Years

Departure from the House of both Sullivan and Abzug left the way clear for remaining congresswomen to create a caucus. And the opportunity was seized by Elizabeth Holtzman and Margaret Heckler.[1]

THE RIGHT CONDITIONS

Holtzman was, like Abzug, an extraordinarily bright, intense lawyer who defined herself as a liberal and a feminist and who had an unshakeable belief in the justness of her causes. She was a conspicuously conscientious House member, as well, and her tenacity and strength of will were endowments she shared with her Manhattan neighbor. Moreover, both women had been part of a mini-group of liberal Democrats which included Patsy Mink and Patricia Schroeder, and which met periodically over coffee and lunch to sign letters and issue statements supporting women's rights and demanding an end to the Vietnam War. But the styles of the two New Yorkers could not have differed more fundamentally. Whereas Abzug was irrepressibly spontaneous, extroverted, thick-skinned, and confident, Holtzman was deliberate, introverted, extremely sensitive, and insecure.

To some observers, the Brooklyn Democrat was a cold, humorless, perfectionist who lacked the human relations skills needed to persuade strikingly diverse female House members to join forces. Critics believed that she was too inflexible and strong-willed to exercise the restraint required to build a women's coalition. But they did not realize just how much Holtzman wanted to create such a group, and she coupled the same dogged determination and penetrating intelligence that had sometimes alienated colleagues to produce a caucus framework that most other women could accept. According to Betty Dooley, the first Executive Director of the Caucus, "If it hadn't been for Liz, it would not have gotten off the ground at all." Someone with her "dynamic interest" was needed to animate the whole program (Lamson 1979, p. 105).

Holtzman's efforts were probably a necessary condition for forming a caucus, but they were not a sufficient condition. Among the other women willing to lead the enterprise, Margaret Heckler was especially important. Heckler's earlier interest in organizing a caucus made her an ideal partner in the venture. Like Holtzman, she very much wanted the caucus to succeed. As a savvy, moderate Republican, she gave the organizing effort the bipartisan orientation needed to convince some of the outnumbered Republican congresswomen that the new group would not be an instrumentality of the Democratic party's liberal wing. Moreover, she and Holtzman worked well together and complemented one another. Heckler was accepted by the business and banking community, while the Brooklyn Democrat had excellent access to labor organizations. They would later turn to both for support.

Also important to caucus formation were the efforts of national feminist groups seeking access to Congress through lawmakers who were inclined to view their entreaties favorably and who were organized to do something about them. Lobbyists from the National Organization for Women (NOW), the National Women's Political Caucus (NWPC), the Business and Professional Women's Clubs (BPWC), among others, encouraged their female contacts in the House to establish an agency through which they could communicate their objectives and which, in turn, would try to make these goals part of the national agenda. One congressional aide (who served as a member's liaison to the Congresswomen's Caucus) said when interviewed in 1978:

> Formation of the Caucus came about almost as much because of the pressure from outside Congress as it did from pressure within. Women's groups wanted more formal entree to the House and they saw a caucus as giving it to them.

Two other congresswomen played key roles in getting the caucus off the ground. One was Shirley Chisholm, the other Barbara Mikulski. Chisholm took an early interest in forming a congresswomen's group and participated actively in preliminary discussions of its structure and purposes. Her involvement also assured observers in and out of Congress that the group's attention would not be confined to matters of interest largely to middle-class, white women.

Mikulski was an important link between outside interest groups and congresswomen. The former Baltimore City Councilwomen, a smart, energetic feminist, had an impeccable credit rating with women's organizations. She was highly regarded by professional politicians in both Baltimore and Washington, as well, and her interest in a caucus gave it the ballast it needed to withstand the suspicion and hostility it was certain to encounter inside and outside the House.

Mikulski also contributed a pragmatism and a flexibility to the group—characteristics which permitted continued viability of an organization whose members held radically different views on some women's issues. Said one Caucus member:

> The Caucus got off the ground because we recognized that we were going to be a pluralistic group. We don't have a shared idea of what women should be. However. we recognize that we are different and because we have decided not to develop a united front on every issue—abortion, for example—we have an effective group in this [the 95th] Congress.

Accordingly, determination to search for a consensus and acceptance of the fact that one would not be found on the more volatile issues were the strategic premises guiding development of the Congresswomen's Caucus.

The energies of these women might have been invested less productively had it not been for the arrival in Washington of an administration sympathetic to most of their goals. President Carter and White House aides provided a receptive environment for Caucus initiatives, one within which new or unorthodox ideas would be taken seriously. True, women's issues were not matters to which they attached highest priority, and communications breakdowns did occur between Capitol Hill and the President's legislative liaisons. But, the relationship between Caucus members and the White House was cordial. More important, scores of Cabinet and sub-Cabinet level Carter appointees were prepared to go out of their way to accommodate Caucus needs. As will be demonstrated, top administrators in the Departments of Commerce, Labor, and Health, Education, and Welfare, among others, gave women's issues an importance they had never had before.

LAYING THE GROUNDWORK

Creation of the Caucus proceeded on two overlapping tracks, one principally inside the House, the other mainly outside. Soon after the November, 1976 election, Holtzman directed staff aide Leah Wortham to list the goals a congresswomen's caucus could realistically fulfill and to suggest a structure it might adopt to help realize these aims. At the same time, an Ad Hoc Coalition of Women's Groups, made up of representatives of more than forty organizations, began to meet with Cabinet nominees of the newly elected, but not-yet-sworn-in Carter administration. Coalition members promoted issues important to them while learning about the priorities these officials expected to give to women's issues.

At a January 13th meeting with Commerce Secretary-designate Juanita Kreps, for example, coalition lobbyists from NWPC, NOW, and BPWC, among other groups, expressed their concern about the number of women that would be holding positions within the Commerce Department and the inordinately large proportion of women, as compared with men, filling low-level government ranks. Also present was newly elected Barbara Mikulski. A few weeks later, other representatives of NWPC, including Elizabeth Holtzman, met with Bert Lance, Director of the Office of Management and the Budget, to urge him to appoint women to high-ranking positions within OMB and to encourage other agencies to do the same.

In the meantime, Mikulski sent a questionnaire to the seventeen other congresswomen asking them to assign priorities to women's issues they thought should receive attention during the 95th Congress. Thirteen responded, and a majority attached highest priority to creating more jobs (and more responsible jobs) for women in the federal government. A less discriminatory social security system was second, with other concerns including child care, displaced homemakers, and health care for women. While the Maryland Democrat was gathering the data, Holtzman and Heckler were sounding out these same women about their interest in a caucus.

On January 26, a "Steering Committee" made up of Holtzman, Heckler, and Chisholm met to discuss the services a Congresswomen's caucus could offer and the issues on which women House members might want to act. They explored the possibility of securing valuable committee assignments for women and the need to monitor all matters affecting women, perhaps by placing at least one female Representative on each standing committee. They agreed on the need to reintroduce measures that had died in the last Congress, Yvonne Burke's bill to aid displaced homemakers, for example, and suggested new bills that should be submitted in the 95th Congress. The Steering Committee also touched on the need to improve administration of measures already on the books.

But perhaps the most important product of the meeting was a shared belief that the caucus, whatever its structure and functions, would be a catalyst for like-minded women, rather than a disciplined unit that tried to forge unanimity on women's issues among its members. The three women agreed that each Representative would decide for herself whether to support other members on an issue-by-issue basis, with action taken in the name of the caucus only when there was complete agreement.

The Steering Committee created the skeleton of a caucus in a series of three meetings held in March. At the first of the three, convened on March 2, Heckler, Holtzman, and Chisholm agreed on the uses to which the caucus would be put. They concluded that its members would keep one another informed about discussions affecting women in their committees, monitor floor action, develop legislative proposals to help women, endorse and support these bills with testimony and by lobbying colleagues, and monitor the administrative behavior of executive branch officials.

The group would have two "chairs" (the term "chairpersons" was rejected as being awkward), and an executive committee made up of the co-chairs, a treasurer, and three other congresswomen. Inasmuch as the Democrats were the majority party, they would hold a committee majority. Later, Heckler and Holtzman were selected as co-chairs, Burke was named Treasurer and Mikulski, Chisholm and Shirley Pettis became members-at-large. The Steering Committee gave the group's officers two-year terms, coinciding with the beginning and end of each Congress, and settled on its formal designation—"The Congresswomen's Caucus."

CAUCUS DELIBERATIONS AND SETTING

The first meeting of the Caucus was held in the Capitol at 12:30, Tuesday, April 19, 1977. Four congresswomen took part in discussions focusing on "battered women" and remedies the Caucus might pursue to deal with the incidence of wife abuse. Continued low turnout for the following week's session prompted members to reconsider the hour and day for meetings, and they settled on 8:30 A.M. every other Tuesday, a decision which was later changed to every other Wednesday after the first quorum call.[2] Frequent shifts in meeting time occasionally left members and their staffs uncertain about just when the group would convene. Notice of a change did not always reach all interested parties, and, on one occasion, Secretary of Labor Ray Marshall appeared in the Capitol at 8:30 A.M. to address the Caucus only to find H235 locked and no one around to tell him why. When he finally reached Holtzman's office, a secretary realized that everyone but the guest of honor had been told that the meeting would be held later than day. Marshall agreed to come back another time.

The change from Tuesday to Wednesday had the intended result, and attendance picked up significantly. Through the remainder of the 95th Congress on average of nine of the fifteen members appeared for each meeting. Executive Board members were almost always present, with Holtzman and Heckler alternately presiding. The group conducted three types of meetings. At the start of the year, meetings were often devoted to establishing a list of legislative priorities. Members stated, sometimes through staff aides, the matters that were important to them and tried to enlist the support of other women. Unanimity was neither sought nor reached, but consensus emerged on most matters, and members left the meetings better informed about the concerns of others and more fully aware of the extent to which their own preferences were shared by colleagues.

An alternative format was followed when administration officials spoke to the Caucus. During the 95th Congress, the Caucus met with Commerce Secretary Juanita Kreps, HEW Secretary Joseph Califano twice, Attorney

General Griffin Bell twice, Labor Secretary Marshall, and Bert Lance and James McIntyre, successive Directors of the Office of Management and the Budget. Sometimes speakers began with a preliminary statement about something in which they knew Caucus members had an interest, but more often congresswomen began the questioning at once. Administrators leaned over backward to be responsive, and attendance at these meetings was slightly higher than it was for those devoted to legislative priorities.

A third type of Caucus meeting centered on Caucus administration. These sessions were relatively infrequent. They touched on fund-raising, staff and equipment needs, and Caucus procedures, and they were likely to be less well attended. Two factors explain the lower turnout. First, most congresswomen were simply not interested in the mechanisms that kept the Caucus going, even though most were satisfied with the information, political advantages, and camaraderie that affiliation brought with it. Second, administrative matters were normally dealt with at the biweekly Executive Committee meetings and by the group's Executive Director.

The meeting site, H235, encouraged informal, thoughtful, unhurried exchanges, among Caucus members and between them and the Cabinet officials who appeared. The "Congresswomen's Suite," as it is officially called, or the "Women's Reading Room" as it is otherwise known, is made up of three rooms—a drawing room which can fit about twenty-five people in chairs around its periphery if they don't mind sitting close to one another, and two small rooms, one of which contains kitchen facilities, the other writing desks and telephones. The Suite was set aside for congresswomen in 1962 to give them a place to handle correspondence, tape broadcasts for use in their districts, hide from constituents, lobbyists, and staff, and kick their shoes off and relax, something which congressmen do in the cloak rooms, but for which congresswomen require more privacy.[3] Thus it was as much of a "retiring room" as a "reading room" before the women began to use it for their meetings, with issues of the *Congressional Record* being the only printed matter available on a regular basis.

The Suite is just a few steps from the House floor, and is across the hall from the "working" office of the House Speaker. Its location makes it ideal as a meeting place for members who don't want to go far either to answer quorum calls or to vote midway through their meetings, and its proximity to the Speaker's office has obvious symbolic virtues. These same factors probably prompted the Black Caucus leaders to use the Suite for their meetings until they were asked by the congresswomen to convene elsewhere.

The drawing room's quiet elegance provides a pleasant atmosphere for Caucus discussions. Its most distinctive piece of furniture, a couch to which former President John Quincy Adams was carried and on which he died of a stroke while completing his political career as a Congressman, gives the room some historical importance. A wall of a corridor leading to the drawing room is covered by photographs of each woman to serve in Congress. A receptionist supervises entry to the Suite, readies it for Caucus meetings, prepares the coffee and refreshments served to visitors, takes messages for the congresswomen who use it, and turns away intruders, including constituents and staff, when Suite occupants do not want to be disturbed.

Caucus membership was reasonably stable throughout the 95th Congress, but did not include all incumbent women Representatives and Senators. Some, notably Barbara Jordan, were members in name only, however. The Caucus began with fifteen of the eighteen Representatives.[4] The number increased to sixteen when, early in 1978, newly appointed Senator Muriel Humphrey was invited to join. Senator Maryon Allen, another appointee to the 95th Congress, declined to affiliate with the group.

ORGANIZATIONAL GROWING PAINS

Soon after the Caucus got underway, three problems emerged to plague its activities. One had to do with the unanimity rule, a requirement that all members had to agree to support statements and proposals before they could be distributed as official Caucus positions. Second, the process devised to determine whether pronouncements did, in fact, have unanimous support was cumbersome and time-consuming. The third and, by far most serious source of concern, was the difficulty the organization had in raising money to pay staff and to support research on women's issues.

Variations in the political and ideological orientations of Caucus members often meant that there were times when consensus, not to mention unanimity, could not be reached on an issue. Fundamental disagreement over abortion had made that subject off limits to Caucus action at the outset. But even when members were in general agreement about a problem, they sometimes differed on an appropriate response—about such things as what action spoke most effectively to the problem and how much money should be spent to finance a program. Most decisions were reached by a handful of officer-activists, but, in the process, Caucus positions were narrowly drawn and more cautious than many believed they should have been. And some matters about which members felt deeply were not dealt with directly. The occasional frustrations liberal members experienced in this regard were nothing compared to what they would face in the 96th Congress, however.

The second problem, the long-drawn-out process of trying to reach agreement among members, was also a product of the unanimity rule. Early Caucus practice was to circulate all documents among the entire membership for their signatures. If one or more members refused to sign, the statement could nonetheless be issued in the names of the signatories, but not as a Caucus document. Unconscionable delays resulted when some members neglected to pass material to other congresswomen in a timely fashion. Caucus staff were forced to call member's offices to learn on whose desk the document was gathering dust. Later, identical copies were sent to all members simultaneously to hasten the process. An additional difficulty inhered in the tendency of some members to alter the language of a statement, producing changes which, if not agreed to, would induce them to withhold their support. But the practice forced recirculation of the document and further delay. Elizabeth Holtzman was a stickler for detail, and, even after submitting a proposal of her own, she often modified it later.

But the unanimity rule and the delay it produced were minor compared with the funding problem the Caucus faced. The Steering Committee had established an annual dues of $50, and it expected members periodically to allocate a portion of their clerk-hire money, funds used to pay their office and district employees, to compensate Caucus staff. The practice was, and is, a common one and it permits members of legislative service organizations collectively to bear the costs of maintaining these agencies. But each woman was expected to determine how much of her staff funds, about $340,000 exclusive of stationery and equipment allocations, would be set aside for Caucus needs, and no mechanism was established to guarantee payment of either the clerk-hire contribution or the annual dues. Only the good faith of the members, their sense of responsibility to one another and to Caucus goals, and the absence of a large number of competing demands for their financial resources would generate salaries and operating revenues for the Caucus staff.

From April to July 1977, the size of the Caucus treasury was of little consequence, inasmuch as the office staffs of congresswomen affiliated with the organization, especially Holtzman's, carried out administrative tasks. Holtzman's Administrative Assistant, Rodney Smith, was, as much as any other aide, a Caucus midwife, present at many of the preliminary meetings early in 1977, representing Holtzman at sessions she could not attend, acting as a trouble-shooter when difficulties arose and, together with another Holtzman staffer, Anne Stone, unraveling the misunderstandings and soothing the hurt feelings that inevitably emerge when an organization is born.

But the need for funds crystallized quickly in July when the Caucus placed Betty Dooley on the payroll as Executive Director. Dooley was an excellent choice for the position. She had, herself, been a candidate for a House district in Texas and for state legislative office, a fund raiser for Robert Strauss when he was Treasurer of the Democratic National Committee, and a lobbyist on health issues in state capitals and in Washington. The year before, she had done advance work for vice presidential candidate Walter Mondale. Dooley's fund-raising and political experience, her knowledge of Washington and her solid connections with socially progressive organizations were precisely the qualities for which the Caucus was looking. One of her first responsibilities was to hire a Deputy Director, and she chose Susan Scanlan, a bright and able young woman who had more than three year's experience on Capitol Hill as a legislative aide. Before long, the two were sharing a mammoth work load. They were responsible for recruiting and supervising Caucus interns, directing research on women's issues, establishing and coordinating a network made up of liaison persons in each Caucus member's office, developing research proposals to submit to Foundations for financial support, issuing press releases, preparing statements and speeches, learning member's positions on legislative proposals, arranging for Caucus meetings with Cabinet and other administration officials, attending all meetings, and following up on directives and suggestions generated by these sessions.

While Dooley and Scanlan were normally able to secure the in-kind services and equipment needed to run their office, money to pay their salaries was another matter. In 1977 and 1978, some congresswomen neglected to pay their dues, and only eight of the fifteen House members contributed clerk-hire funds. Months passed during which Dooley and Scanlan were either not compensated or paid far less than the montly rate called for by the $25,000 and $16,500 annual salaries each was told she would receive. A sum of $12,500 had been initially budgeted for a Secretary/Bookkeeper, but no one bothered seriously to suggest filling that slot. In fact, several congresswomen were either oblivious of the staff's financial needs or simply did not care about them. Feelings ran the gamut from those of Shirley Chisholm, who allocated more than twice the amount of any other Caucus member, to those of Millicent Fenwick, who told the staff that if they really believed in the goodness of what they were doing, they should not want money.

THE CONGRESSWOMEN'S CAUCUS CORPORATION

The growing financial problems facing the Caucus prompted members to decide to hold a fundraising party, a common enough Washington phenomenon, and invite representatives of labor, business, women's, and other organizations which had contributed in the past to congressional candidates and women's causes. The Caucus itself could not sponsor it because donations would then be considered "political" and contributors would be unable to claim them as tax deductions. Instead, the fundraiser would be conducted under the auspices of the Congresswomen's Caucus Corporation, a nonpolitical, educational organization.

Caucus founders had anticipated the need to establish a corporate entity separate from the Caucus itself, but with a link to activities on Capitol Hill through the research and educational programs it carried out at the direction of the Caucus. Accordingly, they directed papers to be drawn up for what came to be called the Congresswomen's Caucus Corporation (CCC). The Articles of

Incorporations were filed in October, 1977, and designated the six-member Executive Committee of the Caucus as the Board of Directors of the Corporation.

The CCC was defined as a charitable and educational agency designed to conduct research, educate the public, and maintain the administrative overhead needed to support these ends. This designation brought the organization within the meaning of paragraph 501(c)(3) of the Internal Revenue Code and permitted it to solicit and collect tax-deductible contributions. Trade unions, for example, were free to offer funds directly from their treasuries, rather than limiting them to volunteer contributions alone. Furthermore, according to amendments to the election Campaign Act of 1971, House members' surplus funds could be given to the tax-exempt organization as long as they were reported to the Federal Election Commission. Later, Dooley was named Executive Director of the CCC and Scanlan became Executive Director of the Caucus.

In the meantime, plans for the fundraiser were laid. At first, the Executive Committee hoped the event would take place in January 1978, but it was not until then that the cochairs selected a professional Washington fundraiser, Scooter Miller, to orchestrate the effort. Heckler and Holtzman met with Miller late that month and tentatively agreed to hold a cocktail-buffet, rather than a sit-down dinner. The event took place in April at the Organization of American States Building, with tickets priced at $100—although some individuals and organizations donated sums of $500 and $250. The formal program would be brief, but included introductions of Rosalynn Carter, ranking elected officials, and other celebrities.

The Caucus netted $30,000, although all but $9,000 went to pay back salaries and operating expenses. More importantly, the April 1978 fundraiser gained publicity for the group and proved the utility of an income-producing device upon which it could rely in the future. Similar gatherings in 1979 and 1980 respectively raised $80,000 and $110,000.

The money was badly needed. Additional staff had to be hired to gather and integrate information Caucus members needed to determine the nature and direction of the initiatives they should take. Their personal staffs were tied up with constituency, legislative, and administrative responsibilities and could not be spared. The General Accounting Office, the Congressional Research Service, and the Congressional Budget Office were already overburdened with requests for information from standing committee staffs and members who had a prior claim on their resources. Consequently, studies produced for Caucus members were often superficial, beside the point, and submitted long after an issue had been disposed of or had lost its visibility. Moreover, executive branch agencies could not always be expected to provide information that left them vulnerable. The Caucus could have relied on research conducted by organizations ouside of Washington but, without a larger staff, it could not easily discover which women's issues were being addressed by which organizations and what implications could be inferred from their findings.

The members agreed, therefore, that a research coordinator and competent investigators were indispensable to the vitality of their organization and, early in 1978, they set out to raise the money to pay for experienced researchers. Among the first sources approached was the Ford Foundation. In February, Caucus members met with Mariam Chamberlain, a Program Director in Ford's Higher Education and Research Division. Chamberlain described Foundation ground rules governing the awarding of grants, the most important of which were that Ford could not itself become involved in pending legislative bills or issues, that it did not make grants for an agency's operations and overhead, and that it did not make un-earmarked contributions. Moreover, given the increasing number of organizations studying women's issues (including a half-dozen universities), Foundation officials would have to be satisfied that this new one would not duplicate research efforts being conducted elsewhere.

Although the Ford Foundation was the first agency with which Caucus members began negotiations for a grant, it was not the first to receive a formal request. That distinction fell to the Rockefeller Family Fund. On May 26, 1978, following preliminary discussions with Family Fund associates, the Caucus asked that organization for $20,000 to support the next four months of its administrative operations. The covering letter and budget statement made clear that this would be "initial funding" to pay the salaries of CCC staff aides and to keep the organization afloat while it sought larger sums. An Appendix contained a laundry list of public policy issues that Caucus members had begun to explore, but, like the request to the Ford Foundation submitted a few weeks later, it neither described in sufficient detail specific projects to be undertaken nor explained why a CCC research staff, rather than agencies already studying these issues, should benefit from the award. In a letter rejecting the request, a Family Fund official noted that the organization focused on "targeted projects" rather than on "general budgetary" requirements.

The same fate awaited the $50,000 proposal submitted to Ford. But the negative decision in this instance was linked not so much to a failure to specify the issues which would receive Caucus attention as much as it was based on the highly political nature of the group requesting the money. True, the Congresswomen's Caucus had put some distance between its members' political identities and the research and educational functions of the Corporation. But the CCC's Board of Directors was the same group of congresswomen making up the Caucus Executive Committee. Furthermore, the Caucus staff and the CCC staff overlapped and occupied an increasingly crowded, top-floor room in the Rayburn building.[5] Thus, if the Caucus hoped to launch its research and coordination activities, it would have to make a more palpable distinction between its political and educational arms. This it did in October 1978, when it created the Women's Research and Education Institute (WREI) to replace the CCC.

The Institute was given a Board of Directors, no member of which was a congresswoman; the terms "caucus" and "Congress" were conspicuously absent from its title; it was assigned a staff distinct from that of the Caucus; and, at the first opportunity, it planned to move from the Rayburn Building into private quarters elsewhere in Washington. As we shall see, the decision to separate the Caucus from its nonprofit educational offspring turned out to be a fortunate one.

THE WOMEN'S RESEARCH AND EDUCATION INSTITUTE

The congresswomen who had made up the CCC Board of Directors were replaced on the Board of WREI by nonpolitical (or no-longer-political) women with national reputations. Former Representatives Martha Griffiths and Shirley Pettis were named respectively President and Vice President, and Dorothy Height, President of the National Council of Negro Women, became Secretary. Washington activist Esther Coopersmith was made Treasurer, and members of the Board included Radcliff President Martina Horner, Sloan-Kettering biochemist Mathilde Krim, AFL-CIO official Jane O'Grady, actress Jean Stapleton, and Sharon Percy Rockefeller, the only woman in the United States whose husband was a Democratic Governor and whose father was a Republican Senator. Betty Dooley, who had been Executive Director of the CCC, was named Director of the Institute. Early in 1980, the Institute staff moved out of the Rayburn office it had been sharing with the Caucus staff and settled in a southeast Washington townhouse, blocks from the Capitol.

In spite of the fact that the Institute's Board was responsible to the Caucus, with the latter influencing the former's agenda, sufficient distance was established between the two to lay to rest trepidations harbored by philanthropic foundations about providing funds to "political" organizations. And the money began to come in. The Ford Foundation reacted favorably to a second proposal and gave the Institute a $150,000, two-year grant to hire a research coordinator. The coordinator was to keep abreast of studies conducted on women's issues, gather information about women's organizations all over the country, integrate these data, and disseminate them to the Caucus, other members of Congress, and the public. The Ford program was renewed for an additional two years in 1982 and increased to $250,000. A $25,000 grant was awarded by the Rockefeller Family Fund to permit the Institute, in cooperation with George Washington University's Women's Studies Program and Policy Center, to undertake a study of the economic problems of older women. This grant, too, was later renewed.

But the largest single sum, $300,000, came from the Charles H. Revson Foundation. The award financed internships for ten women interested in participating in the policy-making process and in generating information calculated to improve legislation. Funds were subsequently made available for four additional internships—two underwritten by R.J. Reynolds Industries, and one each by the Philip Morris Company and the Helena Rubenstein Foundation. These Capitol Hill positions were expected to help the Caucus and WREI determine how policies affect men and women differently, to give more women opportunities to participate in public-policy formulation, to translate research into policy, and to make more people aware that issues defined as "women's issues" are, in fact, of equal importance to women and men.

By the early 1980s, the Institute had increased its staff to a half-dozen, including the Executive Director, a liaison for special projects, and research coordinators. Their goals were to promote exchange of ideas between specialists with technical expertise and policymakers, and to examine policies in terms of their impact on women. They also sought to encourage outside researchers to consider the broader implications of their work and to serve as a link between lawmakers, on the one hand, and scores of women's research, policy, and advocacy centers, on the other. With the help of the foundation grants, WREI produced studies on patterns of employment and unemployment among females, the impact of social security reform on women, and the effects of presidential and congressional budget proposals on women. Financial support from foundations and philanthropic organizations has been barely enough to permit WREI to continue to serve Caucus members' needs. But, as will be made clear in the next chapter, WREI was in clover when compared with the fiscal viability of the Congresswomen's Caucus.

POLITICAL AND PERSONAL USES OF THE CAUCUS

Right from the start, women active in the Caucus enjoyed political and personal advantages traceable directly to group affiliation. Although some of these benefits could have been obtained in other ways, such avenues would have probably required a larger expenditure of members' resources.

First, Caucus participation permitted congresswomen to exchange specialized information economically. Second, it allowed each to articulate her priorities to a sympathetic audience of legislative peers and administrative officials. Third, affiliation allowed members efficiently to distribute the "women's issues" workload among themselves and among their staffs. Unlike their female predecessors—congresswomen who were usually viewed by public, press, and colleagues as experts on all matters affecting women—each Caucus member carved out a relatively narrow range of matters over which she could claim mastery. She shared this knowledge with other group members and felt comfortable referring more challenging queries on matters outside of her expertise to other female House members, without feeling guilty about letting other women down.

Fourth, members' legislative aides specializing in women's problems were integrated into the group's network and educated to the range of issues preoccupying the Caucus. Fifth, Caucus membership tended to improve the representative-image congresswomen cultivated within their districts. Finally, congresswomen gained a measure of personal satisfaction from meeting regularly with other women. The social support derived from this association was an important consequence of affiliation.

Information Generation, Retrieval and Exchange

Meetings among themselves and with Cabinet officials generated information about proposed legislation and administrative practices which Caucus members would not have otherwise so readily obtained. Sessions with the latter produced information which until then was either unknown or unavailable in a form useful to the Caucus. During the first of such meetings, for example, Commerce Secretary Juanita Kreps was asked what proportion of Small Business Administration loans had been secured by women entrepreneurs; whether it was feasible to collect data on alimony and child-support payments in the 1980 census; and how more businesswomen could become regular participants in Commerce Department seminars. Kreps' staff looked into each of these matters and addressed them in a subsequent report to the Caucus.

Perhaps the most ambitious effort to generate data grew out of the group's concern over gender discrimination in the social security system. Next to discrimination in federal hiring and promotion, social security practices received the Caucus's most unremitting attention. And, in May 1978, it asked HEW Secretary Joseph Califano to supply it with comprehensive, detailed information about how the language and implementation of social security laws affected women. Among the questions raised were how often women moved in and out of the labor force; the number of women who were "poor"; and the number not covered by Social Security Disability Insurance. Caucus members were also interested in the statistical techniques employed by the Social Security Administration to estimate the answers to these and other questions, and they asked Califano to compare the strengths and weaknesses of a series of proposed social-security measures then being considered by Congress.

Perhaps the most useful information disseminated was that which the members themselves communicated to one another. Meetings among themselves, in the absence of administration guests, were customarily devoted to the intricacies and expected consequences of bills then being considered by committees on which they served. The legislative stage bills had reached, and indications of congressional and administration support or opposition were also discussed. At a meeting in February 1978, for example, Spellman described her bill to establish life-support centers for pregnant teenagers; Mikulski reported that she had written President Carter asking him to describe the strategy he planned to follow to secure passage of the Equal Rights Amendment; and Oakar reminded Caucus members that her Committee on Banking, Currency, and Housing would soon be holding hearings on the extent to which the Federal Reserve Board was following affirmative action guidelines.

In sum, Caucus activities permitted undiluted concentration on matters affecting women. The information developed and exchanged provided members with knowledge they would not have otherwise obtained and promoted a familiarity with issues which their feminist constituencies expected them to have. Caucus meetings also helped participants estimate more accurately when, if at all, they would be asked to take public stance on a bill, and to learn the implications that a measure and its implementation would have for women. These insights permitted them to adopt more informed positions on matters to which they were expected to react publicly.

Articulation of Political and Personal Priorities

Caucus membership also provided participants with opportunities to express feminist-policy preferences in an audience that was both sympathetic and capable of doing something about them. Congresswomen acted as a sounding board for their colleagues and made constructive suggestions. Members used Caucus meetings to fashion a consensus for pet projects and, together with the Caucus staff, to alert one another to developments that dovetailed with individual interests.

But members' concerns were probably expressed to better purpose when offered in a meeting with a Cabinet member. Oakar, for example, was able to ask Commerce Secretary Kreps whether the Census Bureau was collecting enough information about elderly and single women; Holtzman queried Attorney General Griffin Bell about progress being made by the Justice Department's Task Force on Sex Discrimination; Heckler raised questions about the "sluggish" performance of the Equal Employment Opportunity Commission; Burke asked about guidelines being drawn up by the U.S. Commission on Civil Rights to give publishers cues on how to treat women and minorities in textbooks; and Boggs questioned Bell about the Justice Department's role in a case involving alleged sex discrimination against a House staff member.

Thus, the Caucus facilitated interaction between congresswomen and administrative decision-makers and provided the former with significant opportunities to influence both pending legislation and implementation of measures already enacted. Caucus sessions also permitted members to vent their frustrations before an audience whose members often held a common view but who, in any case, were polite enough to listen.

Division and Specialization of Labor

Members of most political and social groups that are overwhelmingly male often expect the few women in their midst to make informed, "representative" observations whenever a women's issue arises. Male House members are no exception, and for years prior to Caucus formation, virtually all congresswomen were called upon to provide definitive answers whenever questions requiring a "woman's point of view" materialized. Consequently, female Representatives were often expected to have more information at their disposal on a wider range of congressional concerns than their male counterparts, and, given the diverseness and complexity of national issues, they were unlikely to satisfy most expectations—including their own. Moreover, the usefulness of whatever response they gave was likely to be limited, even though those who requested the intelligence were usually prepared to act on it.

Formation of the Caucus made female Representatives more conversant with the intricacies of women's issues and facilitated among them a process that has been institutionalized in the House for decades—namely a division and specialization of labor. With each Caucus member specializing in two or three women's issues, perhaps because they were within the jurisdiction of standing committees upon which each served, and with at least one member developing expertise on every issue, women Representatives relied on one another far more than they did in the past. Questions on women's issues about which a member knew relatively little were passed on to a Caucus member (or her staff) who had already invested the resources sufficient to acquire the anticipated expertise. In the 95th Congress, for example, queries about part-time or flextime jobs in government could be referred to Schroeder; those on displaced homemakers to Burke; and those on domestic violence and protection of rape victims respectively to Mikulski, or Boggs, and Holtzman.

This division of labor among women members relieved them of the prior obligation of trying to know (or seeming to know) everything about all women's issues, and permitted them to make better use of resources that would otherwise be expended in an impossible task. Caucus membership made them better informed about a wider range of issues while, at the same time, relieving them of the responsibility of claiming a range of expertise beyond the grasp of any House member.

Educating a Surrogate Staff

Caucus members were not the only ones whose depth and breadth of knowledge was augmented. Soon after the group came into being, each members' office named an aide to act as liaison to the Caucus staff. These aides became an important link between each member and the Caucus's Executive

Director. Each was expected to be familiar with the entire range of issues with which the Caucus came to grips, as well as with the issues closest to the hearts of his or her employer. At times, liaisons of two or more members worked together to press for congressional action, as Mikulski and Boggs staff aides did in the 95th Congress on the issue of wife abuse and domestic violence. Office liaisons also attended Caucus meetings to represent a member who was unable to attend, to supplement a presentation made before the group, or simply to audit the session. Some aides were designated liaisons to an administrative agency, acting as an arm of the Caucus staff. In May 1978, for example, Sandra Casber, legislative assistant to Martha Keys, was chosen to represent the Caucus in a HEW group studying the treatment of women under the social security system.

Improving Their Representative Image

Affiliation with the Caucus permitted members to be (or appear to be) more responsive to a specialized constituency within their districts. To gain the trust of voters, Representatives must find ways of identifying with them, of showing that they have the same values, needs, and frustrations shared by constituents. For most legislators, service on a standing committee provides opportunities to demonstrate these qualities. Membership on the Veterans' Affairs Committee, for example, gives them a chance to personify ideas and symbols that resonate with meaning for people who serve or once served in the armed forces. Congresswomen wishing to demonstrate a generalized concern for women's needs found no standing committee to which to aspire, and the Caucus gave them an instrument for refining their constituency appeal.

Social and Emotional Support

Congress is a social, as well as a political, institution and virtually all of its members derive satisfaction from the emotional ties they establish among themselves. As has been noted, male Representatives often use the "gym fellowship" and collective ties to interest groups to fulfill social needs. Congresswomen, on the other hand, historically have had few opportunities to establish close personal ties with female colleagues, and the Caucus filled this void.

During its first two years, the Caucus provided a vehicle for conviviality, affection, and good feelings. Members were friendly and considerate of one another, even when they disagreed on substantive issues, and the atmosphere in the "Reading Room" was cordial and occasionally ebullient. For most, meetings were a respite from the heavy pressures under which they labored. One member described Caucus ambience in this way:

> The Reading Room is like a men's smoking room. We stop in and get together in there and we are concerned about reaching a consensus. . . . We share out thoughts with one another and support each other as much as we can. We have developed an affection for each other.

An aide describing the feelings of the congresswoman for whom she worked presented a similar picture:

> She spends a good deal of time on Caucus matters and she enjoys it a great deal. She finds it interesting and has great camaraderie with several of the other women. Some of them have running gags going on all the time. When they all met last week for a picture-taking session, with Muriel Humphrey, the atmosphere was almost electric. All those women together, filled with energy and vitality, generating all sorts of good feelings. They are all supportive of one another, with very little competition among them.

Some of the good feelings referred to had their roots in the early days of the Caucus, when congresswomen traveled to China together. The occasion was both a personal and collective success, and a forty-five-minute film of their sojourn won three television documentary awards and nearly captured an Emmy.

It appears that not all Caucus members were able or willing to derive personal satisfaction from their association with one another. But most extracted considerable pleasure from membership in the all-female group, and the social and personal support they gained from it were not the least important benefits derived from affiliation.

THE CAUCUS AND THE HOUSE

Informal groups in Congress have " . . . assumed a leading role in performing functions historically associated with the party and committee systems" (Stevens et al. 1981, p. 428). They help identify national problems, develop possible responses to these problems, and build coalitions large enough to deal with them. Accordingly, group projects and activities assist the committee and party systems in dealing with issues inherently difficult for them. When, for example, neither party nor committee leaders take the initiative on issues deemed important by rank-and-file members, or when these leaders fail to provide for comprehensive consideration of pressing problems, informal groups often fill the void. In the process, they temporarily usurp the traditional roles of these leaders. But, in the long run, they serve to support those structures which are " . . . primarily responsible for congressional policy output" by responding to pressures which would otherwise get little or no institutional response (Stevens et al. 1981, p. 435).

Thus, informal groups help to identify and deal with problems that fall between the cracks of standing committees and they oversee the administration of programs in which these panels have little interest. At the same time, they may help party leaders establish a legislative agenda, build winning coalitions, or devise legislative strategies. The Congresswomen's Caucus sought to do most of these things during its first two years, but its efforts to perform those tasks normally reserved to the committees were more consistent with its aims and more successful than its attempts to supplement the activities of party leaders.

The Caucus as "Committee"

Unlike committees, informal groups lack the authority to hold hearings, compel the testimony of witnesses, or rely on large appropriations for a skilled staff. Furthermore, they are unable either to act as custodians of bills considered for enactment or report measures for floor consideration. In some respects, however, they are the functional equivalents of standing committees, and the Congresswomen's Caucus carried out responsibilities normally undertaken by committees.

First, it identified and dramatized problems which other congressional instrumentalities tended to ignore. It supported efforts both to look into the plight of displaced homemakers and to respond legislatively to the startlingly pervasive tendency of husbands to beat their wives. It induced federal agencies to produce more information about such matters as the number of single and older women who were "heads of households," the proportion of guaranteed loans distributed to women by the Small Business Administration, and the percentage of women occupying responsible ranks within the federal bureaucracy. Moreover, it helped to amplify agency findings about the high frequency of unnecessary mastectomies, the abnormally high percentage of women addicted to Librium, Valium, and other drugs, and, by sponsoring a seminar on the subject, the problems produced by sexism in the armed forces.

Second, the Caucus established a record of actions taken by government and the private sector to deal with women's issues. Relying upon reports from federal agencies, studies by the Congressional Research Service, testimony of cabinet officials, the research of staff members, and the efforts of private organizations and its own Institute, the Caucus generated a body of information on part-time and flextime job opportunities in the bureaucracy, the treatment of women under the social security system, and the extent to which women were beneficiaries of Comprehensive Employment and Training Act funds.

Activities associated with this second function are not easily isolated from a third committee-like task performed by the Caucus—overseeing bureaucratic implementation of the law—since the former is normally a prerequisite for the latter. Among the matters examined by the Caucus during its first two years were the Commerce Department's implementation of Equal Employment Opportunity and Affirmative Action programs; the extent to which the Federal Reserve Board was encouraging financial institutions to abide by the spirit and letter of the Equal Credit Opportunity Act; and the application of bias-free admission standards by the service academies.

Fourth, Caucus activities helped to redefine and broaden the nature of women's issues, and they began to alter the frame of reference within which these issues were understood. Meetings of Caucus members among themselves and with representatives of women's groups, labor, and business organizations, and federal administrators permitted an exchange of ideas which stretched the awareness participants had of problems affecting women. These sessions institutionalized consciousness-raising, inasmuch as conferees were able to relate to, and build on, one another's experiences and insights. A meeting of labor union leaders, for example, revealed that women were affected more adversely than men by hard times in the retail industry because, as sales personnel and cashiers, the former made up a majority of industry employees. Moreover, many were close to retirement when dismissed and, after years of low wages, they were often left with no nest egg, no health insurance, and no retirement benefits. Unemployment, then, was as much of a women's issue as equal pay for equal work.

Practices which were inequalitarian on their face were simple enough to recognize as such. But patterns of behavior resulting in discrimination not immediately identifiable as gender-based sometimes had to be teased out of empirical observations that had been gathered with little thought to their implications for women. Sources of the discrimination were similarly obscure. As a result, legislative remedies that spoke to problems most citizens believed had nothing to do with gender had to be couched in terms they could understand, accept, and support. The Caucus was an important instrument for defining and generating responses to these public needs, and the years 1977 and 1978 saw a sharp increase in affirmative legislative proposals.

Finally, the Caucus established mutually beneficial links with an interest-group clientele. Feminist organizations gained readier access to Congress than they had before 1977, and congresswomen were better able to take advantage of the systematic support and reinforcement of groups such as NOW and the National Women's Political Caucus—in much the same way as Agriculture Committee members, for example, rely on leaders of the country's farm organizations. This rapport was important for extension of the time limit for approval of the Equal Rights Amendment and for placing the image of Susan B. Anthony (rather than, say, "Miss Liberty") on a newly minted silver dollar. The nexus between Caucus and women's groups provided a clearer voice for a female public that rejected some traditional views of women and thereby made Congress a more representative institution than it would have been in the absence of a Congresswomen's Caucus.

The Caucus as Supplement to Party Structure

Caucus activities of the kind normally undertaken by party leaders was much less in evidence than was its committee-like behavior. Apart from the President and congressional leaders, few individuals and groups can legitimately claim principal credit for affecting the legislative agenda, for promoting integrated consideration of policy proposals, for creating winning coalitions, or for devising successful legislative strategies. The Congresswomen's Caucus was not among the exceptions to this generalization. Compared with the more numerous Democratic Study Group or the less formal Chowder and Marching Society, it had little success in seizing the prerogatives of legislative leaders. More than that, it was simply unable to generate the opportunities for doing so. Its initial decision to act as a catalyst, rather than as a ramrod, in the policy-making process imposed realistic limitations on what it could do and still remain a viable organization.

From time to time the Caucus had an impact on policy. Surely the attention it gave to the bill prohibiting employer discrimination against pregnant women contributed to the measure's passage. And the spotlight it threw on gender disparities in federal employment and social security arrangements helped the discriminatory character of these practices penetrate the consciousness of many who had no direct stake in the alteration of either policy.

But, the Caucus had only limited success in shaping the legislative agenda and in persuading their colleagues that important women's issues were not only linked to one another but also intimately interwoven among the programmatic threads of policies which, on their face, seemed to be unrelated to the special needs of women. During the early years of the Carter administration, Caucus members tried to establish the position that welfare policy was connected to the availability of child-care services, job-training programs for women, rural development, part-time and summer jobs, counseling for pregnant teenagers and the ground rules governing distribution of food stamps. This approach had little lasting effect. An attempt to treat social security and private pension rights of women within the framework of rapidly changing trends in spousal relationships met an even less auspicious fate.

During its formative years, the Caucus made few attempts to build coalitions, or to plan legislative strategies, and when it did, its efforts were superficial. Holtzman tried to bring together the Department of Labor, the Office of Management and the Budget, and the Civil Service Commission for consciousness-raising sessions with Caucus members to explore ways of providing more federal service opportunities for women. And the Caucus had little difficulty establishing close ties with women's groups and leaders of the AFL-CIO. But internal coalitions that congressional groups are sometimes able to forge with party leaders and one another were not readily evident. Individual Caucus members were able to urge a Caucus position on other groups with which they were affiliated, as, for example, Chisholm and Schroeder were able to do respectively in the Black Caucus and the Democratic Study Group. But the Congresswomen's Caucus as a group did not build even intermittent coalitions with other congressional or administration organizations.

Caucus attempts to fashion and implement legislative strategies were similarly infrequent and superficial. From time to time the group asked a House or Senate colleague to expedite hearings on a women's issue, as it did in the case of displaced homemakers bills. And amendments to bills under consideration sometimes received the benefit of Caucus discussion and endorsement, as in the case of Holtzman's measure to protect the privacy of rape victims. But, for the most part, the Caucus did not formulate steps to shepherd desirable bills through the legislative process. To the extent that such strategies were pursued, they were likely to be based on the initiatives of individual Caucus members acting with the implicit support of their female colleagues, the sympathies of ideological soulmates on the committees upon which they served, and the tacit acceptance of party leaders.

During the 95th Congress, there was one important exception to this generally unimpressive leadership pattern. The Caucus's effort to extend the life of the Equal Rights Amendment was a tour de force, and Holtzman, Heckler, and other Caucus members scored a victory many thought unlikely when they first undertook the battle.

BUYING TIME FOR THE ERA

When Congress approved a constitutional amendment granting "equal rights" to women in March 1972, there seemed little doubt that three-quarters of the state legislatures would approve it within the stipulated seven-year limit.[6] The votes in the House and Senate were overwhelming, 354 to 24 and 84 to 8 respectively, and most believed that the public sentiment expressed in these huge margins would be reflected in the states, as well. Before 1972 ended, 22 of them had given the amendment their endorsement, and, in 1973, eight others followed suit. With only eight more needed to reach the number required for adoption, however, remaining states, mostly from the south and west, seemed less enthusiastic. Three legislatures approved the measures in 1974, and one each acted favorably in 1975 and 1977, but, in the meantime, four which had supported the amendment (Idaho, Nebraska, Tennessee, and Kentucky) rescinded their earlier affirmation.

With just two years left, then, only three more states were needed for the proposed amendment to become part of the Constitution—assuming that the action taken by rescinding states was discounted by Congress. Yet, in spite of intensive efforts by women's groups, and irrespective of ERA support by a new Democratic administration, the approval of three additional states before March 1979, was considered unlikely. Much opposition to the amendment had crystallized since its first blush of success. The Eagle Forum, an organization created and administered by Phyllis Schlafly, was the most visibly active force working against the Amendment, but it was assisted by many conservative groups throughout the country, groups able to exercise influence with legislators in less urban, less industrialized states who represented constituencies which held a more traditional view of women's place in society. As a result, ERA proponents decided to seek an extension of the seven-year limit to permit additional pressures to be brought to bear in the remaining fifteen hold-outs. And, in October 1977, Elizabeth Holtzman introduced a Joint Resolution adding seven years to the period during which states could endorse the measure. A companion Resolution was introduced in the Senate by Indiana Democrat Birch Bayh.

Obstacles to the Resolution were formidable. In the first place, there was no precedent for extension of a proposed amendment's time limit. Ever since 1917, when Congress began to impose such limits, none had been seriously challenged. Even some lawmakers who supported the ERA regarded the extension as a precedent they would prefer not to set. Second, many conservatives in Congress believed that approval of the Holtzman Resolution should require a two-thirds vote in both House and Senate, the same extraordinary majority needed for all constitutional amendments and, of course, for the ERA passage in 1972. Third, some House and Senate members concluded that if Congress gave the states which *had not* voted for the amendment more time during which to do so, it ought to give states which *had* adopted the measure the option of rejecting it upon reconsideration. Permission to rescind an endorsement would implicitly recognize the decisions reached by the four states nullifying earlier approval, although many argued that Congress should heed only those rescissions passed during the extended time period.

The potentially killing effect of any one of these objections, left the most ardent ERA proponents pessimistic about its chances. Even Holtzman was uncertain about her Resolution's fate, and, while the Speaker and House Majority Leader pledged their cooperation, they told Caucus members that they were not hopeful. For a time, it appeared as if the measure would be rejected by the House Judiciary Committee, and even more doubtful Senate leaders considered the possibility of by-passing their own Judiciary Committee because that panel was unlikely to produce an ERA majority.[7]

In fact, the House Judiciary Committee reduced the proposed extension from seven to little more than three years, giving additional states until June 30, 1982, to approve the amendment. Otherwise it reported out a measure which met its supporters terms. The Committee rejected the demand that legislatures which had approved the proposed amendment be given the opportunity to rescind it during the extension period, and it asked the Rules Committee to adopt a rule permitting passage by a simple majority. The Rules Committee compiled; efforts to change the rule and the Resolution on the House floor failed; and the House passed the extension, 230–189. Days before the 95th Congress adjourned, ERA supporters scored a 60–36 Senate victory. Moreover, the Senate Resolution was identical to the House-passed measure, thereby obviating the need for a conference which, late as it was in the session, could have prevented passage of an identical Resolution in both chambers before adjournment.

The shifting sentiment in Congress was as much a product of Caucus Leaders' efforts as it was of any other factor. Once the House Judiciary Committee called for hearings, Caucus members launched an intensive drive to build support for extension. They regularly called in women's groups leaders and pleaded with them to become involved. According to one source, they "nagged and cajoled and literally begged some who didn't think the drive would succeed."

Some militant women's organizations did not need much prodding, and they participated in massive demonstrations on Capitol Hill. But it was Caucus members primarily who mobilized and gave direction to the torrent of energy and emotion generated by the issue. Holtzman, Heckler, Schroeder, Mikulski, and Spellman, particularly, met with women's groups in their own offices, in the Caucus office, and elsewhere in Washington, although Holtzman's Longworth Building suite was probably the principal hub of activity. They coordinated the efforts of the groups, explored legislative strategies, and suggested lobbying tactics. Before the battle was over, they were meeting with women's groups three and four times a week. Leaders from such feminist organizations as NOW and NWPC appeared regularly on Capitol Hill, but so, too, did leaders of associations less identified with feminist causes, including the Girl Scouts of America and the YWCA.

The Caucus had not met and determined that it would consciously devote its attention to passing the Resolution. No such formal decision had to be made. The ERA was one of a handful of measures on which all Caucus members shared enthusiastic, even passionate, agreement. Some were prolife, others prochoice on the abortion issue. And they might disagree on how much federal money to spend to aid wives who are victims of spousal abuse. But the ERA was the litmus test of whether you were for women or against them, and only four congresswomen expressed reservations about unrestricted extension of the time limit, three of whom were not Caucus members. Only one of the four, Marilyn Lloyd, did not vote for final passage. She was "paired against" the Resolution.[8]

Caucus leaders pursued standard practices in building a winning coalition. They counted the number of "sure" votes, designated which House and Senate members were either undecided or capable of being persuaded to alter negative predispositions, and turned on the charm and the heat. They lobbied face to face when personal rapport with members permitted, and they pressured colleagues indirectly by encouraging delegations of women's groups to visit m mbres' offices. They also asked other Washington lobbyists to urge interest-group members whom they represented to request their own lawmakers to support the Holtzman-Bayh Resolution. Holtzman capitalized on her access to labor leaders, Heckler on her acquaintances in the business community, and Spellman on her contacts among state and local government officials. Before long, the Resolution's prospects brightened. Legislators from states with powerful labor unions announced in favor of the measure, and even some from states that had not approved the ERA came around.

The White House played a role, as did House and Senate leaders and representatives of women's groups. But the successful coalition was largely the product of a campaign orchestrated by Caucus activists. It was a consequence of shrewd legislative manuevering. Congressmen concerned about anti-ERA sentiments in their states and districts would have to vote against the measure to satisfy constituency opinion—no matter what their personal feelings about the women's movement. But they did not necessarily have to vote against the rule permitting passage by a simple majority, or in favor of a floor amendment allowing states on record supporting the ERA to rescind action already taken.

Accordingly, Holtzman and other Caucus leaders pointed out the opportunity these lawmakers had to retain constituency support while, at the same time, helping female Representatives fashion the most important women's legislation they would face in the 95th Congress. "Vote against final passage if you must," they told male members, "but support us with votes to bar rescissions by state legislatures and vote down the motion to require a two-thirds majority." Among the 189 congressmen voting against final passage, fifty supported the pro-ERA positions on at least one of the three roll call votes that preceded it. The closest tally was on a motion by Illinois Republican Tom Railsback to allow states to rescind their earlier approval of the ERA. Thirty-four of those voting against final passage also chose to reject the Railsback proposal. More than half of that number, eighteen, were southern and border Democrats. A switch of sixteen votes would have changed the result.[9]

Adoption of ERA extension was the legislative high point of the 95th Congress for most Caucus members. First, they had forced the White House, as well as Congress, to deal with an issue which many believed was, if not dead, then not high on most leaders' lists of public priorities. Second, they had turned a problematic outcome into a signal victory, and they had done it on an issue which more than any other reflected their raison d'etre. Third, it was a legislative success for which they could take much of the credit. As women, they represented, more than any other lawmakers, the intensive, pervasive pro-ERA sentiment throughout the country. Fourth, against formidable odds, they had built a congressional coalition sufficient to extend the time limit, and they had devised a legislative strategy to permit that coalition to work its will. In this one instance, then, the group carried out an array of tasks normally performed by House leaders.

The victory was short-lived, however. The additional time bought by the Resolution saw not a single state added to the thirty-five that had already approved the ERA. In the meantime, Caucus leaders who saw their success as a portent of better things to come were sorely disappointed. Events turned their exhilaration into frustration and despair, and it is with the circumstances that produced this state of mind that we deal in the next chapter.

NOTES

1. Information in this chapter and the next about the formation, development, and activities of the Caucus was gathered from interviews with congresswomen and staff members, and from the Caucus minutes, memoranda, letters, press releases, and newsletters they provided.

2. The Caucus altered this routine to suit the convenience of Cabinet members and others invited to speak to the group. During the second session of the 95th Congress, it settled on the first and third Wednesday of each month at 3:30 P.M. after first experimenting with Tuesdays at 11:30 A.M. Obviously the Caucus was casting about for a time which would be least inconvenient for its members and, given the fact that the House had chosen Wednesday as the day it would normally convene early and continue into the evening if necessary, that was the day on which Representatives were most likely to be on Capitol Hill, close to the House floor.

3. Prior to 1962, female members searching for a room of their own had little choice but to use H311, the "Ladies Retiring Room" located on the relatively inconvenient gallery floor of the Capitol and accessible to the wives and families of all members of Congress.

4. Congresswomen declining Caucus membership at the time were Marjorie Holt, Virginia Smith, and Marilyn Lloyd.

5. The uncertain status of the Caucus was revealed, in part, by the fact that its office door had no permanent number on it (a piece of cardboard taped to it with the number "2471" seemed to suffice), and no placard outside the door telling visitors what agency was inside. Memoranda distributed to announce meetings in the room often stated: "Room 2471 Rayburn Building is directly across the hall from 2400. PLEASE NOTE THIS LOCATION as room is hard to find."

6. The text of the proposed amendment read as follows: "Equality of rights under the law shall not be denied or abridged by the United States or by any state on account of sex. The Congress shall have the power to enforce, by appropriate legislation, the provisions of this article. This Amendment shall take effect two years after the date of ratification."

7. Accounts of the legislative history of the extension Resolution appear in the following *Congressional Quarterly Weekly Reports*, vol. 36: May 27, 1978, p. 1347; July 15, 1978, p. 1833; August 19, 1978, pp. 2214, 2226, 2227; October 7, 1978, p. 2724; and October 14, 1978, p. 2983. Information about the role played by the Caucus in extending the ERA time limit was developed through interviews with several Caucus members and with staff aides of both male and female House members in 1978 and 1979, and through observation of two meetings of representatives of women's groups in 1978, during their most intensive lobbying efforts.

8. The one Caucus member to vote in favor of the rescission motion was Republican Shirley Pettis of California. Pettis voted for final passage, however. Non-Caucus members Marjorie Holt and Virginia Smith voted as Pettis did.

9. The Railsback motion was rejected 196–227. Among the sixteen other Representatives voting against both his motion and final passage, eight were Republicans and eight were northern Democrats.

11 / The Congresswomen's Caucus: Decline and Transformation

Congress adjourned a week after the ERA extension passed, and members hurried home to conduct reelection campaigns. Caucus leaders were reasonably pleased with the progress made during the first two years and were hoping to improve on it in the 96th Congress. Before leaving Washington, they gave their blessings to a joint meeting of their staff liaisons and representatives of national women's organizations, the purpose of which was to determine legislative and administrative priorities for the coming year.

Conferees met on November 1, 1978, a few days before the mid-term election, and one by one they read off the issue areas they believed deserved congressional attention. Among the women's groups represented were NOW, AAUW, NWPC, BPWC, and the Women's Lobby. Also present was an assistant to Sarah Weddington, President Carter's Special Advisor on Women's Issues. The White House aide began the meeting with a long list of administrative objectives. It included a National Health Insurance program, social security reform, stricter enforcement of Title IX, legislation aiding victims of domestic violence, measures to help displaced homemakers, a recodification of rape laws, an improved child-care program, revision of veterans' preference regulations, bills promoting reproductive freedom, and new funding for the Women's Educational Equity Act.

Additional proposals were offered by others present, and when they had finished, a sizeable accumulation of goals were ready for Caucus consideration, objectives which the group's leaders would sort out when they came back to Washington to begin the next Congress. But when they returned, prospects for successfully pressing women's issues had changed significantly for the worse, and the next three years saw limited Caucus activity. Reasons for the inertia had to do with membership changes, an unfortunate strategic decision by Caucus leaders at the start of the 96th Congress, insufficient financial resources, political and personality clashes among members, and the election in 1980 of Ronald Reagan.

THE 96TH CONGRESS: DECLINE OF THE CAUCUS

Retirements, a bid for another public office, and 1978 election defeats meant that six women who had been members of the Caucus in the 95th Congress would not be back for the 96th. One of the six had lent prestige to the group simply by having her name on the letterhead, but a lack of interest in most women's issues had minimized her contributions to the Caucus. This was Barbara Jordan. The other five who did not return would be missed, some significantly so. Muriel Humphrey had given the Caucus a presence in the Senate and she had been a loyal and faithful member. Most thought she would not seek election to the remainder of her husband's Senate term after she was appointed to replace him, and the conventional wisdom was borne out. Soon after taking the Senate seat she announced that she had no desire to remain in Congress and she vacated her position at the first opportunity.

Retiring Republican Shirley Pettis took her cues from party leaders as a rule, but her membership on the Caucus Executive Committee improved the group's bipartisan image, a useful contribution in an organization so top-heavy with moderate and liberal Democrats. Helen Meyner had also been a faithful Caucus supporter, and her unsuccessful reelection campaign deprived the Caucus of an eminently sensible, intelligent, even-tempered foreign policy specialist with a keen insight into discriminatory practices affecting women. Yvonne Burke's decision to run for California Attorney General meant that the Caucus would have to find a new Treasurer, and that it would lose a politically experienced, articulate lawyer. The departure of both Burke and Pettis stripped the group of female Representatives from the country's most populous state and the House's largest delegation.

In some ways, the defeat of Martha Keys was the most damaging to the Caucus. Keys, only the second Democratic woman ever to serve on the Ways and Means Committee, had become the Caucus specialist on social security matters. Much of what the Caucus had done in these areas was done through her and informed by her expertise and that of her staff. Moreover, she was the only Caucus Democrat from the country's agricultural midsection and her perspective as a moderate Democrat from a moderate to conservative area would be missed. Her loss was also difficult to accept because many attributed it to her marriage to another House member. Some of her Kansas constituents believed that she was abandoning them in favor of her new husband's district residents in Indiana and that the quality of her representation would suffer. True, she had won reelection two years earlier, after Kansans were already aware that this mother of four had divorced her husband upon coming to Washington and had remarried soon after arriving there. But 1976 was not a strong Republican year, and the residual ill-feeling about her domestic life, when coupled with the GOP tide in 1978, was probably a powerful enough issue to make the difference.

These losses were offset in part by the election of three new congresswomen who were willing to join the Caucus. Democrat Geraldine Ferraro and Republican Olympia Snowe lost little time in affiliating with the group, and they were soon making valuable contributions to it. For Beverly Byron, the third new female Representative in the 96th Congress, joining the Caucus was not as high a priority and, as we shall see, she left when the annual fee for members was increased and standardized.

Another important addition to the Caucus in 1979 was the lone woman Senator, newly elected Nancy Kassebaum. The Kansas Republican was not known for dramatizing women's causes and she had opposed extension of the time period for approving the Equal Rights Amendment. But she favored the ERA itself and generally sought to establish moderate positions on most issues. Kassebaum was appointed to the CC Executive Committee and became a major asset to the group, especially after her party gained control of the Senate in 1981. She developed excellent rapport with the Senate leadership, became a knowledgeable member of the Budget, Foreign Relations, and Commerce Committees, and held down two subcommittee chairs.

Thus, the loss of loyal and constructive members was partly offset by the arrival of a few reinforcements. But the gains were diminished by a serious miscalculation on the part of Holtzman and Heckler. It occurred when they decided to persuade the three women who had declined Caucus membership in the 95th Congress—Marjorie Holt, Virginia Smith and Marilyn Lloyd—to join the organization in the 96th. From the time the Caucus had been established in 1977, the cochairs had been embarrassed by questions from the press about why some congresswomen were not members. They drew the obvious conclusion that affiliation by all congresswomen would end the need to make defensive replies to these queries. It would also present the House, the public, and foundations from which they planned to solicit research grants with a united front, and end any lingering doubts about the organization's viability. And so, they set out in January 1979, to bring the remaining congresswomen into the fold.

Acting in tandem, they approached Holt, Smith and Lloyd on the floor of the House and asked them to join. The three conservative congresswomen were told about the unanimity rule—that nothing with which they disagreed would be endorsed by the Caucus—and that they would be under no obligation to attend even a minimum number of meetings. They were further advised that they would not be pressed for financial contributions (after all, even women who were already members had managed to ignore this requirement), and that their names would be on the letterhead. In the meantime, they could identify with the Caucus to a greater or lesser degree, as their political needs dictated.

The cochairs were quick to note that identification with the group had many positive features. They pointed out that the Speaker of the House, Tip O'Neill, had been impressed with the CC's contributions, that many of their male colleagues were equally impressed, and that Nancy Kassebaum had joined the Caucus at her first opportunity. Holtzman and Heckler added that in its first two years the Caucus had done nothing radical, and nothing which appeared to have damaged a member's standing with her constituents. Apparently the three women found the arguments persuasive, inasmuch as they accepted the offer. But it was an offer hard to resist. They were asked to join an organization whose meetings they did not have to attend, whose financial needs they could ignore, and over whose decisions each exercised an absolute veto. And should the Caucus score a notable achievement, they could join in claiming credit for it.

Caucus activists, on the other hand, soon found the benefits of 100 percent female membership more than offset by the difficulties of trying to lead a strikingly heterogeneous group of congresswomen. The three new members rarely attended meetings, even when administration representatives were scheduled to speak. They introduced few ideas for the Caucus leaders and staff to develop, and they were not notably active in trying to persuade colleagues, individually or in testimony before committees, to support Caucus positions. Unsurprisingly, they allocated no clerk-hire funds to pay Caucus expenses. But they did exercise the right to veto proposals, refusing to sign letters and statements that had been drafted for membership endorsement. They were especially disinclined to support measures that involved an expenditure of funds. True, Caucus leaders could now claim that all women were members, but their chances of securing consensus on most women's issues and of generating an innovative legislative program were sharply reduced.

As the 96th Congress progressed, meetings were held much less frequently than they had been in the 95th, and a legislative agenda simply never emerged. The ambitious proposals offered by the White House aide and others attending the November, 1978 meeting were supported intermittently thereafter, with little concrete effort made systematically to mobilize Caucus support behind them. Leaders' efforts to prod House colleagues to cosponsor legislation aiding women, to hold hearings on these matters, or to testify at hearings declined significantly. Staff members drafted letters and arranged for meetings, but did little else, and there was often no coordinated follow-up on reactions generated by either. Caucus meetings became dull affairs and a few participants seemed simply to go through the motions.

In keeping with past practices, the Caucus invited Cabinet and sub-Cabinet officials to talk to them about subjects falling within the jurisdiction of the agencies they headed. These appearances slowed to a trickle compared with the number in the 95th Congress. Health and Human Services Secretary Patricia Harris had a useful meeting with the Caucus early in the first session. And Social Security Commissioner Stanford Ross came to Capitol Hill a few months later to explore further some of the issues raised with Harris and to describe the status of social security reform. In October, Chairman of the Joint Chiefs of Staff General David Jones agreed to meet with the CC, after months of being unavailable, and, in 1980, Chairman of the Federal Reserve Board Paul Volcker, and William Driver, the new Social Security administrator, spoke to the Caucus.

General Jones discussed the uses to which women were being put in the armed forces and the desirability of lifting prohibitions on the responsibilities they could be asked to carry out. He did not necessarily favor placing them in combat roles, but he believed that each service should decide for itself how servicewomen should be utilized. Under Secretary of the Air Force Antonia Chayes accompanied Jones, and it was during this meeting that the groundwork was laid for banning topless dancers from officer's clubs on military installations. Volcker was advised about discrimination against women in a tight credit market (inasmuch as they were not as likely to be established customers for business loans and mortgages, and financial institutions were more apt to terminate or reduce their credit opportunities). And Driver tried to explain an earlier statement he had made that there was no discrimination against women in the social security system, an assertion about which he developed second thoughts when he met with the Caucus.

These sessions provided CC members with opportunities directly to affect administrative practices, but they were few and far between. One reason for their decline was the inertia gripping the Caucus. It was able to dramatize few policy priorities, social security and the plight of aging women being notable exceptions, and Caucus leaders felt no overwhelming pressures to invite other speakers. A second reason was that the Caucus's reputation had diminished. The difficulty leaders had in persuading General Jones to meet with the group reflected this loss of influence. When the General was asked to discuss discrimination against women in the armed forces, an aide phoned to say that the General did not feel qualified to talk about the subject because he did not favor discrimination against servicewomen. When the Caucus persevered and established a specific meeting date, a colonel called the Executive Director to say that "the General is unable to come to your party." After Betty Dooley repeated the reply to Marjorie Holt, ranking Republican on the Military Personnel subcommittee, Holt called Jones directly and the General changed his plans.

Caucus leaders were aware that they had lost momentum and some expressed their frustration openly. Mikulski and Schroeder complained bitterly to other members and to the CC staff. But still the Caucus seemed rudderless. The group cosponsored a series of seminars with George Washington University's graduate program in Women's Studies and it highlighted the close relationship between the University program and the Women's Research and Education Institute. Hearings on women in business were undertaken by the Small Business Committee at the prompting of the Caucus. And it threw its support behind selected legislative proposals, among them Cardiss Collins' effort to continue to celebrate a Working Mother's Day, established initially in 1978.

Caucus leaders took satisfaction, as well, in helping to enact legislation providing the ex-wives of Foreign Service officers with a pro-rata share of their husbands' pensions in divorce settlements. This Caucus-backed effort was particularly significant in that the law became a model for subsequent pension reforms, including benefits for ex-military wives and proposals aimed at ex-wives of civil servants. Other initiatives prompted by the Caucus were a law requiring the sums awarded to female-owned businesses on federal contracts exceeding $10,000 be reported, and a measure providing financial aid to nontraditional and half-time students. But these successes fell far short of the goals staff liaisons had defined before the 96th Congress convened.

Another factor leading to the decline of the Caucus was related to differences in the personal and political styles of its members. Partisan, ideological, and regional differences explain a good deal of what happens in Washington, but important developments often turn on differences in personalities. Thus, Caucus inertia during the 96th Congress was partly the result of Margaret Heckler's hesitant leadership and the annoyance it provoked among the group's activists. Having cochairs promoted a bipartisan spirit, but it inhibited expeditious, decisive action. The unanimity rule was a drag on CC initiatives, but even before a statement was circulated for members' reactions, the two chairs had to approve it. And Heckler was notoriously slow about making decisions.

Her hesitancy on Caucus matters was a reflection of the same uncertainty she exhibited on the House floor. During roll calls, for example, she was often among the last to cast a vote, waiting to see what other members of the mostly Democratic Massachusetts delegation would do, and concerned about the consequences of breaking ranks too frequently with Republican colleagues. She seemed to change her vote more than most House members and appeared always to be struggling to beat the fifteen minute time limit during which decisions had to be made. One observer said that he could not blame her. She was a moderate Republican from a liberal state and represented a district which leaned Democratic. She had no choice but to exercise caution when casting votes on issues salient to her constituents. But this caution carried over into Caucus activities and the only time limit she had to heed was the one dictated by her internal clock.

As a result, she delayed for days signing even the most innocuous letters, producing cries of outrage from staff members and, especially, from Patricia Schroeder when the Colorado Democrat replaced Elizabeth Holtzman as cochair. On one occasion it took her six weeks to sign a luncheon invitation to labor leader Douglas Fraser, so long, in fact, that the date of the luncheon had to be changed.

It was during the 96th Congress, as well, that an open break developed between Caucus leaders and one of their peripheral members. Relations between them had not been good during the 95th Congress, but the differences seemed unimportant because of the constructive Caucus activities in which members were engaged. Few achievements emerged during the 96th Congress, however, and the congresswomen began to magnify irritants they had ignored in the past. The woman who was seen as out of step was Millicent Fenwick, and her adversaries included almost all of the Caucus members who were carryovers from the 95th Congress.

For many people inside and outside of the House, Millicent Fenwick was the model Representative. Tall, slender, and with aristocratic bearing, her statements both on and off the floor defined the moral and ethical dimensions of important issues. She established a reputation for being scrupulously honest and for shunning the behind-the-scenes deals and trade-offs that precede many congressional decisions. She believed in social justice with all her heart, but was terrified about the possible excesses of a too-powerful government and she frequently resolved conflicts between admirable social goals and limited government in favor of the latter.

If her imposing stature, penetrating wit, noble causes, and pleas to do "the right thing" annoyed her less-patrician colleagues, that, she concluded was their problem. She was much admired by others, not because she was an effective legislator—she neither excelled nor wished to excel at the skills useful for creating legislative majorities—but because she sometimes served as the conscience of the House.

But the New Jersey Republican often played politics by appearing not to play politics. She chided other members for accepting campaign contributions from Political Action Committees, and vigorously opposed the salary increases they voted themselves (one critic noting that he would have voted against the increase if, like Fenwick, he, too, had inherited $5 million). These actions endeared her to voters who believed that many politicians were venal and to those who held that the honor and opportunity of serving the people are rewards enough for the conscientious legislator. While campaigning, she was refreshingly candid and unequivocal. When seeking a Senate seat, for example, she supported busing for racial integration before an audience of conservative Republican suburbanites; called for reduced government pensions at a meeting with postal workers; and opposed the death penalty, school prayer, and tuition tax credits, staples of the conservative Republican's diet, in an address to a small town Republican club (Geist 1982). Perhaps this behavior cost her the election, but she had never lost one before and, given the strength of her convictions, she would have had it no other way.

From the time she joined the Caucus, the New Jersey congresswoman had been uncomfortable with her affiliation. In fact, Fenwick believed that all caucuses do more to divide lawmakers than they do to unite them for the common good. Social and economic problems have to be worked out for the society as a whole, she contended, and caucuses institutionalize special, rather than national, interests. It should come as no surprise that this attitude affected her relations with other Caucus members. They were intent on defining, dramatizing, and dealing with women's needs. She was preoccupied with national problems which she believed were not divisible by gender. Thus, her colleagues sometimes saw her as subverting Caucus goals. She raised subjects that were not on the official agenda, and had to be reminded regularly to stick to the topic. She asked visiting officials questions that had little to do with the reasons they had been invited, she patronized other members, and she was loath to support most proposals that had to do with spending more money, regardless of how favorable an impact they might have on women. On one occasion, she astounded some congresswomen by expressing outrage because the Caucus had taken a position supporting female beauty shop employees in the House who were asking for the same fringe benefits already available to men who worked in congressional barber shops.

One of the first to take offense to Fenwick's behavior was Shirley Chisholm. The circumstances under which the break between the two occurred have been reconstructed from the acounts of three witnesses. One day at a Caucus meeting Fenwick expressed her dislike for caucuses and the divisiveness they produced. Chisholm remarked that they were useful for groups that had not yet been integrated into the society. For blacks, especially, said Chisholm, caucuses mobilized resources that otherwise might never be brought to bear on their behalf. When we have a completely fair society, the Brooklyn Democrat continued, we won't need caucuses. When asked by Fenwick what achievements the Congressional Black Caucus could claim, Chisholm mentioned legislation requiring the Small Business Administration to set aside loans for firms owned by members of minority groups. Fenwick dismissed the example as insignficant, told Chisholm that she, personally, did not discriminate against people because of their color and that she had been active in the civil rights movement since Brown v. Oklahoma [sic], longer, in fact, than Chisholm had. The assertions may well have been true, but Chisholm was incensed by Fenwick's patronizing manner and made it a point thereafter to avoid meetings at which she believed Fenwick would be present.

Fenwick's attack on Helen Meyner had further alienated her from other Caucus members. When congresswomen traveled to China together, most invited a spouse or some other companion. Elizabeth Holtzman, for example, was accompanied by her mother. Meyner brought her husband, former New Jersey Governor Robert Meyner, and Fenwick paid the way of her physician, inasmuch as a pacemaker had recently been implanted in her chest and its efficacy had not been fully tested. While traveling in China, the Meyners had been particularly solicitous of their New Jersey neighbor, remaining behind with her when she did not keep up with the rest of the group and generally being helpful to a tour member who was less agile than other travelers. But when they returned to the United States, Fenwick publicly denounced Meyner for taking her husband to China at the taxpayer's expense. Whatever the merits of the claim; Fenwick's behavior was viewed as unnecessarily mean-spirited and she further lost the respect of Caucus members.

The strained relations continued to surface from time to time, but Fenwick did not mention them when she finally resigned from the organization. Instead, she chose to emphasize the source of the group's financial support to explain her decision. Even before the Congresswomen's Caucus Corporation had been reorganized and replaced by the Women's Research and Education Institute, Fenwick questioned the propriety of a group of House members soliciting funds from special interest groups for the purpose of furthering the policy goals of congresswomen who, in turn, ultimately help decide the future of these same groups. The objection was a reasonable one and, in fact, had been raised by the Ford Foundation when considering a grant proposal from the CCC. The same demurrer would lead in 1981 to significant changes in House rules governing legislative service organizations. But even when WREI replaced the CCC and set up separate quarters with a separate staff and a Board of Directors containing no congresswomen, the fact that it sought tax deductible contributions from groups affected by legislation on which congresswomen who were served by WREI had voted was unacceptable. Said Fenwick, "I don't think it's appropriate for members of Congress to form a group and get deductability for contributions made to that group" (*New York Times* July 16, 1981).

But Fenwick's departure was only the first of several that occurred during this period. Other women left the Caucus in the 97th Congress, defections which its leaders encouraged, and which were followed by a transformation of the Congresswomen's Caucus.

STALEMATE AND PURGE

When the 97th Congress convened in 1981, Caucus leaders were as intent as ever on increasing their membership. One reason for their concern was the loss of two former Caucus officials, Elizabeth Holtzman and Gladys Spellman. Holtzman had given up her House seat to run, unsuccessfully, for the Senate, and the CC was forced to carry on without one of its founders and moving spirits. A more devastating blow, perhaps because it was tragic and so unexpected, occurred when Spellman, on her way to easy reelection, suffered a heart attack and became comatose. She won the contest in spite of her condition, but the House declared her seat vacant after physicians concluded that there was no hope of recovery.

Spellman's loss was hard to overestimate. She had served as Caucus Secretary in the preceding Congress, and her excellent rapport with colleagues was matched by valuable contacts with public officials all over the country. While serving as Prince George's County Commissioner, the Maryland Democrat was appointed to the Advisory Commission on Intergovernmental Relations by

President Johnson. She was unusually active in national organizations of local and state officials and was later elected President of the National Association of Counties, the first woman to hold the position. When she came to the House, she already knew a good many of her new colleagues, inasmuch as they had been state and local officials before serving in Washington and had participated with Spellman in national organizations and conferences. She was chosen vice chairman of the 94th Democratic Class when that swollen group of "Watergate babies" met to organize themselves,[1] and she was active in planning the ouster of three Democratic committee chairmen who had seemed unresponsive to the policy preferences of rank and file party members. Thus Spellman's illness and Holtzman's defeat deprived the Caucus of two of its ablest women.

The 1980 elections sent four new Republican women to the House, Bobbi Fiedler, Lynn Martin, Marge Roukema, and Claudine Schneider, and one, Paula Hawkins, to the Senate. Heckler and Schroeder lost no time in calling a Caucus meeting to brief the newcomers, but only Fiedler, Martin, and Schneider attended. The cochairs were joined by Lindy Boggs, and the three veterans highlighted the virtues of Caucus membership. Heckler presented a short history of the organization, and stressed the benefits of affiliation—the forums, briefings, research from WREI, newsletters, and the sense of common purpose. Schroeder described Caucus-sponsored events to be held in the next two months, and urged the new congresswomen to feel free to employ Caucus resources to realize their own legislative objectives, so long as they were consistent with Caucus goals. The three first termers were also told that each member was expected to contribute $2,500 to the Caucus each year, a requirement which had often been ignored in the preceding Congress. The names of the four new House members soon appeared on the Caucus letterhead, but neither affiliation on paper nor the sales pitch in January persuaded any of them to join at the time.[2]

Rejection by all four came as a surprise to many observers and as a painful disappointment to Margaret Heckler. It was a surprise because they had seemed interested in women's issues, although some more so than others, and none appeared to represent a district in which affiliation with the CC would be viewed as a liability. Moreover, they all supported the Equal Rights Amendment, and Martin and Schneider, especially, had run with strong support from women's groups. It seemed only natural, therefore, for them to have become a part of the Caucus, even if unable initially to take an active role.

Heckler's reaction grew out of a belief that these other Republican women would help her maintain the Caucus as a bipartisan organization. Republicans Olympia Snowe and Nancy Kassebaum gave her a good deal of support in promoting the Caucus as a vehicle for protecting women's rights. But as one of its founders and as cochair, Heckler, much more than they, was torn between the conservative orthodoxy pressed on her by other members of her party and the liberal orientations of Caucus activists who believed, as she did, in aiding women. The prospects of recruiting four other moderate Republicans who would move the Caucus consensus closer to the political center were enormously appealing.

The explanations the four gave for not joining were clear enough, although each woman probably weighed the reasons differently. First, the financial contribution to the organization was larger than was warranted by the advantages they could expect to derive from Caucus membership. The sum of $2,500 was more than they were prepared to part with in their freshman term, even though it represented roughly four-tenths of one percent of the clerk-hire, stationery and equipment allowances to which they were entitled annually. Second, their preoccupation with other projects that were more important to them would leave insufficient time and energy to do justice to Caucus affiliation. Unstated, but implicit in the comments of some, was a reluctance, shared by most new members, to identify with groups and issues when the political consequences of such associations are uncertain. Electoral vulnerability is greatest during the early years of service and many members are inclined to delay affiliation with organizations deemed marginal to their service until they have established a stronger political base in their districts.

Fourth, at least one of the four was disinclined to view issues as "women's issues." She may have believed that separate economic and regional interests lent themselves to explicit representation, but the same was not true about gender. There were no "men's" or "women's" issues. These same sentiments were shared by Paula Hawkins, who maintained that she did not believe " . . . in a women's caucus, black caucus, or any special interest caucuses," and she too, declined to join the CC (*New York Times* July 16, 1981).

Fifth, some of the Republican women were concerned about the political style and motives of Patricia Schroeder. Although she and her predecessor as cochair, Elizabeth Holtzman, were both Harvard-trained lawyers, they had very different legislative styles. Whereas Holtzman was deliberate and painstaking in preparing herself on issues and legislative measures, Schroeder worked quickly and spontaneously. At times, she appeared impulsive. She spent little time agonizing over the precise language to use to express her views and gave minimum attention to considering the appropriate time to introduce them into discussion. Holtzman believed in slowly, systematically building her case and then overwhelming the opposition with a mountain of evidence; Schroeder in using her ammunition as soon as it became available. The Denver Democrat also invested her energies in many different causes thereby limiting her ability to master the subtleties of more than one or two.

As a result, critics concluded that Schroeder did not do her homework and was predisposed to shoot from the hip. She also had a reputation as a publicity seeker—more because she readily agreed to requests for interviews and was always good for a wisecrack than because she consciously sought the exposure— and some first term Republicans voiced reservations about being identified with an organization led by a liberal Democrat whose legislative behavior was not always predictable and whose goals seemed inextricably linked to generating press coverage. Said Lynn Martin when asked why she decided not to join the Caucus: "The dues were too high, and I don't need to pay that for a Pat Schroeder show" (Glaser and Elliot 1983, p. 160).

But casting a shadow over all of these explanations was another concern these women shared, a concern more important than any they offered publicly. It was a fear that affiliation with the Caucus would place them at odds with the Reagan administration. Ronald Reagan was opposed to the Equal Rights Amendment and had persuaded a Republican national convention to deny support for the Amendment after forty years of calling for its enactment. He had also promised to reduce the federal government's role in promoting the public welfare and to cut back programs and dollars directed toward that end. Legislative measures of interest to the Congresswomen's Caucus, on the other hand, normally called for a greater federal role and larger expenditures of federal funds. The four first-termers were too new seriously to consider opposing the administration on these issues, and they turned the Caucus down rather than chance offending the President and his constituency. Margaret Heckler might have the seniority and the electoral security to risk opposing the White House on women's issues. As freshmen, they had neither.

Having missed a golden opportunity to replenish its membership, the Caucus, nonetheless, had some reason for optimism as the 97th Congress began. True, the new women had not accepted the invitation to join the group, but their names would appear on the letterhead for a few months, and there was always the chance that they would affiliate later in the session. Furthermore, some believed that the new administration would be more sympathetic to women's needs than most critics were predicting it would be. Before his inauguration, the President-elect, accompanied by Vice President-elect George Bush, Max Friedersdorf, who would head his congressional liaison office, former Ambassador Anne Armstrong, and Jeane Kirkpatrick, who was about to become U.S. Ambassador to the United Nations, held a reception for congresswomen. Mr. Reagan made clear that he opposed the ERA because he preferred other ways of ending discrimination against women, and he said that he would work diligently toward achieving that goal.

The Caucus referred to the event as a "working" luncheon and, indeed, some important items of business were explored. The President-elect assured the women that they would have regular access to Cabinet members, that he strongly approved of meetings between the Caucus and executive branch officials, and that all they had to do was let him know with whom they would like to meet and he would be happy to arrange it. He also listened to the congresswomen spell out their priorities and, in a press release issued later that day, Caucus leaders observed that the President elect was " . . . obviously open to suggestions and ideas." The meeting showed his " . . . sensitivity to the role of American women and the problems we face." Skeptics called this reaction unrealistically optimistic, but many of the women were prepared to give the President, this charming, gentle man, the benefit of the doubt.

A second reason for the upbeat mood among Caucus members was the improvement in the administrative and financial arrangements governing Caucus operations. Through the spring of 1980, the staffs of the Caucus and the Women's Research and Education Institute occupied the same cramped quarters in the Rayburn Building. The space and facilities were simply insufficient for both simultaneously to hold meetings, conduct briefings, and carry out administrative and clerical functions without getting in one another's way. The efficiency of the two operations was bound to be adversely affected. In January, China Jessup joined WREI to look into research projects being carried out on women. In February, the Caucus hired Ann Charnley Smith to succeed Susan Scanlan, who moved over to WREI, and the tightly packed office produced a highly charged atmosphere. Staff members of both agencies had difficulty keeping their responsibilities, facilities, resources, and interns straight.

In April, WREI moved out of the Rayburn Building and settled in a town house several blocks from Capitol Hill. Its departure gave Smith some breathing room and an opportunity to deal with the increasing difficulties facing the Caucus. She brought to her task a rich background of teaching, foreign travel, and administrative, organizational, and public relations experience—qualifications useful for a Caucus Director who had to be a self-starter.

One of the two important problems with which she had to come to terms was the inertia characterizing Caucus behavior during the remaining months of the 96th Congress. With Holtzman out of the picture and most other leaders increasingly diverted by presidential politics and their own reelection efforts, it was difficult to mobilize Caucus members' energies to a level sufficiently intense to promote orchestrated legislative initiatives. The second vexing and persistent problem Smith had to confront was that of financing staff activities. Some members continued to delay payment of their dues.

It was partly in response to these financial difficulties that Smith worked with Caucus leaders to create UPDATE, a biweekly newsletter. The principal objective of this new organ was to provide timely information on the status of legislation affecting women, information which until then was unavailable in a single, easily accessible source. UPDATE summarized recent bills, announced hearings soon to be held, alerted readers to action taken by House and Senate committees, provided special reports on issues that had come to a head within the last few months, and reported federal regulations that government agencies had adopted or were about to adopt.[3] The newsletter was carefully conceived to keep Caucus members, their liaison persons, and other interested parties informed about current and pending developments. But the publication was also expected to solve the Caucus's financial woes. UPDATE would be free to members, but other lawmakers, along with interest groups active in women's issues, would be charged an annual fee. If enough subscribers signed on, the newsletter could be the CC's salvation. Cost of the biweekly was set at $125 per year, but corporate recipients were asked to pay $1,000.

By December, 1980, with the distribution of the second issue, more than twenty Representatives, two Senators and one subcommittee (on Civil and Constitutional Rights) had subscribed, and all congressional offices had begun to receive it. Not long after, business, labor, philanthropic, and public interest lobbyists sent checks. Among them were the American Council of Life Insurance, Bendix, Atlantic Richfield, Johnson and Johnson, RCA, the United Auto Workers, the American Federation of State, County and Municipal Workers, and the Women's Division of the United Methodist Church. By devising a means of transmitting information more effectively, the Caucus simultaneously took a step closer to solvency. UPDATE subscriptions could yield up to $20,000, which, together with help from interns, and funds from the congresswomen who fulfilled their financial responsibilities, would be enough to sustain Rayburn office activities.

Possible support from the newly elected President, a resourceful staff director, and financial viability were the three most important reasons for Caucus optimism, but they were not the only ones. Another good sign was the scores of women's bills introduced and highlighted by both Caucus members and nonmembers. These measures called for fundamental social security reform, changes in pension systems that discriminate against women, protection of reproductive rights, aid to women specializing in math and the sciences, creation of a breast cancer task force in the National Institutes of Health, an Economic Equity bill, and more rigorous enforcement of Title IX and other anti-discriminatory provisions of laws passed in the last fifteen years. At the same time, congresswomen were receiving strong moral support from women's groups. Late in January, the National Women's Political Caucus and the Capitol Hill Women's Political Caucus held a luncheon reception to honor the twenty-one women in the House and Senate, and the CC later joined with representatives of women's organizations to hold a briefing on legislative highlights in women's issues from 1973 to 1980.

But as the 97th Congress wore on, the fragile optimism initially character-izing Caucus members' spirits began to crumble. Failure to reach consensus on many issues, a serious problem in 1979 and 1980, arose again in 1981. Fenwick had resigned from the group, but the three women who Heckler and Holtzman had tried so hard to recruit refused to support measures which might be objectionable to the new administration. Members gave up trying to convene regularly at a specific time on a stipulated day, relying instead on ad hoc arrangements. As a result, meetings were few and far between, and whatever progress was made on proposals helpful to women was the product of Caucus members acting in their individual, rather than their collective, capacity.

Especially disappointing was the refusal of administration officials to honor Caucus requests for meetings. Only two high-ranking administrators accepted invitations throughout 1981, Health and Human Services Secretary Richard Schweiker, and Social Security Administrator John Svahn. David Stockman, Director of the Office of Management and the Budget, ignored repeated calls to appear. When Carter advisors had come to Capitol Hill in 1977 and 1978, a candid, free-flowing exchange of ideas took place, with administrators agreeing to conduct a survey, write a report, look into a questionable practice, consider counterproposals, and come back for another session. The meeting with Schweiker was useful, but the one with Svahn seemed to generate hostility. Caucus members took pains to point out that social security reform to help women was not a partisan issue and Svahn expressed regret on several occasions that it had become one.

If the infrequent meetings with the President's top advisors was a disappointment to Caucus members, the President's budgetary priorities were considered a calamity. After he released his proposed 1982 budget, the Caucus asked WREI to prepare a report detailing the budget's impact on women. WREI distributed its study at the end of March and Caucus leaders found it sobering (Rix and Stone 1981). More than ninety percent of recipients of Aid to Families with Dependent Children were women and children and, according to administration figures, more than 650,000 of these families would lose some or all of their aid. To Caucus members, this was a high price to pay to try to reduce fraud, minimize abuse, eliminate families that were not needy enough, and improve incentives to work.

The President's proposals to place a cap on Medicaid and reduce eligibility for food stamps were also expected to place a greater burden on women than on men. At the time, sixty-one percent of all Medicaid recipients were women, and thirty-six percent of all households covered by Medicaid were headed by a female with no spouse present. In addition, six of every ten households receiving food stamps were headed by a woman, and as many as 700,000 women could be eliminated from the Women, Infant and Child program if the budget remained unchanged. Cuts in the social security minimum benefit program would also fall disproportionately on women, inasmuch as three-quarters of the 2.3 million recipients were female. And reductions in funds for the Legal Services Corporation (two-thirds of whose clients were women) and for guaranteed student loans were also expected to have an especially deleterious impact on women. What was clear to Caucus leaders was that this President, who had promised to be sensitive to women's needs, had fashioned a budget which would have a disastrous effect on those women least able to protect themselves—the poor, the elderly, the widowed, and the isolated. He seemed to be in the process of accelerating the feminization of poverty.

In the meantime, there was little the Caucus could do. A strong negative response would be vetoed by more conservative members. Consequently, the criticism leveled at the Reagan administration was issued either individually or through the collective voices of smaller combinations of women. For Caucus liberals these circumstances were intolerable, and they reacted in two ways. First, they placed some of the better-known equalitarian women's issues on the back burner and began to give more of their attention to economic equity for women. Said one staff member, "You can't think much about more vigorous enforcement of Title IX when medical benefits for women and children are being threatened." Second, they decided to change the ground rules that defined the obligations of members and their organization's mode of doing business.

The Economic Equity bill was a comprehensive measure targeting women whose traditional roles and responsibilities had left them economically disadvantaged with respect to pensions and annuities, employment opportunities and wages, capital for investment, and social security and insurance benefits. It reflected an affirmative effort by lawmakers to respond to the deprivations women suffer because society asks them to perform certain roles, because they dutifully carry out these roles, because little or no monetary value is attached to the tasks they fulfill, and because they usually live longer than men. Caucus leaders joined three senators in cosponsoring the bill and they made it their highest priority during the remainder of the 97th Congress.

For liberals, inability to use the Caucus as a more active, positive force had gone on for too long. The inertia was especially galling in the face of the Reagan administration's efforts to blunt many of the victories women had won since the 1960s. "We had no idea," said one Caucus activist, "just how creative they [the Reagan administration] would be in undoing rights for women." In July, the Executive Committee met and adopted a set of bylaws, the first collection of written rules governing Caucus operations and member responsibilities. Provisions approved put an end to the unanimity rule, limited to seventy-two hours the length of time members could take to approve or reject a letter circulated for Caucus endorsement, and required each member to contribute $2,500 to the Caucus annually. After adoption of the bylaws, it would take rejection by two persons, rather than a single member, to withhold the Caucus imprimatur on a letter.

The reaction was immediate and predictable. Republicans Marjorie Holt and Virginia Smith, and Democrats Marilyn Lloyd and Beverly Byron resigned. Byron asserted that the fee was excessive relative to the services the Caucus provided. Schroeder, on the other hand, explained why the decision had been made: "The ten of us carrying it [the Caucus] said 'this is really aggravating. They [those who make no contributions] run on the fact that they belong to the Congresswomen's Caucus and they ask us to write speeches'" (*New York Times* July 16, 1981). Caucus leaders also ended the pretense that the four new Republican women were members, and their names, too, were dropped from the letterhead. With the adoption of bylaws and the purge of marginal members the Caucus entered a new phase. It became more aggressive and more inclined to reveal its strongly progressive orientation. Its smaller size made consensus more likely and unanimity easier to engineer.

Rapport between the cochairs became more problematical, however, because the pressures on Heckler's middle position between liberal Democrats and orthodox Republicans intensified once the organization was reduced to ten members. The indecision and delay that had characterized her past behavior worsened, in fact, and Schroeder and the Caucus staff sometimes waited weeks for her to sign a letter. The most exasperating instance of this behavior occurred when the Senate approved the nomination of Sandra Day O'Connor to the Supreme Court and Caucus members agreed to send her a note of congratulations and good wishes. The staff drafted a simple letter to that effect and forwarded it to Heckler for approval. Concerned about the vigorous opposition to O'Connor's nomination by anti-abortionists, and anticipating a difficult reelection campaign in 1982, Heckler revised the draft and lengthened the message stating, among other things, that the Caucus took positive note of the new justice's strict constructionist, conservative views. The changes were unacceptable to other Caucus leaders, and Heckler produced a second, shorter version, which suggested that the Caucus would be reviewing with interest O'Connor's judicial record in Arizona. This, too, was unacceptable and, ultimately, the initiative died. Congresswomen did, indeed, extend best wishes, but several letters were sent, none of which conveyed sentiments on behalf of the Caucus.

In the end, Heckler's devotion to the Caucus and her belief in its usefulness as an instrument for helping women were not as appreciated as her supporters hoped they would be. Critics who thought she was being used to give a bipartisan facade to what was really a Democratic sideshow must have felt vindicated when, during the 1982 campaign, Caucus Democrats campaigned for her opponent. Democratic Congressman Barney Frank and she were placed in the same district as a result of reapportionment and redistricting, and Geraldine Ferraro, Barbara Mikulski, and Schroeder told Massachusetts residents "You don't have to be a woman to be a feminist." Women's groups, too, supported Frank. But Heckler's difficulties and dilatory behavior became less important when, toward the end of 1981, the Caucus was faced with a crisis. The crisis threatened its survival and forced its leaders to change the organization's structure and composition. It also led to a Caucus more effective than it had ever been before.

TRANSFORMATION: THE CONGRESSIONAL CAUCUS FOR WOMEN'S ISSUES

The decision forcing the Caucus to change its character was made official on October 21, 1981, but members had been expecting it for weeks. It was issued by the House Administration Committee and it changed the rules governing the operations and funding of all House caucuses.

Among the more than fifty such groups, twenty-six, including the Congresswomen's Caucus, were officially registered with the House. Under the old guidelines, they could occupy space in House office buildings, use congressional office supplies and equipment, lay claim to House telephone numbers, and raise funds from sources both inside and outside of Congress. Under the new rules, these legislative service organizations could receive office space, furniture, furnishings, telephones and other goods and services from the House. And they could be financed by contributions of members through dues and assessments from clerk-hire and expense allowances. But they could not receive outside funding from, say, corporations and foundations, and, at the same time, retain their entitlements to public benefits.

The Congresswomen's Caucus was, for the most part, already in compliance with the new rules. When it set up the Women's Research and Education Institute, moved the corporation out of House facilities, established it as an entity separate and distinct from the Caucus, and made it the sole recipient of foundation and other grants, the Caucus had insulated itself from direct outside funding. But one of the new rule's changes affected indirect contributions, as well, including newsletter subscriptions, the Caucus's principal mode of raising money for its own operations. UPDATE was expected to bring in about $20,000 annually, but with subscriptions, too, defined as an outside source of revenue, the Congresswomen's Caucus could no longer sell UPDATE to private customers and continue to rely on House resources and facilities and on members' financial contributions.

Under the new rules, all caucuses had to inform the Administration Committee by no later than January 1, 1982, whether they planned to give up that source of outside income, and, if not, they had to vacate public premises by January 1, 1983 (*Congressional Quarterly Weekly Report* Vol. 39, October 24, 1981, p. 2074). Anticipating the Committee's decision, the Caucus met the day before it was handed down to consider its implications and review their options. They agreed that if UPDATE subscriptions were discontinued, the Caucus would have to be disbanded. On the other hand, if the newsletter moved off Capitol Hill in order to keep its outside funding, it would lose its usefulness as a resource for members. Faced with the unpleasant choice, the Caucus decided to expand its membership, admitting male Representatives, and replace the funds from subscriptions with the annual dues of congressmen who joined the Caucus.

The idea of permitting men to affiliate was not new. It had been broached early in 1977, when the Caucus was first being formed, and had been considered often since then. Most congresswomen acknowledged that many male colleagues were more authentic feminists than some female Representatives, that half the country's population deserved to be represented by more than a handful of House members, and that by inviting men to join, the Caucus would gain better access to the House power structure. But most Caucus leaders regularly rejected the suggestion. They thought that a male presence would dilute the thrust of

Caucus concerns about women, and that men might try to seize control of the organization for their own purposes. The subject was raised again after male Representatives helped bail out the Caucus by subscribing to UPDATE when it began publication. But with newsletter fees from corporate, labor, and other interest groups now ruled out, the Caucus decided it had no alternative but to permit male members to make an even greater contribution—this time as members.

Six weeks after adopting the change, forty-six men had affiliated with the group. On March 2, 1982, it changed its name to the "Congressional Caucus for Women's Issues" and, by the middle of the month, sixty-six congressmen had signed on. Before long, male membership reached 100 and included House speaker Tip O'Neill. What kind of "members" they might become was not immediately certain. When the transformation was being considered, Schroeder and others supported "auxiliary" membership, allowing congressmen to pay something less than the full $2,500 dues in force at the time, but giving them a reduced role in determining policy and running the organization. One proposal suggested charging men $1,000, allowing them to attend quarterly meetings, and permitting participation in press conferences and hearings sponsored by the Caucus.

Some who were less enthusiastic about admitting men held out for a smaller role, and Caucus members finally decided to charge males $600 annual fees, for which they would receive UPDATE. Furthermore, their names would appear on press releases and all correspondence. Under Caucus bylaws adopted May, 1982, congressmen are ineligible to hold Caucus office or vote for officers or on policy matters. But many congresswomen believed at the time that males in the Caucus would soon play an active role in running it, and, for them, nothing has happened since to change that expectation.

One critic of the Caucus commenting on the transformation, stated: "The men are allowing themselves to be used. They are adding their names but they have no power in the Caucus. It's tokenism in reverse." But a staff person close to the Caucus stated:

> The men would have been admitted sooner or later. When they were taken in, it was out of financial necessity, but it was politically expedient, as well, and the men will reap some benefits among women's groups in their own districts. Some congresswomen were invited to these districts in 1982 to campaign for fellow Caucus members.

Cochair Pat Schroeder commented, shortly after male Representatives were admitted: "We've known for some time that we had to broaden our base of support. We knew that separatism was not the way to go. We need partnership with men in the women's movement" (*New York Times* December 14, 1981).

It is possible, of course, that, in the absence of change, the CC would have nonetheless served the personal and political needs of its members. If the financial crunch had not made expansion necessary, the original Caucus might have gone on providing congresswomen with information, a more rational distribution of the work load on women's issues, a better-informed staff, emotional satisfaction derived from affiliation, and greater attractiveness to feminist organizations in their districts. Moreover, the purge had resolved, for a time, its two most serious problems—the tentativeness or, in some cases, the meaninglessness of Caucus membership, and policy differences among members on a broad range of basic issues.

Nevertheless, Caucus efforts before its transformation fell short of the expectations shared by its most committed members. Apart from extending the time period for the Equal Rights Amendment, the Congresswomen's Caucus had been unable to build majorities in Congress, effectively devise political strategies, or significantly affect the legislative agenda. One reason for these failings was its size. Until membership went beyond a handful of activist congresswomen, its value as a voting bloc and as a surrogate for House leadership was bound to be limited. Moreover, few of its members had sufficient seniority to control legislation within their committee's jurisdiction and the leverage to exchange such control for favorable treatment of measures supported by the Caucus. Their numbers and their peripheral positions within the structure of influence often left them at the mercy of colleagues who were disinclined to view women's problems as legitimate concerns of Congress.

But the characteristic which made long-term success most unlikely was the organization's principal criterion for membership. Unlike the great majority of other House groups, the Congresswomen's Caucus recruited members because of who they were rather than because of the nature of their constituencies. House members who today join the Steel or Textile Caucuses, for example, do so because their districts rely significantly on the manufacture or processing of these products. Regional, ideological, and partisan groups similarly unite House members whose districts' residents share a demonstrable cultural, programmatic, or political orientation. The CC, on the other hand, was made up of people whose membership depended on their gender, rather than on discernible commonalities shared by their districts. Since its priorities were often incompatible with policy preferences in some members' districts, its viability was always in doubt.

The now defunct Blue Collar Caucus bore an important similarity to the Congresswomen's Caucus. Its membership was limited to those who had worked in blue-collar jobs before being elected to the House. Begun by house painter Edward Beard of Rhode Island, it never grew to more than a half-dozen members and it disbanded after Beard was defeated for reelection. During its short life, the Blue Collar Caucus was sustained by the shared vocational background of its members, rather than by the common experiences and orientations of a preponderant, sharply visible proportion of district residents. The same fate may well have been in store for a caucus made up of Representatives whose only qualifications for membership was their gender.

Admission of men has given feminist congresswomen allies who think much as they do on women's issues and who are advantageously enough placed within the House power structure to do something about these issues. In the meantime, Representatives unsympathetic to the women's rights movement have been denied affiliation. As a result, opportunities to force the House to consider matters which the Caucus thinks are important have increased.

One instance of Caucus clout occurred weeks after the transformation, and may have been a portent of things to come. In December 1981, a federal district court in Idaho declared the extension of the ERA time period unconstitutional, and upheld the right of states to rescind prior approval. At the time, six months remained during which three additional legislatures could have acted to bring to three-quarters the number of states approving the proposed Amendment. When the National Organization for Women called for an expeditious appeal of the judge's verdict, inasmuch as the decision itself might negatively affect the ERA's chances, the Justice Department rejected the NOW request and announced that it would ask the Supreme Court to allow the case to follow "the normal appeals process." The Department's response virtually assured high-court inaction until after expiration of the extension period.

Incensed by the Attorney General's decision, Caucus leaders helped frame a telegram to President Reagan urging the Justice Department to reconsider its position. The telegram, signed by eighty-eight Representatives and thirty-one Senators, had the effect sought by the signatories. It is worth noting that among the seventy-eight male House members whose names were on the telegram, fifty-nine, more than three-quarters, soon became, or were already members of the Congressional Caucus for Women's Issues.

During 1982, Caucus activities expanded significantly. It introduced and organized support for the House version of the Economic Equity Act. Portions of the measure enacted into law provided pensions for ex-wives of armed services personnel and augmented child-care opportunities. The fight to restore minimum social security benefits to elderly Americans, millions of whom are older women with no other source of support, was also led by Caucus members. This success was followed by extension of flextime for federal workers who juggle both employment and child-rearing responsibilities. And a massive jobs bill was amended at the behest of Caucus members to include funds to create employment opportunities in the field of child care.

Finally, the growing reputation of the Caucus as an effective congressional organization led to establishment of strong ties with national womens' groups, and Caucus headquarters became a home away from home for group representatives working on the Hill.

NOTES

1. When the 94th Class of Democrats met to select officers, Berkley Bedell of Iowa nominated Spellman for Secretary, but she reacted with mock horror, saying that the Women's Liberation Movement would not approve. Spellman then nominated Bedell as Secretary and Max Baucus of Montana submitted her name as Vice Chairman, adding that he thought women's liberation would approve of her serving in that office.

2. Caucus leaders generally listed congresswomen on the letterhead unless and until they were asked explicitly to remove a name.

3. UPDATE was not the first House newsletter specializing in women's issues. Several years before, Congressman Charles Rose of North Carolina launched "The Congressional Clearinghouse on Women's Issues." Rose's staff wrote it, printed it, and published it without aid of other members, and it was more of an advocacy periodical than UPDATE became. In 1978 he decided that it was draining his resources and he decided to give it up. He approached the Caucus staff to see if they wanted to assume its publication, but when they learned that production costs, including in-kind expenditures, were $140,000 a year, they told him that they could not possibly accept his offer. At the time, the Caucus staff considered itself fortunate if they were paid when they were supposed to be.

Part V
Past, Present, and Future

12 / Changing Gender and Legislative Roles

The recruitment, treatment, and behavior patterns revealed in the preceding chapters are closely linked. Pathways congresswomen followed en route to the House affected the treatment they received and the activities in which they engaged once they arrived in Washington. Of course, their congressional experiences were colored by other factors, notably the prior attitudes male members held about women in general and congresswomen in particular. But male attitudes and behavior were not immune to the influence of female aspirations and achievement. They, too, were linked to changes in the recruitment and behavioral patterns described here.

LINKAGES

Although a great majority of widows of congressmen who died in office earlier in this century did *not* succeed their husbands, those who did constituted a large proportion of the women who served during that period. They and many other congresswomen of their era did not have the political or occupational experience possessed by most male colleagues, having secured their seats by relying upon family connections and substantial wealth. By and large, they were recruited and elected because of characteristics ascribed to them rather than because they had evidenced either political skill or public achievement.

Women who came to the House with no political experience were usually accorded gentlemanly deference but little professional respect by male House members. Moreover, their access to important committee and party leadership positions was either denied or delayed. They invested their energies in subjects deemed peculiar to the interests and capacities of members of their gender, and they did not go out of their way to identify themselves with issues directly affecting women. Their limited political experience served to reinforce an existing male bias against women in politics, and their activities in the House were sharply curtailed. Thus, recruitment through ascription contributed to unequal treatment and circumscribed behavior.

Women elected after World War II and through the 1950s and 1960s brought considerably more political and vocational experience with them, and, while they were by no means treated as equals by congressmen, they were given a greater measure of responsibility and respect than their female predecessors had received. Past achievements made more credible their search for policymaking opportunities on committees once all but closed to women. And party leaders began to distribute secondary, mostly integrative leadership positions among them. They tended to be younger than earlier congresswomen, better prepared to serve in Washington for an extended period, and willing (and able) to join the increasing number of informal House groups.

During this period, Congress was no less a male institution than it had been in earlier years, but female Representatives were as disinclined to abdicate important legislative responsibilities as they were to ignore the interests of constituents. Moreover, they began to provide the House with leadership on legislation dealing with equal-rights issues, sharing with congressmen the credit for securing approval of these measures.

Most of the congresswomen elected since the mid-1960s and early 1970s brought with them even more politically relevant experience than their immediate predecessors. They were also younger, more interested in establishing a career in Congress, and more numerous than female contemporaries who had gained House seats by virtue of ascriptive qualities. Political achievements and increased seniority made requests for assignment to important House committees more difficult to refuse, and these women became more conspicuous among members holding middle-level strategic, as well as integrative, party positions.

Although not all obstacles to informal groups disolved, most did, and an increasing number of women gained access to important internal communications channels. Fuller participation in House activities brought increased respect from male colleagues. And precongressional achievements, along with the confidence and purposiveness such success fosters, induced congressmen to take more seriously the feminist orientations most of these women brought with them or acquired once in Washington. At the same time, 1970s congresswomen established a Caucus to help them represent American women and "feminize" the legislative agenda. In 1981, the Caucus gave limited membership to male Representatives, men who expected affiliation with what was once an exclusively women's group to reap legislative and political rewards.

The implications of these developments are significant. They suggest, first of all, that the electorate has become sufficiently impressed with the political skills and experiences of female candidates, choosing women whose qualifications speak to the job responsibilities House members normally undertake. They also indicate that today's voters find tolerable female candidates' inability to boast of substantial personal wealth or a well-known family pedigree. Thus, palpable achievements, rather than ascriptive attributes (so important in the years before World War II) contributed to the victories of most contemporary female Representatives. More important, changes in the criteria the electorate has been applying to evaluate successful women candidates have expanded the limits of the political opportunity structure and established new role models for women aspiring to House seats. They have also produced a more democratic political recruitment process.

Democratization of the process would not have had a demonstrable impact on public policy if the newly recruited women had been unwilling to become champions of a population component long denied a direct voice in the House. The same is true if these women had neglected to formulate legislative and administrative remedies that addressed the needs of women not much different from themselves, and if they had been unable to convert electoral success into legislative effectiveness. But, as has been argued in preceding chapters, congresswomen have come to be treated as equals by a majority of the men with whom they serve, and male chauvinism has become an institutional as well as a political liability. Congresswomen have also begun to acquire influence within the political parties with which they affiliate, in the committees on which they serve, and in the informal groups with which they identify.

Thus, an expanded political opportunity structure and fuller integration into the House have led to a more equalitarian system of mutual obligations. Congresswomen have also contributed to the adoption of programs designed explicitly to help women—to promote their economic well-being, to augment their social options, and to nourish their physical and mental health. Female House members today represent not only the more than 500,000 people who live in their districts. They also serve the tens of millions of other women who make up more than fifty percent of the country's population. The benefits they provide are fashioned by perspectives and values which, although currently shared by many male Representatives, were absent from the congeries of views held by virtually all former members of Congress.

It is possible that some institutional responses (formation of the Caucus for Women's Issues, for example), some policy initiatives (extension of the ERA time period, for example), and, particularly, the changing character of women's issues (the Economic Equity bill, for example) would have materialized even if the recruitment, treatment, and behavior patterns described here had not evolved as they did. But it is more reasonable to believe that these responses, initiatives, and emerging issues would have been retarded at the very least if the democratizing impulses resonating through the body politic had stopped short of congressional women.

Moreover, changes in congresswomens' backgrounds and in the treatment they received from male colleagues are important even if their impact on public policy has been more modest than is claimed here. Changes in recruitment and treatment of congresswomen produced and accompanied alterations in gender role orientations. These shifts in the way male and female House members interact with one another constitute developments more fundamental than the policy reorientations reflected in Congress's handling of women's issues. This is the case because policy reorientations are vulnerable to counterattack by leaders who hold contrary views and who are in a position to redefine national priorities. Role orientations, on the other hand, are likely to be more durable.

Consequently, the last major task of this study will be to explore changes in the way House members have come to identify themselves as men and women and as lawmakers. A broader perspective within which to view changes in gender and legislative role orientations—a perspective that takes into account the source of gender roles and the stages through which these roles undergo alteration—helps illuminate not only where the House had been with respect to the relationship between male and female members, but also where the House may be going in this regard.

MYTH AND GENDER ROLES

In 1923, when the newly elected Idaho state legislature convened in Boise, the handful of women legislators present were told how they might avoid tarnishing their image as lawmakers. "Never carry a pocketbook or bag," they were advised, and "never point to an audience with a lorgnette or pencil." They were warned not to wear skirts so short that colleagues would look at their ankles instead of listening to what was being said, and they were instructed, above all, to avoid wearing flapper earrings (Swank 1923).

If male lawmakers were given a similar set of guidelines, the strictures were certainly of a different sort. Furthermore, we can be reasonably confident that sartorial pointers were not the only ones communicated to either group. Legislative leaders must have surely reinforced the already learned differences in the expected comportment of men and women, driving home to their apprentices more comprehensive behavioral norms for each.

The principal source of these norms, then as now, are the myths embodied in our culture. These myths shape and reinforce our values and provide a framework for understanding the world around us. They define and enforce our morality, express and codify our beliefs, and generate and legitimize the rituals and practices that constitute our behavior. Myths serve our needs by reinforcing our convictions, by justifying our resentments, and by providing bonds of common feeling (Janeway 1971, p. 42). They also promote roles for people to play, and we come to understand who we are and what we do in terms of mythically inspired role delineations. Moreover, our behavior is perceived and evaluated by others within the perspectives of these role prescriptions: "... what people *are* can only be understood in terms of [what we believe] ... they *ought* to be" (Parsons 1953: 18. The emphasis is Parsons').

The social order in the United States, like that in virtually all other countries, prescribes different patterns of behavior for men and women. As a result, the expectations we have for each vary considerably, and gender roles, unlike, say, occupational roles, are ascribed to men and women rather than adopted by them. These assignments are distributed among members of each group according to physical characteristics. Elizabeth Janeway maintains that gender roles are of some use in that "... we find in them definitions for living which we feel to be deeply needed" (1971, p. 74). But she is far more concerned about the negative consequences of calculating and inferring behavior on the basis of ascribed roles, and she takes pains to distinguish between them and roles which are "based upon activities and the relationships that grow out of these activities" (1971, p. 83). Being a woman is not the same thing as being a teacher or a lawmaker. The role of the first is assigned and its occupants have virtually no say in accepting or rejecting it. The expectations others share about their behavior emerge from a stereotype, and those to whom it is ascribed are judged by a set of criteria that has no necessary relationship to their full range of skills and talents.[1] Adoption of occupational roles on the other hand, involves some discretion for those who fill them, and these roles are defined by what these people do rather than who they are.

Occupants of ascribed roles are often pigeon-holed not only with respect to the behavior in which they are expected to engage, but also with regard to the psychological orientations they hold. Thus, expected predispositional differences between men and women are a part of our mythology. According to this mythology, men are purported to be confident, self-reliant, and serious; women are expected to be insecure, dependent, and frivolous. The former are viewed as assertive, rational, and objective, the latter as tentative, emotional, and subjective. Males are perceived as deliberate and original, females as impulsive and reactive. From the constraints of the mythology flow important consequences. Men are customarily evaluated in terms of instrumental success; women are measured by expressive standards. Thus, the former are supposed to be task-oriented, employing their managerial skills, competitive proclivities, physical aggressiveness, and thirst for power to achieve material, economic goals—goals pegged to survival. Women, on the other hand, are perceived as people-oriented. They manifest a sensitivity to those around them, a kindliness toward the deprived, a desire to please others, and an inclination to reduce tensions and establish bonds of affiliation. Their goals are social.[2]

As should be clear from this summary of mythically inspired variations between men and women, observers are inclined to place different values on typically male and typically female behavior, and there is little doubt that they see the former as preferable to the latter. "Masculine initiative and activity are valued more highly than feminine decorum and passivity," says Janeway (1971, p. 97). Women are regarded as the "second sex," and they are experienced by men as "other" rather than as equals (de Beauvoir 1953). Moreover, they are likely to be more conscious of their subordinate role and its restrictions than men are aware of the advantages they enjoy by being perceived as possessing the preferred attributes. "The fence around women's place is more apparent to the people who live inside it than to those outside in a man's world" (Janeway 1971, pp. 97–98). Once women recognize their subordinate state, they acquire those characteristics which permit them to give expression to their relative inferiority. Among them are patience, endurance, and, above all, the ability to please (Janeway 1971, p. 114).

To the extent that women live up to those expectations that are linked to their ascribed role, they are considered normal females, even if subordinate human beings. If they leap "the fence" and adopt behavior patterns perceived as male, they are considered aberrant women, even if normal human beings. They cannot be both normal women and admirable people, however, and, as a result, they find themselves in what some have called the "double bind" (Janeway 1971, p. 104; and O'Leary 1974, p. 812).

Historically, distinctions in gender roles have been the most important impediment to women's full participation in the American political system (Kirkpatrick 1974, p. 239). Denial of the right to vote still rankles the memory of many older women and, in spite of the increasing political success of contemporary females, relatively few have gained important public office. Even when women overcome deterrents to public life, however, they still must hurdle gender-related obstacles within the political settings in which they find themselves. Some of the difficulties encountered by congresswomen have been described in the preceding chapters.

ASCRIBED AND ASSUMED ROLES

When women Representatives come to Washington, they are perceived by others as fulfilling two very different types of roles. One is "assumed" and is linked to legislative politics, with all of the representational, political, and constitutional obligations this occupation implies. The other is "ascribed" and emerges out of those anticipated differences between male and female behavior which are nourished by stereotypes and embodied in our cultural mythology. Male Representatives have little difficulty performing the two simultaneously. The qualities, orientations, and goals they, as men, are expected to possess are the very same attributes which are most valued in the House, an institution which is defined as "male" by lawmakers of both genders. (See Chapter 4.) The confident, assertive demeanor of unselfconscious and rational males—congress-men who are determined to solve the fundamental problems affecting the economy and national security and who work in an arena in which male hegemony is the norm—is precisely the behavioral mode most admired by House members generally.

Congresswomen, on the other hand, have, until recently, been much more cautious in managing their behavior. Like most women, they were taught to be sensitive to the feelings of others, to demonstrate kindliness, concern and affection, and to please men—qualities useful for producing social amelioration. They are, moreover, mindful of the stereotypical traits ascribed to them, just as men are alert to the qualities assigned to males. While determined to exhibit characteristics which will convince colleagues and constituents that they are capable lawmakers, they are aware (sometimes painfully so) that there is a repertoire of gender-role items which most people accept as appropriate to the identities of women. Many of these items are believed to be incompatible with the legislative role. Thus, they confront the double bind, a reluctance on the part of others to define them as both normal women and successful legislators.

One of the earliest evocations of the problem in the House was provided by a male Representative, former Congressman Jerry Voorhis of California. In 1947, he observed:

> In recent years an increasing number of women have been elected to Congress, particularly the House. As I watched their work I could see how difficult is the problem they face, for they must steer a course midway between two fatal mistakes. The woman member must take care that she does not base her appeal for the cause in which she is interested on the fact of her womanhood. She cannot expect chivalry from the male members when it comes to casting their votes. Neither, on the other hand, can she hope to gain a strong position for herself if she attempts the role of hail fellow well met and tries to be like a man. What she has to do is to be simply a member of the House who quite incidently happens to belong to the female sex (1947: 35).

The tactic proposed by Voorhis, then, was to "steer" a middle course between legislative role demands, on the one hand, and behavior that was expected of a woman by virtue of her gender, on the other. Some congress-women followed that course, others did not. Even though no two of them responded to the challenge in precisely the same way, it is possible to distill a few common patterns of adaptation that emerged over time. As will be made clear, some ignored or were unable to fulfill their legislative responsibilities. Others tried to mask their identities as women, while, at the same time, adopting a professional orientation toward lawmaking. And some recent women have brought about changes in conventional role orientations.

STAGES OF ROLE CHANGE

To describe and analyze the adaptive responses of these women, it is useful to conceive of role change as occurring in four stages, stages defined by the repertoire of role items a role occupant is prepared to exhibit.[3] In the beginning stage, role behavior is *undifferentiated*. Persons holding a position in the social structure are but dimly aware of the role requirements or the expectations of others, and they proceed either to neglect their responsibilities or fulfill them in a diffuse and unspecialized fashion. They may organize components of the role (components which include orientations, activities, and expectations, for example) in the most general of ways and offer inconsistent or superficial responses to demands made upon them. At stage two, role behavior becomes *differentiated*. It reflects an awareness of the demarcation between appropriate and inappropriate action, and an inclination to abide by the constraints normally imposed upon the role occupant. The nature of the responsibilities undertaken, the limitations observed, the privileges claimed, and the rewards accepted conform to expectations about what constitutes appropriate behavior for persons holding such positions.

The third stage of role development, role *de-differentiation*, occurs when some items of one or more role components are abandoned, or when items which heretofore were found exclusively in the component or components of another role, become part of the first role's repertoire. Both may occur at the same time. Stage four of the transformation process is the *reconfiguration* period. During reconfiguration, the " . . . major role elements of a given role, redefined under the process of de-differentiation, may become stabilized or rigidified." Thus, the cycle is returned to stage two (or stage one if persons unfamiliar with the role requirements are suddenly asked to live up to them), and the groundwork is laid for circumstances and events to bring about another role de-differentiation (Lipman-Bluman 1973, p. 116).

GENDER AND LEGISLATIVE ROLE TYPES

This conceptualization of role change is useful for explaining shifts that have taken place in the way congresswomen have identified themselves—as both females and lawmakers—while trying to reconcile these identities with one another and with the expectations they knew others held about them. Moreover, our understanding of these shifts is substantially improved when distinctions are made among gender role types and among legislative role types.

Over the years, female Representatives' identities as women have been reflected in three different *gender* role types. At the same time, their behavior as elected officials has been exhibited in three *legislative* role types. Variations in both roles are summarized in Table 12.1. One gender role type is associated with

Table 12.1. Gender and Legislative Role Types

Gender Role		Legislative Role	
Type	*Brief Description*	*Type*	*Brief Description*
Lady	Accustomed to performing subordinate, traditionally female responsibilities.	Amateur	Lawmaking orientation: undifferentiated Career aspiration: negligible Policy concerns: superficial
Neutral	Inhibited about exhibiting behavior calling attention to her identify as a woman	Professional	Lawmaking orientation: differentiated Career aspiration: developed Policy concerns: truncated
Feminist	Unselfconsciously proud of her identity as a woman and insistent on equality with men	Colleague	Lawmaking Orientation: de-differentiated Career aspiration: integrative Policy concerns: comprehensive

a woman's precongressional career as wife, mother, and homemaker, and is defined largely by a status most recognize as subordinate to that of men. This role type is referred to here as "Lady." A second role type linked to gender is revealed in a congresswoman's efforts to mask her identity as a woman by avoiding those items of her ascribed role which are too easily interpreted as typically female. This woman is labeled "Neutral." Role behavior which exhibits pride in being a woman and which openly challenges the mythic superiority of males is referred to as "Feminist."[4]

The legislative role type defined as "Amateur" applies to congresswomen whose grasp of the lawmaking role is undifferentiated, whose career aspirations are virtually nonexistent, and whose policy concerns are superficial. A congresswoman who satisfactorily fulfills lawmaking responsibilities normally carried out by a House member, who contemplates and often serves an extended House career, and whose policy interests are broad, but exclude those which threaten to place her in a position of representing women's interests, is referred to as a "Professional." And a congresswoman whose behavior promises to alter the traditional legislative role, whose career aspirations include not only extensive House service, but full integration into the life of the House, and whose range of policy interests knows no necessary limits is defined as a "Colleague."

Accordingly, most of the widows who succeeded their husbands in the years before World War II, along with some who came to Washington later, constitute one of the three combined gender and legislative role types. Their relationships with male Representatives were significantly influenced by their previous identities as congressional wives, and they were treated by male House members as "ladies," with all the deference and condescension the term implies. Furthermore, they possessed an "undifferentiated" understanding of their legislative role and were either unable or disinclined to take their lawmaking responsibilities as seriously as most other members. Accordingly, the term *Lady Amateurs* is an appropriate one to describe their combined gender and legislative roles.

Many of the women who came to the House through the early 1970s had had political experience, and they adapted to their responsibilities differently than did most widows. Unlike the ladies, these women had carved out independent lives and careers. Their identities were distinct from those of their husbands or other relevant males, and they sought the acceptance of congressmen as equals. Moreover, their experience in public life (or, if widows, in positions proximate to public life) had given them the opportunity to become familiar with the lawmaking role and to "differentiate" between appropriate and inappropriate behavior associated with that role. They harbored behavioral and career orientations that were "professional" and this professionalism added to their effectiveness as legislators. As will be demonstrated, however, these *Neutral Professionals* were inclined to hedge and repress their behavior in the House so as to avoid threatening the men with whom they served.

Most congresswomen belonging to the third combined gender and legislative role type began to arrive in the House in the 1970s, although a few who came to Washington before that period also qualify. A major difficulty in defining this role type is that its contours are still being shaped in the 1980s. Unlike the women who were Neutrals, members of this group often go out of their way to accentuate their identities as women. They are not nearly as concerned as most of their female predecessors about "rocking the boat," nor do they take extraordinary pains to please the men with whom they work. Rather they have been inclined to adopt a "feminist" perspective, even if it means that their behavior is unacceptable to some Representatives. At the same time, they have altered the lawmaking role by adding a set of attitudinal and behavioral items to it.

This ongoing "de-differentiation" is reflected in the increased tendency for both male and female House members to represent women as a discrete constituency, to promote and organize groups in and out of Congress to serve that end, and to evaluate legislative proposals, no matter how gender-free they may seem on their face, in terms of their impact on women. It has also had the effect of increasing the frequency with which women are elevated to secondary leadership positions and assigned to valued committees. Thus, female Representatives in this category are referred to as *Feminist Colleagues*.

Further elaboration of the three combined role types makes possible a fuller account of changes in the contributions women have made to the legislative process, as well as a more comprehensive description of how women elected to the House have changed over time.

Lady Amateurs

Not all women elected to succeed their husbands were objects of exaggerated deference, and a number were conscientious and serious about their legislative responsibilities. Edith Nourse Rogers, Frances Bolton, and Margaret Chase Smith are three who were among the exceptions. But most who reached the House through the matrimonial connection were lady amateurs, and, according to some Representatives interviewed during the 95th Congress, at least one congresswoman fitted comfortably into that category as recently as 1978.

For many of these widows, the responsibilities of congressional office were understandably inconsistent with their identities as women. They had neither held public office nor, indeed, had they even contemplated the prospect. They were wives, social secretaries, and mothers. Their brief congressional tours filling vacancies entitled them to the remainder of their husbands' wages, and the sympathy and support of male Representatives. It is difficult to imagine House members and their spouses treating these women differently than they had when the new congresswomen were wives of living Representatives. Politicos in Washington and in home districts were likely to offer these fledgling House members little more than the respect due a grieving widow.

At the same time, most of these women were disinclined seriously to adopt well-developed legislative role orientations. They either neglected or rarely exhibited role items associated with lawmaking. They introduced few legislative proposals, and participated in committee and floor deliberations infrequently. Constituency service was a task with which they were likely to be more familiar, but even this function was performed in a relatively unspecialized, diffuse fashion. Congresswomen who succeeded husbands with whom they had worked closely were likely to be better able and more willing to carry out legislative responsibilities. Their grasp of the requisite role behavior was almost certain to be more fully developed than those of widows whose familiarity with their husbands' vocation was minimal. But even the former depended heavily upon their deceased husbands' staffs and the *Lady Amateurs* left Congress at the first opportunity.[5]

Neutral Professionals

Most of the women elected to the House who did not succeed their husbands were experienced politicians. Many brought mature political and legislative role orientations with them to Washington, and a few had compiled outstanding records as public servants. They were independent, career officeholders who had managed to overcome community prejudice against politically ambitious women. And they had developed a self-confidence and sense of purpose to which the heady experience of election victory contributes so materially.

But these women knew that as members of a small, conspicuous minority, they would be operating within a goldfish bowl. Behavior that would be overlooked or quickly forgotten if engaged in by a male Representative would trigger derision or worse if enacted by a congresswoman. There were simply too many House members and constituents who did not need much of an excuse to interpret their activities within the framework of a female stereotype. Lady Amateurs faced no such threat. They had never claimed expertise as politicians and they had retained their reputations as normal women. But the "professionals" had no intention of relinquishing a rare opportunity to be effective lawmakers and they were determined to persuade colleagues, constituents, and themselves that they were both successful women and able House members, characterizations which for many observers represented a contradiction in terms.

Individual responses to the challenge varied, but most can be reduced to a single dominant pattern—that of stripping their public images of features which could be interpreted by others as typically female. Some of these Neutral Professionals resolved the identity problem by limiting their House careers to a few terms, thereby reducing the period during which they would be compelled to cope with the contradiction. These women served long enough to leave a small imprint on the House and on our political history, but not long enough to suggest pretensions to a career in Congress or to gain sufficient seniority to warrant consideration for leadership positions.

Jessie Sumner, for example, left the House after four terms at the age of forty-eight even though she probably could have been reelected in the same district for as long as she cared to serve. Iris Blitch also settled for early retirement, relinquishing her seat during a period when most Representatives left the House only because the voters insisted upon their departure.[6] And Clare Boothe Luce declined to run again after serving only two terms, a decision influenced in part by personal tragedy.

But Luce was unusually sensitive to the burden of the female stereotype and she and Representative Helen Gahagan Douglas agreed to avoid public disagreement, or even the semblance of a rivalry, lest the press interpret the dispute as a "hair-pulling," "fingernail-scratching catfight" (Shadegg 1970, pp.

122–123). Differences in their foreign policy views led the press to feature prospective legislative performances of the two as a "battle of the glamour queens," and reporters found it useful to suggest that Luce and Douglas would "claw one another," once the 80th Congress convened. "The implication was that we were frivolous, vacuous women rather than serious, committed politicians," Douglas observed, and she decided " . . . to clear the air of such insulting innuendo . . . " as soon as possible (Douglas 1982, p. 198).

Efforts to deal with ascribed and assumed roles were also reflected in the objections some congresswomen raised to their being called "Gentlelady," or "Congresswoman." Both Mary Norton and Frances Bolton preferred to be referred to as "Congressman," and they chastized male House members who did otherwise. Bolton, who spent twenty-nine years in Congress, also became the unofficial guardian of female deportment, cautioning other female House members about chewing gum and wearing curlers on the House floor (Lamson 1968, p. 44). Certainly there were times when women tried to use feminine charm to achieve their ends, but they were more likely to mask their sexuality. An attractive widow serving in the 95th Congress described the precautions she took to retain a professional demeanor. "I work hard, and I don't run around with the men here. I don't flirt with anyone," she added, "and I have gained the admiration and respect of all my colleagues."

Attempts to improve their reputations as lawmakers took other forms. Several actively sought influence in policy areas traditionally viewed as beyond the competence of women, while systematically avoiding association with "feminist" issues. Positions on the Armed Services, and Science Committees, among others, were aggressively pursued, even if not always secured. Margaret Chase Smith, for example, fashioned an image as a frugal, defense-minded member of the Naval Affairs and (later) Armed Services Committees. At the same time, she scrupulously avoided being identified as a feminist. Many Neutrals 'shunned the ERA until massive male support for the Resolution weakened claims that it was exclusively a woman's issue. Exceptions to this practice in the late 1940s and early 1950s included a handful of mostly conservative female Representatives who had established reputations of indifference to most women's issues and who had stockpiled credit as Neutral Professionals among male Representatives by rejecting radical, "bleeding-heart" causes.

Many of these Professionals also aspired to party leadership positions, vacancies on the more prestigious standing House committees, and membership in selected informal groupings. Marjorie Holt's bid for a Republican leadership post was rebuffed, but Katharine St. George was assigned to the Rules Committee, even though she had to wait fourteen years before receiving the appointment. And the highly respected Julia Butler Hansen did not allow the uneasiness she perceived among Appropriations Committee members to affect her leadership as chair of an Appropriations subcommittee (*Congressional*

Quarterly Weekly Report July 10, 1970, p. 1748). To be sure, some of these women wrote off informal groups as unimportant and as having little impact on their influence as House members. On the other hand, other Professionals found affiliation with the more structured groups useful for fulfilling lawmaking responsibilities.

A common tactic employed by some Neutrals was to maintain a low profile, remaining as inconspicuous among their colleagues as legislative goals and continuation in office would permit. They thereby reduced the frequency with which they would have to choose publicly between risking, on the one hand, the disapprobation of male members by appearing too "womanly," and, on the other hand, denying their integrity and spontaneity as people by masking their identities. When taking the initiative or when forced to react, they sought to steer the path recommended by Congressman Jerry Voorhis in 1947, that is, to "be a member of the House who quite incidently happens to belong to the female sex."

Thus, many tried to avoid appearing emotional, tentative, or impulsive on the one hand, while, on the other, dispelling suspicions that they were in competition with male House members. After her 1962 interviews with male and female House members, Gehlen (1969) noted that the women most accepted by men were those who were " . . . rational rather than emotional, articulate, intelligent, and not too prudish; that is, the men did not have to modify their own behavior greatly to accommodate them." The most competent women, she added, had " . . . moved the most toward changing their ascribed role behavior from women to a pattern much more nearly like that of men."

Sometimes they were caricatures of congressmen, never more than when they resorted to cliché-ridden House rhetoric, the language used *ad nauseum* to impose a dispassionate, impersonal cloak over fundamental disagreements. At the same time, they emphasized constituency service at the expense of lawmaking activities because the former, exercised outside the ken of other members, did not entail the risk of rubbing male Representatives the wrong way. Moreover, it gave female members more opportunities to reflect a sensitive, caring image without appearing "soft" (and, therefore, vulnerable) in the eyes of other Washingtonians.

But, by maintaining a low profile, by masking their identities as women, and by trying to balance assigned and achieved roles, most Neutrals were, in effect, opting for the subordinate status that females have traditionally held in their relationships with males. For underlying these efforts carefully to manage their behavior and avoid calling attention to their gender was the more fundamental objective of pleasing men. They wanted to be effective legislators, and they could not gain that reputation by "rocking the boat." They did not want to sacrifice the interests of their constituents, but neither did they challenge institutional norms and leadership prejudices which defined them as "other."

By and large, Neutrals suffered the inequitable distribution of House rewards in silence and patiently waited for the seniority rule to elevate them to subcommittee chairs on less-sought-after standing committees. They took credit for successful policy initiatives, many of which were important, but they eschewed the dramatic claims and grandstanding of some male colleagues. And they were inclined to be more flexible, more willing to compromise, and less insistent about imposing their own vision of "the good, the true, and the beautiful," on legislation. One exception to this pattern was Oregon's Edith Green, whose strong views on education contributed ultimately to her leaving the Education and Labor Committee and relinquishing her subcommittee chair after eighteen years in the House. Some informants serving in the 95th Congress believe she was hounded off.

Feminist Colleagues

Green's aggressive style foreshadowed that of other women who began to come to the House in the early 1970s, about the time she left. They were just as sensitive to the potential contradictions implicit in their roles as women and lawmakers, but, unlike Neutrals, they felt little obligation to make concessions in order to adjust to these conflicts.

The new type of congresswoman saw herself as a representative of both her constituents and American womanhood. She adopted feminist causes and she did not necessarily abjure or dilute behavior which could be defined as typically female by those who were of a mind to do so. Neither did she go out of her way to please men with whom she worked—expecting rather than seeking equal treatment, and objecting when she did not get it. Thus, the latest group of congresswomen has begun to alter expectations males have about their behavior while, at the same time, modifying the role that all House members, male as well as female, are fulfilling as lawmakers. The process defies precise description, however, because role de-differentiation has not yet run its course. As a result, the new gender and legislative roles that will emerge are impossible to depict with certainty. Their origins and some of their manifestations are worth exploring, however.

Women who qualify as *Feminist Colleagues* began to come to the House before the 1970s but the woman who, more than any other, heralded and facilitated the role change was Bella Abzug. The Manhattan Democrat conceived of women as having a policy orientation which was unique to their gender and which was more humane, more civilized, more liberated, and more desirable than any combination of public policy visions men could possibly conjure up. Her feminism and her belief in the superiority of women's policy orientations were articulated often and unambiguously. She was, in fact, Congress's first unembroidered female chauvinist, and in the journal she kept during her first year in the House, she indulged her fantasies about how the United States and the world would be better places if women were represented in Congress in proportion to their numbers in the population.

> Just imagine for a moment what life in this country might have been like if women had been properly represented in Congress. Would a Congress where women in all their diversity were represented tolerate the countless laws now in the books that discriminate against women in all phases of their lives? Would a Congress with adequate representation of women have allowed the country to reach the 1970s without a national health care system? Would it have permitted the country to rank 14th in infant mortality among the developed nations of the world? Would it have allowed the situation we now have in which thousands of kids grow up without decent care because their working mothers have no place to leave them? Would such a Congress condone the continual butchering of young girls and mothers in amateur abortion mills? Would it allow fradulent packaging and cheating of customers in supermarkets, department stores, and other retail outlets? Would it consent to the perverted sense of priorities that has dominated our government for decades, where billions have been appropriated for war while our human needs as a people have been neglected? Would it vote for ABMs instead of schools, MIRVs instead of decent housing and health centers? Does anyone think that a Congress with large numbers of women would ever have allowed the war in Vietnam to go on for so long, slaughtering and maiming our children and the people of Indochina? (Abzug 1971, pp. 30–31).

Many House members first viewed Abzug's behavior with surprise and amusement. Her likes had never quite been seen in the House chamber and male Representatives exchanged knowing winks and nods whenever she was recognized in committee or on the House floor. Before long, congressmen who found her behavior objectionable turned to ridicule, and her detractors said that when she rose to speak, she cost her side twenty-five votes. For some, there seemed to be no limits to the lengths to which she would go to persuade the House to accept her views. Her criticism of other Representatives and of Congress as an institution seemed unrelenting and there was simply no way of predicting what she would do next. She, thus, became an object of hostility among congressmen who were accustomed to a reasonably predictable network of professional interactions. Now they had to deal with a woman whose aberrant behavior made them uneasy about their own identity and about what responses they were expected to make.

One consequence of Abzug's behavior was legitimation of the Feminist gender orientation of congresswomen whose personal styles were not quite so threatening. Male Representatives who agreed with Abzug's goals, but found her tactless, were now more willing to support the objectives of women who were as feminist in their orientations, but less controversial. Unlike some Neutral

Professionals who preceded them, many of these women did not ask other Representatives to call them "congressman," but insisted, instead, that they be referred to as "Ms." They were not interested in making male House members forget they were women. Rather, they tried to reinforce their image as politicians and legislators in order to gain acceptance as women colleagues.

Some who did not arrive in Washington as feminists soon defined themselves as such when they realized that men came to Congress with " . . . a presumption of competence," but that women came with "a burden of proof" (Plattner 1983, p. 784). And if the new breed of congresswomen were not as aggressive as Abzug had been, the difference was not a substantial one. Millicent Fenwick maintained that women should not go into politics unless they were " . . . prepared to take a perfectly firm stand like anybody else—just the way men do and the way all successful women do . . . without being afraid of being called aggressive" (Lamson 1979, p. 32).

While they did not go out of their way to bait male Representatives, they were not especially anxious to please them, either. If Neutrals were flexible, willing to compromise, prepared to settle for less rather than more, Feminists were more insistent upon achieving their goals. They were sometimes openly critical of the House and its members and less willing to "go along" if it meant only that they would "get along." During a legislative session that was particularly unproductive and rancorous, Patricia Schroeder suggested that the Congress hire "nannies for the boys," aides who would serve warm milk and cookies—nourishment which would contribute to better House decorum and more attention to business. Hiring nannies would improve the employment situation, as well, she argued, while encouraging " . . . this body to deal with substance once again" (*Congressional Record* March 14, 1978, p. H 2001).

Younger and physically attractive feminists harbored fewer inhibitions about exhibiting their sexuality. The romantic relationship between a congresswoman and a divorced first term Representative became an open secret soon after the latter took his seat in the 97th Congress. A few years earlier Martha Keys had married Indiana's Andy Jacobs after her first year in Washington. They met while serving together on the Ways and Means Committee. She had been divorced for less than a year and was cautioned to postpone marriage until after the 1976 election lest it affect the contest's outcome. But she refused to " . . . apply a political test to her personal life," and she went ahead just as male Representatives in similar circumstances might have (Kronholz 1976, p. 1).[7]

Meanwhile, social and professional relationships between male and female House members became less strained, more natural, with males increasingly prepared to accept women as equals (even as "one of the boys") and women convinced that, no more than any male colleague, they were under no obligation to do and say things simply to gain the approbation of congressmen. And if the strains, anxieties, and frustrations of legislative life prompted them to utter expletives, some people began not to notice.

Changes in gender orientation were accompanied by changes in legislative role behavior. In the House, women increasingly began to stake out leadership positions on feminist and other issues, insisting, unlike some predecessors, that their identities as women made them better qualified to write laws addressing the needs of women. Several devoted large shares of time to mobilizing support for the Equal Rights Amendment and, later, for extension of the time period during which states could approve the measure. Most of these same women joined House caucuses to help them frame and pursue issues that were important to them.

At the same time, they began to evaluate legislative measures within a feminist perspective. They asked how even apparently innocuous bills might affect poor women, pregnant women, married women, widowed women, handicapped women, military women, bureaucratic women, and women in general.

Acquaintance with the details of a broad range of legislation alerted them to the fact that bills most important to women were not necessarily those which mentioned women's rights directly. Proposals dealing with pensions, jobs, taxes, savings, insurance, and welfare were critically important. They proceeded to exploit the rationalization that Neutrals and antifeminists had used to justify their contempt for feminist issues. For years, the latter had maintained that legislation which singled out women as beneficiaries either ignored the fact that all bills ultimately affect all people, or that women were not the only ones deserving special treatment. Now feminists were saying that bills which did *not* single out women for benefits had a profound effect on women as a class and that a feminist perspective was indispensable to any lawmaker worth his or her salt. In the process, they raised the consciousness of male colleagues, politicized issues which had until then been considered private rather than public in character, and began to alter the national agenda.

Increased activity, greater visibility, and readier male acceptance led to more appointments to valued House and party leadership positions.[8] Not all who benefitted were Feminist Colleagues, but all capitalized on the drive for broader representation of women on important House instrumentalities. After a while, congresswomen invited males to join their Caucus, perhaps as much to preserve the organization's financial viability as to foster a spirit of colleagueship. Over 100 accepted the offer and began contributing annual dues. Mixed membership helped awaken and reinforce dormant feminist sympathies of congressmen who had not been sensitive to the breadth of issues affecting women as a constituency. In the meantime, the Democratic House leadership began regularly to consult with Caucus leaders, increasing their influence and agreeing at the start of the 98th Congress to assign the number "1" to the reintroduced ERA Resolution.

Inaccessibility to the Chowder and Marching Society and its functional equivalents constitutes one of the remaining obstacles to the colleagueship some women are currently trying to create. Admission of women to these all-male social and political organizations could be a signal of further role de-differentiation, although, in the case of the Society, it may prompt more traditional GOP members to resign and form other bastions of male exclusivity. The importance of such groups would depend upon whether House leaders also became members.

Incremental change in the lawmaking role of Feminist Colleagues has been no small achievement. Many male Representatives continue to define virtually all congresswomen as aberrations. For them, female refusal to accept a subordinate status or to shape behavior to please men is puzzling, at best. They are troubled as much by the fact that women are doing something new and different, as they are by the fact that women are not doing something old, something expected.

Moreover, de-differentiation of gender and legislative roles has not been made easier by decisions of some congresswomen to reject the Feminist Colleague role orientation. Beverly Byron attributed her more traditional view to the fact that she had never run into inequity in her own experience and, therefore, "It's hard for me to understand people who have doors closed on them" (Plattner 1983, p. 785).

But, for many male Representatives, female members have found a way to change the ascribed identity of women by engaging in behavior that is both new *and* familiar. Most congressmen had difficulty accepting the style of an Abzug, but many find that the gender orientations of women House members in the 1980s are not terribly different from those of women with whom they went to college and graduate and professional school. Moreover, it is identical to that of the women who lead feminist groups within their own districts. Thus, just as contemporary congresswomen are reflecting the values of a growing number of such groups, their own legitimacy is being validated in the expectations of male colleagues by the activities and the ubiquity of these same organizations.

In the meantime, the legislative role orientations of many contemporary congresswomen are having an effect on the lawmaking role generally. Private social relationships once considered beyond the authority or jurisdiction of Congress, are increasingly being introduced into its deliberations. More and more male, as well as female, lawmakers are acting on the belief that power relationships in private, domestic arenas have significant public consequences. Subject matter once deemed inappropriate for congressional consideration has been added to the national agenda and the spectrum of legislative inquiry has been broadened.

Male members' understanding of their representative responsibilities has also been undergoing change. Congressmen have become less likely to ignore or treat cursorily the women's constituency and they are much less diffident today about identifying with and even dramatizing their support for feminist causes. As

Republican William Gradison has said: "It's a new ballgame. Anyone who fails to consider the impact of legislation on women does so at his or her peril" (*New York Times* March 3, 1983).

Congressmen who once treated the women's movement as a source of humor and its goals as insignificant, are now less likely to exchange wise cracks and locker room jokes about matters which women have always taken seriously. Although the term "legislator" may not conjure up images of male *and* female lawmakers for some House members, they are a dying breed, inasmuch as congresswomen have begun to shed their subordinate status in the eyes of most male Representatives. If "colleagueship" has not quite been established among male and female members, the groundwork has been laid for them to begin to ignore gender differences when dealing with one another professionally.

THE FUTURE OF CONGRESSIONAL WOMEN

Predicting the future of women in the House is tempting, but difficult. It assumes that the factors affecting patterns of recruitment and behavior are known beyond doubt, and that their impact is understood well enough to forecast future developments. But all these factors are not well known, and the manner in which many of them influence one another is more uncertain still. Nevertheless, what happened in the past and what is happening today permit formulation of a few contingent generalizations.

First, the number of women who enter public life is likely to increase if we continue to encourage young women to aspire to and train for vocations heretofore dominated by men. The precongressional career convergence of female and male Representatives found by Thompson (forthcoming) is worth noting in this connection.

Second, the increase is especially likely to occur if women pursue those vocations whose skills and orientations are valued in a political setting. The legal profession comes to mind, but it is by no means the only one. Business administration, the communications field, and sales are also useful.

Third, the number of prospective female candidates having palpable qualifications for national office will increase if the number of women elected to state, county, and local offices continues to grow. Not all women officeholders will want to run for Congress, but by increasing the number with an effective political opportunity, it stands to reason that more will aspire to House office.

Fourth, women elected to Congress are more likely to possess the legislative and political virtuosity valued in that body if voters, would-be candidates, and those who recruit them place a significantly higher priority on achievement in public life than they do on contestants' ascribed characteristics.

Fifth, the highly developed political ambitions and skills that contribute to congresswomen's elections are likely to lead, in time, to selection for top leadership positions in the House.

Sixth, all of these developments are likely to make more imminent the interaction of men and women House members on a basis of equality.

Changes suggested by these generalizations are unlikely to take place rapidly, assuming, of course, that they will occur at all. There is good reason to believe, with Kirkpatrick, that a revolution in the numbers of women who seek public office and in the attitudes people hold about these women is simply not in the offing (1974, p. 249). As she points out, many fewer women than men reflect an interest in contesting elections and the traditional views about the appropriate (i.e. traditional) role of women dies hard. Nonetheless, barring retrogression in the more liberated sociopolitical expectations many now share, the ratio of female to male House members is apt to grow more rapidly than it has to date. As Rule (1981, p. 76) notes, " . . . the critical stage of women's recruitment precedes formal nomination." Once they secure party endorsements, their chances of victory become much more promising. And the number of nominations they have received in recent years has risen steadily. With substantially more women House members, the gender-related orientations of Representatives are likely to change more noticeably than they did during the sixty-six years after Jeanette Rankin first took her seat in Congress.

It seems reasonable to believe that an increase in the number of women elected to the House, perhaps more than most factors, will promote female colleagueship. But social changes contributing to role de-differentiation are still at work, and the nature and implications of such colleagueship will not be fully understood until it has been acted out and accepted by both the role players and those with whom they interact. Consequently, no one can say when or in what form "role reconfiguration" will emerge. Furthermore, the full integration of women into congressional life will not take place until myths about women's subordinate social role are rejected. Only then will it be possible for ascribed qualities to be peeled away from the identities of men and women, for women's identities as "other" to be discarded, and for gender differences to become irrelevant while men and women are undertaking the public's business together.

NOTES

1. This is not the place to explore the nature v. nurture controversy, but recent literature on the subject suggests that there are relatively few characteristics that are inherently female or inherently male, and that even with respect to these traits, differences between men and women are more matters of degree than of kind. Furthermore, men and women often possess in significant measure characteristics attributed to the other gender. As a result, we can make few if any reliable predictions about the orientations and behavior of individual men and individual women solely on the basis of gender.

2. Attributes purported to be peculiar to members of each gender (and which they are often expected to learn because of their gender) are defined by Bardwick (1976, p. 31), Iglitzin (1975, p. 26); Janeway (1971, p. 8), and Kelly and Boutilier (1978, p. 31), among others.

3. Lipman-Bluman (1973) defines these stages while discussing role change during crisis. They lend themselves nicely to gradual, or evolutionary change, as well, however, and to variations in the role behavior that congresswomen have exhibited over time.

4. The term "feminist" has been defined differently both among those who call themselves by that name and among those for whom the word produces revulsion. It is employed here in much the way most dictionaries define it: "One who advocates social and political rights of women equal to those of men" (*The Random House Dictionary of the English Language* 1967).

5. These women did not always leave willingly. Some were forced by party leaders at home to alter their intentions to run for reelection. That they refused to put up a fight, as some "professionals" did, may further mark them as "amateurs."

6. The average length of a House career peaked during the 1950s and 1960s (Polsby 1967). The retirement rate was lower than the rate of incumbent defeat, although the incidence of each tended to be low. From 1945 to 1964, retirements averaged twenty-nine per Congress, general election losses thirty-five. Incumbent defeats in primary elections averaged nine for each Congress (Bibby et al. 1980, p. 14).

7. Keys survived the 1976 election, but was defeated two years later following a campaign in which the opposition tried to capitalize on the fact that she was married to a man who lived in, and represented, a district in Indiana. Doubts about her loyalties were raised and her campaign in a highly competitive Kansas district could not have been helped by this kind of innuendo.

8. In the 98th Congress, for example, Olympia Snowe was chosen Republican Deputy Whip, and Lynn Martin was named Assistant Whip and a member of the GOP Policy Committee. Among Democrats, both Geraldine Ferraro and Patricia Schroeder were appointed to the Steering and Policy Committee, with the latter joining Mary Rose Oakar as an "At-Large" Whip. The year 1983 also saw three women on the coveted Budget Committee, Republicans Martin and Bobbi Fiedler, and Democrat Ferraro, and one Democrat, Barbara Kennelly, on Ways and Means.

Appendixes

Appendix A. Women Elected to the House of Representatives, 1916–1982 (in order of election)

Congresswoman	Date of First Election	Term Expired	Political Party	State
Jeannette Rankin	Nov. 7, 1916	Mar. 4, 1919[a]	Republican	Montana
	Nov. 5, 1940[b]	Jan. 3, 1943		
Alice M. Robertson	Nov. 2, 1920	Mar. 4, 1923	Republican	Oklahoma
Winnifred S.M. Huck	Nov. 7, 1922	Mar. 4, 1923	Republican	Illinois
Mae Ella Nolan	Jan. 23, 1923	Mar. 4, 1925	Republican	California
Mary Teresa Norton	Nov. 4, 1924	Jan. 3, 1951	Democratic	New Jersey
Florence P. Kahn	Feb. 17, 1925	Jan. 3, 1937	Republican	California
Edith Nourse Rogers	June 30, 1925	Sept. 10, 1960[c]	Republican	Massachusetts
Katherine G. Langley	Nov. 2, 1926	Mar. 4, 1931	Republican	Kentucky
Ruth Hanna McCormick	Nov. 6, 1928	Mar. 4, 1931[d]	Republican	Illinois
Ruth B. Owen	Nov. 6, 1928	Mar. 4, 1933	Democratic	Florida
Ruth B.S. Pratt	Nov. 6, 1928	Mar. 4, 1933	Republican	New York
Pearl P. Oldfield	Jan. 9, 1929	Mar. 4, 1931	Democratic	Arkansas
Effiegene L. Wingo	Nov. 30, 1930	Mar. 4, 1933	Democratic	Arkansas
Willa McCord Eslick	Aug. 4, 1932	Mar. 4, 1933	Democratic	Tennessee
Virginia E. Jenckes	Nov. 8, 1932	Jan. 3, 1939	Democratic	Indiana
Kathryn O'Loughlin McCarthy	Nov. 8, 1932	Jan. 3, 1935	Democratic	Kansas
Isabella S. Greenway	Oct. 3, 1933	Jan. 3, 1937	Democratic	Arizona
Marian W. Clarke	Dec. 28, 1933	Jan. 3, 1935	Republican	New York
Caroline L.G. O'Day	Nov. 6, 1934	Jan. 3, 1943	Democratic	New York
Nan W. Honeyman	Nov. 3, 1936	Jan. 3, 1939	Democratic	Oregon
Elizabeth H. Gasque	Sept. 13, 1938	Jan. 3, 1939[e]	Democratic	South Carolina
Jessie Sumner	Nov. 8, 1938	Jan. 3, 1947	Republican	Illinois
Clara G. McMillan	Nov. 7, 1939	Jan. 3, 1941	Democratic	South Carolina
Margaret Chase Smith	Jan. 3, 1940	Jan. 3, 1949[f]	Republican	Maine
Frances P. Bolton	Feb. 27, 1940	Jan. 3, 1941	Republican	Ohio

Florence R. Gibbs	Oct. 1, 1940	Jan. 3, 1941	Democratic	Georgia
Katharine E. Byron	May 27, 1941	Jan. 3, 1943	Democratic	Maryland
Veronica G. Boland	Nov. 3, 1942	Jan. 3, 1943	Democratic	Pennsylvania
Clare Booth Luce	Nov. 3, 1942	Jan. 3, 1947	Republican	Connecticut
Winifred C. Stanley	Nov. 3, 1942	Jan. 3, 1945	Republican	New York
Willa L. Fulmer	Nov. 7, 1944	Jan. 3, 1945	Democratic	South Carolina
Emily Taft Douglas	Nov. 7, 1944	Jan. 3, 1947	Democratic	Illinois
Helen Gahagan Douglas	Nov. 7, 1944	Jan. 3, 1951[d]	Democratic	California
Chase Going Woodhouse	Nov. 7, 1944	Jan. 3, 1947	Democratic	Connecticut
	Nov. 2, 1948[b]	Jan. 3, 1951		
Helen D. Mankin	Feb. 2, 1946	Jan. 3, 1947	Democratic	Georgia
Eliza Jane Pratt	May 25, 1946	Jan. 3, 1947	Democratic	North Carolina
Georgia L. Lusk	Nov. 5, 1946	Jan. 3, 1949	Democratic	New Mexico
Katharine P.L. St. George	Nov. 5, 1946	Jan. 3, 1965	Republican	New York
Reva Beck Bosone	Nov. 2, 1948	Jan. 3, 1953	Democratic	Utah
Cecil M. Harden	Nov. 2, 1948	Jan. 3, 1959	Republican	Indiana
Edna F. Kelly	Nov. 8, 1949	Jan. 3, 1969	Democratic	New York
Marguerite S. Church	Nov. 8, 1950	Jan. 3, 1963	Republican	Illinois
Ruth Thompson	Nov. 8, 1950	Jan. 3, 1957	Republican	Michigan
Maude Elizabeth Kee	July 16, 1951	Jan. 3, 1965	Democratic	West Virginia
Vera D. Buchanan	July 24, 1951	Nov. 26, 1955[c]	Democratic	Pennsylvania
Gracie B. Pfost	Nov. 4, 1952	Jan. 3, 1963[d]	Democratic	Idaho
Leonor K. Sullivan	Nov. 4, 1952	Jan. 3, 1975	Democratic	Missouri
Iris F. Blitch	Nov. 2, 1954	Jan. 3, 1963	Democratic	Georgia
Edith Green	Nov. 2, 1954	Jan. 3, 1975	Democratic	Oregon
Martha W. Griffiths	Nov. 2, 1954	Jan. 3, 1975	Democratic	Michigan
Coya G. Knutson	Nov. 2, 1954	Jan. 3, 1959	Democratic	Minnesota
Kathryn E. Granahan	Nov. 6, 1956	Jan. 3, 1963	Democratic	Pennsylvania

(Continued on next page)

Appendix A. *(continued)*

Congresswoman	Date of First Election	Term Expired	Political Party	State
Florence P. Dwyer	Nov. 6, 1956	Jan. 3, 1973	Republican	New Jersey
Catherine D. May	Nov. 4, 1958	Jan. 3, 1971	Republican	Washington
Edna O. Simpson	Nov. 4, 1958	Jan. 3, 1961	Republican	Illinois
Jessica McCullough Weis	Nov. 4, 1958	Jan. 3, 1963	Republican	New York
Julia Butler Hansen	Nov. 8, 1960	Jan. 3, 1975	Democratic	Washington
Catherine D. Norrell	Apr. 18, 1961	Jan. 3, 1963	Democratic	Arkansas
Louise G. Reece	May 16, 1961	Jan. 3, 1963	Republican	Tennessee
Corrine B. Riley	April 10, 1962	Jan. 3, 1963	Democratic	South Carolina
Charlotte T. Reid	Nov. 6, 1962	Oct. 1, 1971[g]	Republican	Illinois
Irene B. Baker	Mar. 10, 1964	Jan. 3, 1965	Republican	Tennessee
Patsy T. Mink	Nov. 3, 1964	Jan. 3, 1977[a]	Democratic	Hawaii
Lera M. Thomas	Mar. 26, 1966	Jan. 3, 1967	Democratic	Texas
Margaret M. Heckler	Nov. 8, 1966	Jan. 3, 1983	Republican	Massachusetts
Shirley A. Chisholm	Nov. 5, 1968	Jan. 3, 1983	Democratic	New York
Bella S. Abzug	Nov. 3, 1970	Jan. 3, 1977[a]	Democratic	New York
Ella T. Grasso	Nov. 3, 1970	Jan. 3, 1975[h]	Democratic	Connecticut
Louise Day Hicks	Nov. 3, 1970	Jan. 3, 1973	Democratic	Massachusetts
Elizabeth B. Andrews	Apr. 4, 1972	Jan. 3, 1973	Democratic	Alabama
Yvonne Brathwaite Burke	Nov. 7, 1972	Jan. 3, 1979[i]	Democratic	California
Marjorie S. Holt	Nov. 7, 1972	[j]	Republican	Maryland
Elizabeth Holtzman	Nov. 7, 1972	Jan. 5, 1981[d]	Democratic	New York
Barbara Jordan	Nov. 7, 1972	Jan. 3, 1979	Democratic	Texas
Patricia Schroeder	Nov. 7, 1972	[j]	Democratic	Colorado
Corinne (Lindy) Boggs	Mar. 20, 1973	[j]	Democratic	Louisiana
Cardiss Collins	June 7, 1973		Democratic	Illinois
Millicent Fenwick	Nov. 5, 1974	Jan. 3, 1983[d]	Republican	New Jersey
Martha Keys	Nov. 5, 1974	Jan. 3, 1979	Democratic	Kansas
Marilyn Lloyd	Nov. 5, 1974	[j]	Democratic	Tennessee

Name	Date		Party	State
Helen Meyner	Nov. 5, 1974	Jan. 3, 1979	Democratic	New Jersey
Virginia Smith	Nov. 5, 1974	j	Republican	Nebraska
Gladys N. Spellman	Nov. 5, 1974	Feb. 24, 1981[k]	Democratic	Maryland
Shirley N. Pettis	Apr. 29, 1975	Jan. 3, 1979	Republican	California
Barbara Mikulski	Nov. 2, 1976	j	Democratic	Maryland
Mary Rose Oakar	Nov. 2, 1976	j	Democratic	Ohio
Beverly Byron	Nov. 7, 1978	j	Democratic	Maryland
Geraldine Anne Ferraro	Nov. 7, 1978	j	Democratic	New York
Olympia J. Snowe	Nov. 7, 1978	j	Republican	Maine
Bobbi Fiedler	Nov. 4, 1980	j	Republican	California
Lynn M. Martin	Nov. 4, 1980	j	Republican	Illinois
Margaret S. Roukema	Nov. 4, 1980	j	Republican	New Jersey
Claudine C. Schneider	Nov. 4, 1980	j	Republican	Rhode Island
Barbara Bailey Kennelly	Jan. 12, 1982	j	Democratic	Connecticut
Jean Ashbrook	June 29, 1982	Jan. 3, 1983	Republican	Ohio
Katie Hall	Nov. 2, 1982	j	Democratic	Indiana
Barbara Boxer	Nov. 2, 1982	j	Democratic	California
Nancy L. Johnson	Nov. 2, 1982	j	Republican	Connecticut
Marcy Kaptur	Nov. 2, 1982	j	Democratic	Ohio
Barbara Vucanovich	Nov. 2, 1982	j	Republican	Nevada

a. Unsuccessfully sought party's nomination for the Senate.
b. Served two nonconsecutive terms.
c. Died in office.
d. Secured party's nomination for Senate, but lost the general election.
e. Never sworn in to the House.
f. Secured party's nomination for Senate and won the general election.
g. Resigned to accept appointment to an independent regulatory agency.
h. Ran successfully for Governor.
i. Ran unsuccessfully for state Attorney General.
j. Serving in the 98th Congress.
k. Seat declared vacant following a disabling heart attack.

Sources: Women in Congress, 1917–1976. U.S. Congress Joint Committee on Arrangements for the Commemoration of the Bicentennial, 1976; Schwemle (1982), *Congressional Quarterly Weekly Report*, Vol. 41, No. 1, January 8, 1983.

Appendix B. Southern and Nonsouthern Widows Receiving Major Party Nominations, 1916–1982

Southern Widows

Widow	Year of First Nomination	Husband's Seniority Status	Husband's Leadership Status	Competitiveness of District	Primary or General Election Opposition	Renominated	Age	Worked Closely with Husband
Langley	1926	High	Leader	Competitive	Yes	Yes	38	Yes
Oldfield	1929	High	Leader	Safe	No	No	52	No
Wingo	1930	High	Leader	Safe	No	No	47	Yes
Eslick	1932	Moderate	Nonleader	Safe	No	No	53	No
Kemp	1933	Moderate	Leader	Safe	No	*	N.A.	N.A.
Gasque	1938	High	Leader	Safe	No	No	42	N.A.
McMillan	1939	High	Leader	Safe	No	No	45	N.A.
Gibbs	1940	Low	Nonleader	Safe	No	No	50	No
Fulmer	1944	High	Leader	Safe	No	No	60	No
Norrell	1961	High	Leader	Safe	Yes	No	60	Yes
Reece	1961	High	Leader	Competitive	Yes	No	62	Yes
Riley	1962	High	Nonleader	Safe	Yes	No	68	No
Baker	1964	Moderate	Nonleader	Safe	No	No	62	Yes
Thomas	1966	High	Leader	Safe	No	No	65	Yes
Pool	1968	Low	Nonleader	Competitive	Yes	*	51	N.A.
Andrews	1972	High	Leader	Safe	No	No	61	Yes
Boggs	1973	High	Leader	Safe	Yes	Yes	57	Yes
Lloyd	1974	**	**	**	Yes	Yes	45	Yes

Nonsouthern Widows

Widow	Year of First Nomination	Husband's Seniority Status	Husband's Leadership Status	Competitiveness of District	Primary or General Election Opposition	Renominated	Age	Worked Closely with Husband
Huck	1922	Moderate	Nonleader	Competitive	Yes	No	40	Yes
Nolan	1923	Moderate	Leader	Safe	Yes	No	36	Yes

Name	Year							
Kahn	1925	High	Leader	Safe	Yes	Yes	56	Yes
Rogers	1925	Moderate	Leader	Safe	Yes	Yes	44	Yes
Clarke	1933	Moderate	Leader	Competitive	Yes	No	53	Yes
Bolton	1940	Moderate	Nonleader	Competitive	Yes	Yes	54	Yes
Smith, M.C.	1940	Low	Nonleader	Competitive	Yes	Yes	42	Yes
Schwert	1941	Low	Nonleader	Competitive	Yes	*	50	N.A.
Byron, K.	1941	Low	Nonleader	Competitive	No	No	37	Yes
Boland	1942	Moderate	Leader	Competitive	Yes	No	43	N.A.
Barry	1946	Moderate	Nonleader	Competitive	Yes	*	37	Yes
Church	1950	Moderate	Nonleader	Competitive	Yes	Yes	58	Yes
Kee	1951	High	Leader	Competitive	Yes	Yes	57	Yes
Buchanan	1951	Moderate	Leader	Competitive	Yes	Yes	49	Yes
Sullivan	1952	Moderate	Nonleader	Competitive	Yes	Yes	49	Yes
Granahan	1956	Moderate	Nonleader	Competitive	Yes	Yes	60	Yes
Smith, E.J.	1958	High	Nonleader	Competitive	Yes	*	62	Yes
Simpson	1958	High	Leader	Competitive	Yes	No	67	Yes
Reid	1962	**	**	**	Yes	Yes	49	N.A.
Collins	1973	Low	Nonleader	Safe	Yes	Yes	41	Yes
Pettis	1975	Moderate	Nonleader	Safe	Yes	Yes	50	Yes
Byron, B.	1978	Moderate	Nonleader	Safe	Yes	Yes	46	Yes
Ashbrook	1982	High	Leader	Competitive	Yes	No	47	Yes

Note: "N.A." indicates information not currently available.

* indicates woman was never elected.

** indicates inapplicable because husband never served.

259

Appendix C

QUESTIONNAIRE ADMINISTERED TO TWENTY-FOUR REPRESENTATIVES IN THE 95TH CONGRESS*

First I would like to ask you some questions about the character of the House as an institution, and about the personal and professional relationships between the men and women who serve in it.

1. One political scientist has said that state legislatures have strongly "masculine" traditions, that these masculine traditions affect the relationships of their members, and that the legislatures share a macho culture—the same macho culture one finds in a locker room, a smoker, and a barracks. Would you characterize the House in the same way?

2. Why do you think the House is similar to (or dissimilar from) state legislatures in these ways?

---

*Every effort was made to conduct the interviews in a relaxed, conversational manner. They usually lasted between thirty and forty-five minutes, but some took one hour, and one, with a congresswomen, continued for three hours. Representatives were informed at the outset that their observations would not be attributed to them and that, if they wished, I would withhold the fact that they had discussed these subjects with me. Not all questions were asked of all interviewees. If an answer to one or more of them had been provided in responses to preceding questions, they were omitted. Many queries were raised that were not part of the questionnaire. They were prompted by responses to questionnaire items.

Respondents included thirteen female and eleven male House members. Interviews were requested from all eighteen female Representatives in the 95th Congress. Four refused to see me. The fifth was absent from Washington so often that a mutually convenient time for an interview could not be found. The eleven male Representatives were part of an original pool of twenty-five who were reputed to be sensitive to personal and professional relationships among House members. The other fourteen declined my request for an appointment, a few indicating that they did not believe that they could make a positive contribution to this study.

3. Can you give me some concrete examples of what you're talking about?

4. Back in the mid-1940s, a congressman made a speech on the House floor, part of which went like this:

"I have my anxieties about the present Congress and the future and, as an older member, I am anxious to know what the new members will bring to us in abilities and opinion. As I look to my left, I see the face of a new lady member. I wish that all other lady members were present. May I say to her, one of the great worries I have in Congress itself is lest we have too many of you. Although I say this in a somewhat jocular way, still I am a little serious about it. The lady members are extremely satisfactory to us. But they, like all women, can talk to us with their eyes and their lips, and when they present us an apple it is most difficult to refuse. Even old Adam could not resist. Women have a language all their own. . . . They are dangerous in that they may influence us too much. Suppose we had fifty of them. Seemingly I note flirtations enough now, but what would there be with fifty of them?"

Are there members of the House today who might express these same sentiments?

5. Are there members who think that way even though they may not say this sort of thing publicly or in mixed company?

6. What sort of reactions, if any, do you think other members would have if a congressman said something like that today?

7. State legislators say that they often witness discrimination against women and that it takes four general forms. First, routine conversation, legislative debate and language in bills refer to "men" and "male" legislators, with women thought of as part of neither the legislature nor the public affected by legislation. Second, women lawmakers are subjects of excessive deferrence, they are patronized or condescended to. Third, women are expected to concentrate on a limited range of subjects, like welfare and education, but are routinely prevented from dealing with things like banking and tax regulations. And, fourth, women are victims of snide or insulting remarks and are put down by men. Have you witnessed or heard about instances of these kinds of behavior?

8. (If "yes") Do they occur often?

9. (If answer to question 7 was "yes") Can you give me some examples?

10. (If answer to question 7 was "yes") How have the people present responded when these things occurred?

Next, I would like to ask you some questions about the extent to which women are members of House caucuses and other informal groups, some of which do not have a formal title.

11. Do you belong to any informal groups or caucuses in the House?

12. (Asked of males only) Do women belong to the groups of which you are a member?

13. Do you find membership in these groups valuable?

14. (If "yes") How?

15. As far as you know, are there groups from which women are excluded?

16. (If "yes") Why is this so?

17. Have you ever heard of Sam Rayburn's Board of Education?

18. As far as you know are there groups like that in the House today?

19. Have you ever heard of the Chowder and Marching Society?

20. Do you believe that exclusion from one or more of these groups affects a person's ability to be an effective House member?

Now I would like to ask you some questions about the extent to which women have access to top leadership positions.

21. Do you think that it is likely that a woman will be selected for a top leadership position, say, Speaker, floor leader, or chief whip, in the foreseeable future?

22. What makes you think that?

23. Can you visualize the circumstances or conditions under which a woman would be selected for such a position?

24. What obstacles, if any, do you think limit a woman's access to a top leadership position?

25. (Asked of males only) Would any of these factors affect your thinking about the matter?

26. (Asked of females only) Are you interested in sometime securing a top leadership post?

Respondents included thirteen female and eleven male House members. Interviews were requested from all eighteen female Representatives in the 95th Congress. Four refused to see me. The fifth was absent from Washington so often that a mutually convenient time for an interview could not be found. The eleven male Representatives were part of an original pool of twenty-five who were reputed to be sensitive to personal and professional relationships among House members. The other fourteen declined my request for an appointment, a few indicating that they did not believe that they could make a positive contribution to this study.

Appendix D

COMMITTEES AND SUBCOMMITTEES CONSIDERING ISSUES
TYPICALLY REGARDED AS BEING OF INTEREST TO WOMEN AND
TO WHICH WOMEN WERE ASSIGNED, 1917–1983

1917–1946

Committees

Accounts
Disposition of Useless Papers in the Executive Branch
District of Columbia
Education
Election of President, V.P., and Representatives in Congress
Civil Service
Enrolled Bills
Expenditures in Government Departments
Foreign Affairs
Indian Affairs
Insular Affairs
Invalid Pensions
Labor
Library
Memorials
Milage
Pensions

Printing
Reform in the Civil Service
Territories
Woman Suffrage
World War I Veterans Legislation

1947–1964

Committees*

District of Columbia
Education and Labor
Expenditures in Executive Departments
Foreign Affairs
Government Operations
House Administration
Post Office and Civil Service
Veterans' Affairs

Subcommittees

Agriculture

Family Farms

Banking and Currency

Consumer Affairs
Housing

District of Columbia

Health, Education, Recreation
Special Study for Civic Center

Education and Labor

General Education

General Labor
Impact of Imports
National Labor Relations Board
Select Education

Foreign Affairs

Far East and Pacific

Government Operations

Executive and Legislative Reorganization
General Government Activities
Government Activities
Intergovernmental Relations

House Administration

Printing
Enrolled Bills

Interior and Insular Affairs

Insular Affairs
National Parks
Territorial and Insular Affairs

Merchant Marine and Fisheries

Fisheries and Wildlife Conservation

Post Office and Civil Service

Civil Service
Manpower Utilization
Postal Operations

Veterans' Affairs

Education and Training
Hospitals
Spanish War

1965–1983

Committees*

Government Operations
Post Office and Civil Service
Standards of Official Conduct

Subcommittees

Agriculture

Domestic Marketing and Consumer Relations
Domestic Marketing, Consumer Relations and Nutrition

Appropriations

District of Columbia
Foreign Operations
HUD and Independent Agencies
Labor and HEW

Armed Services

Human Relations
Military Compensation
Military Personnel
Military Personnel and Compensation

Banking, Finance and Urban Affairs

Consumer Affairs
Historic Preservation and Coinage

Housing
Housing and Community Development
The City

District of Columbia

Bicentennial, the Environment, and the International Community
Education
Education, Labor and Social Services
Fiscal Affairs and Health
Government, Budget and Urban Affairs

Education and Labor

Agricultural Labor
Elementary, Secondary and Vocational Education
Employment Opportunities
Equal Opportunities
Farm Labor
General Education
General Labor
Labor-Management Relations
Labor Standards
Manpower, Compensation, Health and Safety
Post-Secondary Education
Poverty War
Select Education
Select Labor
Special Labor

Energy and Commerce

Telecommunications, Consumer Protection and Finance
Health and Environment

Foreign Affairs

Africa

Asian and Pacific Affairs
Europe and Middle East
Inter-American Affairs
International Operations
International Organization
International Resources, Food and Energy
Oversight

Government Operations

Commerce, Consumer and Monetary Affairs
Conservation and Natural Resources
Donable Property
Environment, Energy and Natural Resources
Foreign Operations and Government Information
Government Activities
Government Activities and Transportation
Government Information and Individual Rights
Intergovernmental Relations and Human Resources
Manpower and Housing

House Administration

Accounts
Contracts and Printing

Interior and Insular Affairs

Energy and Environment
Environment
Indian Affairs
National Parks and Recreation
Public Lands and National Parks
Territorial and Insular Affairs

Merchant Marine and Fisheries

Fisheries and Wildlife Conservation
Maritime Education and Training

Post Office and Civil Service

Civil Service
Compensation and Employee Benefits
Employee Ethics and Utilization
Employee Political Rights and Intergovernmental Programs
Human Resources
Postal Facilities, Mail and Labor Management
Postal Operations and Service
Retirement and Employee Benefits

Small Business

Minority Enterprise and General Oversight

Science and Technology

Natural Resources, Agricultural Research and Environment

Veterans' Affairs

Education and Training
Education, Training and Employment
Hospitals
Hospitals and Health Care
Housing
Insurance
Medical Facilities and Benefits

Ways and Means

Public Assistance and Unemployment Compensation

---

* No substantively defined subcommittees established, or no subcommittee assignments designated in individual cases.

Bibliography

BOOKS

Abzug, B. 1972. *Bella: Ms. Abzug goes to Washington*. New York: Saturday Review Press.

Almond, G. A. and Coleman, J. S. eds. 1960. *The politics of developing areas*. Princeton: Princeton University Press.

Amundsen, K. 1971. *The silenced majority: women and American democracy*. Englewood Cliffs: Prentice-Hall.

de Beauvoir, S. 1953. *The second sex*. New York: Knopf.

Becker, S. D. 1981. *The origins of the Equal Rights Amendment: American feminism between the wars*. Wesport: Greenwood Press.

Bibby, J. F., Mann. T. E., and Ornstein, N. J. 1980. *Vital statistics on Congress*. Washington: American Enterprise Institute.

Breckinridge, S. P. 1933. *Women in the Twentieth Century: a study of their political, social and economic activities*. New York: McGraw-Hill.

Brookes, P. 1967. *Women at Westminster: an account of women in the British Parliament, 1918–1966*. London: Peter Davies.

Brownson, C. B. (ed.), 1983. *Congressional Staff Directory*. Mount Vernon: Congressional Staff Directory, Ltd.

Chamberlin, H. 1973. *A minority of members: women in the U.S. Congress*. New York: New American Library.

Clarke, I. C. 1925. *Uncle Sam needs a wife*. Philadelphia: The John C. Winston Co.

Congressional Quarterly Inc. 1976. *Guide to U.S. elections*. Washington: Author.

Currell, M. 1974. *Political woman*. London: Croom Helm.

Douglas, H. G. 1982. *A full life*. Garden City: Doubleday.

Diamond, I. 1977. *Sex roles in the state House*. New Haven: Yale University Press.

Duverger, M. 1955. *The political role of women*. Paris: United Nations Educational, Scientific and Cultural Organization.

Engelbarts, R. 1974. *Women in the United States Congress, 1917–1972: their accomplishments; with bibliographies*. Littleton: Libraries Unlimited.

Epstein, L. 1958. *Politics in Wisconsin*. Madison: University of Wisconsin Press.

Fenno, R. 1966. *The power of the purse: appropriations politics in Congress*. Boston: Little, Brown.

Galloway, G. B. 1953. *The legislative process in Congress*. New York: Crowell.

Gladieux, L. E. and Wolanin, T. R. 1976. *Congress and the colleges: the national politics of higher education*. Lexington: Lexington Books.

Gruberg, M. 1968. *Women in politics*. Oshkosh: Academia Press.

Hess, S. 1966. *America's political dynasties: from Adams to Kennedy*. Garden City: Doubleday.

Jacobson, G. C. 1983. *The politics of congressional elections*. Boston: Little, Brown.

Janeway, E. 1971. *Man's world, woman's place: a study in social mythology*. New York: William Morrow.

Jones, C. O. 1964. *Party and policy-making: the House Republican Policy Committee*. New Brunswick: Rutgers University Press.

_____. 1965. *The Republican Party in American politics*. New York: MacMillan.

Kelly, R. M., and Boutilier, M. 1978. *The making of political women: a study of socialization and role conflict*. Chicago: Nelson-Hall.

Kirkpatrick, J. J. 1974. *Political woman*. New York: Basic Books.

Lamson, P. 1968. *Few are chosen: American women in political life today*. Boston: Houghton Mifflin.

_____. 1979. *In the vanguard: six American women in public life*. Boston: Houghton Mifflin.

Lemons, J. S. 1973. *The woman citizen: social feminism in the 1920s*. Urbana: University of Illinois Press.

Lewis, W. C. ed. 1972. *Declaration of conscience: Margaret Chase Smith*. New York: Doubleday.

McNeil, N. 1963. *Forge of democracy: The House of Representatives*. New York: David McKay.

Mandel, R. B. 1981. *In the running: The new woman candidate*. New York: Ticknor and Fields.

Manley, J. F. 1970. *The politics of finance: The House Committee on Ways and Means*. Boston: Little, Brown.

Mann, J. 1962. *Women in Parliament*. London: Odhams Press.

Margolis, D. R., and Stanwick, K. 1979. *Women's organizations in the public service*. New Brunswick: Center for the American Woman and Politics, Eagleton Institute.

Martin, J. 1960. *My first fifty years in politics*. New York: McGraw-Hill.

Matthews, D. R. 1960. *U.S. Senators and their world*. Chapel Hill: University of North Carolina Press.

Mooney, B. 1964. *Mr. Speaker: four men who shaped the United States House of Representatives*. Chicago: Follett.

Paxton, A. 1945. *Women in congress*. Richmond: The Dietz Press.

Peabody, R. L. 1976. *Leadership in congress: stability, succession and change*. Boston: Little, Brown.

Prewitt, K. 1970. *The recruitment of political leaders: a study of citizen-politicians*. Indianapolis: Bobbs-Merrill.

Putnam, R. D. 1976. *The comparative study of political elites*. Englewood Cliffs: Prentice-Hall.

Rix, S. E., and Stone, A. J. 1981. *Impact on women of the administration's proposed budget*. Washington: Women's Research and Education Institute.

Seligman, L. G.; King, M. R., Kim, C. L., and Smith, R. E. 1974. *Patterns of recruitment: a state chooses its lawmakers*. Chicago: Rand McNally.

Shadegg, S. 1970. *Clare Boothe Luce: a biography*. New York: Simon and Schuster.

Sorauf, F. J. 1963. *Party and representation: legislative politics in Pennsylvania*. New York: Atherton Press.

Swank, G. R. 1978. *Ladies of the House (and Senate), Idaho 1899–1978*. Boise: author.

Tolchin, S., and Tolchin, M. 1974. *Clout: womanpower and politics.* New York: Coward, McCann and Geoghegan.

Vallance, E. M. 1979. *Women in the House: a study of women members of Parliament.* London: Athlone Press.

Voorhis, J. 1947. *Confessions of a congressman.* Garden City: Doubleday.

Wiley, A. 1947. *Laughing with Congress.* New York: Crown Publishers.

ARTICLES IN EDITED WORKS AND PROFESSIONAL JOURNALS

Bardwick, J. M. The great revolution. In *New Research on Women and Sex Roles*, ed. D. G. McGuigan, pp. 25–34. Ann Arbor: University of Michigan Center for Continuing Education of Women.

Bone, H. A. 1956. Some notes on the Congressional Campaign Committee. *Western Political Quarterly* 9: 116–137.

Buchanan, C. 1978. Why aren't there more women in congress. *Congressional Quarterly Weekly Report* 36: 2108–110.

Bullock, C. S., III, and Heys, P. L. F. 1972. Recruitment of women for Congress: a research note. *Western Political Quarterly* 25: 416–23.

Clubok, A. B., Wilensky, N., and Berghorn, F. J. 1969. Family relationships, congressional recruitment, and political modernization. *Journal of Politics* 31: 1035–62.

Comstock, A. 1926. Women members of European parliaments. *American Political Science Review* 20: 379–84.

Czudnowski, M. M. 1975. Political recruitment. In *Handbook of Political Science, Vol. II.* Greenstein, F. I., and Polsby, N. W. eds. 155–242. Reading: Addison-Wesley.

Dodd, L. C. 1979. The expanding role of the House Democratic whip system: The 93rd and 94th Congresses. *Congressional Studies* 7: 27–56.

Dreifus, C. 1972. Women in politics: an interview with Edith Green. *Social Policy* 2: 16–22.

Ferraro, G. 1979. Women as candidates. *Harvard Political Review.* 7: 21–24.

Fiellin, A. 1962. Functions of informal groups in legislative institutions. *Journal of Politics* 24: 72–91.

Gehlen, F. L. 1969. Women in Congress. *Transaction* 6: 36–40.

Gelb, J., Palley, M. L. 1979. Women and interest group politics: a comparative analysis of federal decision making. *Journal of Politics* 41: 362–93.

Gertzog, I. N., and Simand, M. M. 1981. Women and 'hopeless' congressional candidacies: nomination frequency, 1916–1978. *American Politics Quarterly* 9: 449–66.

Githens, M., and Prestage, J. 1978. Women state legislators: styles and priorities. *Policy Studies Journal* (Winter, No. 2): 264–70.

Iglitzin, L. B. 1974. The making of the apolitical women: feminity and sex stereotyping in girls. In *Women in Politics*, Jaquette, J. ed.: 25–35. New York: John Wiley.

Jaquette, J. S. 1974. Introduction. In Jaquette, J. *Women in Politics*, author ed.: XIII–XXXVII. New York: John Wiley.

Kincaid, D. D. 1978. Over his dead body: a positive perspective on widows in the U.S. Congress. *Western Political Quarterly* 31: 96–104.

Lasswell, H. D. 1954. The selective effect of personality on political participation. In *Studies in the Scope and Method of the Authoritarian Personality*, Christie, R., and Jahoda, M. eds.: 197–225. Glencoe: The Free Press.

Lee, M. M. 1977. Toward understanding why so few women hold public office: factors affecting the participation of women in local politics. In *A Portrait of Marginality*, Githens, M., and Prestage, J. eds.: 118–38. New York: David McKay.

Lipman-Blumen, J. 1973. Role De-Differentiation as a system response to crisis. *Sociological Inquiry* 43: 105–29.

Loomis, B. A. 1981. Congressional caucuses and politics of representation. In *Congress Reconsidered* (2nd edition), Dodd, L. C., and Oppenheimer, B. I. eds.: 204–20. Washington: Congressional Quarterly Press.

Lynn, N. 1975. Women in American politics: an overview. In *Women: A Feminist Perspective*. Freeman, J. ed.: 264–85. Palo Alto: Mayfield.

O'Leary, V. 1974. Some attitudinal barriers to occupational aspirations in women. *Psychological Bulletin* 11: 809–26.

Oleszek, W. 1969. Age and political careers. *Public Opinion Quarterly* 33: 100–02.

Parsons, T. 1953. The superego and the theory of social systems. In *Working Papers in the Theory of Action*, Bales, R. F., Shils, E., and author, eds.: 13–29. New York: The Free Press.

Plattner, A. 1983. Various legislative styles, philosophies . . . found among Congress' 23 Women. *Congressional Quarterly Weekly Report* 41: 784–85.

Polsby, N. W. 1968. Institutionalization of the U.S. House of Representatives. *American Political Science Review* 62: 144–68.

_____. 1969, The growth of the seniority system in the U.S. House of Representatives. *American Political Science Review* 3: 787–807.

Rule, W. 1981. Why women don't run: the critical contextual factors in women's legislative recruitment. *Western Political Quarterly* 34: 60–77.

Stevens, A. G., Jr., Mulhollan, D. P., and Rundquist, P. 1981. U.S. Congressional structure and representation: The role of informal groups. *Legislative Studies Quarterly* 6: 415–37.

Sullivan, W. E. 1975. Criteria for selecting party leadership in Congress: an empirical test. *American Politics Quarterly* 3:25–44.

Thompson, J. H. 1985. Career convergence: election of women and men to the House of Representatives, 1916–1975. *Women and Politics* (forthcoming).

Van Hightower, N. R. 1977. The recruitment of women for public office. *American Politics Quarterly* 5: 301–14.

Werner, E. E. 1966. Women in Congress, 1917–1964. *Western Political Quarterly* 19: 16–30.

_____. 1968, Women in the state legislatures. *Western Political Quarterly* 21: 40–50.

ARTICLES IN POPULAR MAGAZINES AND NEWSPAPERS

Anderson, G. E. 1929. Women in Congress. *The Commonweal*, March 13: 532–34.

Anderson, J., and Cappaccio, T. 1980. Jack Anderson rates the Congress. *The Washingtonian*, October: 166–71.

Auletta, K. 1975. 'Senator' Bella—seriously. *New York Magazine*, August 11: 27–34.

Blair, E. N. 1925. Are women a failure in politics? *Harper's*. October: 513–22.

_____. 1927. Are women really in politics? *The Independent*, December 3: 541–44.

_____. 1931, Why I am discouraged about women in politics. *The Woman's Journal*, January: 20 ff.

Brenner, M. 1977. What makes Bella run? *New York Magazine*, June 20: 54–64.

Davis, F. 1943. Beauty and the East. *Saturday Evening Post*, July 17: 216.

Dudar, H. 1967. Women in the news—Representative Leonor Sullivan: if I want something bad enough. *New York Post Weekend Magazine*, September 2.

Geist, W. E. 1982. Millicent Fenwick: marching to her own drum. *New York Times Magazine*, June 27: 21 ff.

Gilfond, D. 1929. Gentlewomen of the House. *The American Mercury*, October: 151–60.

Glaser, V. and Elliott, L. 1983. Woman power. *The Washingtonian*, May: 156–64.

Huck, W. M. 1923. What happened to me in Congress. *Woman's Home Companion*, July: 4

Kronholz, J. 1976. For congresswoman, issue in Kansas race is a 'messy' divorce. *Wall Street Journal*, October 7: 1.

Lockett, E. P. 1950. FDR's Republican cousin in Congress. *Colliers*, August 19: 26 ff.

Owen, R. B. 1933. My daughter and politics. *Woman's Home Companion*, October: 27–30.

Payne, L. 1982. Mrs. Chisholm calls it quits: a conversation with Shirley Chisholm. Essence, August: 72 ff.

Porter, A. 1943. Ladies of Congress. *Colliers*, August 28: 22.

Pratt, R. S. (Baker). 1926. Plea for party partisanship. *Woman Citizen* March: 23.

Winifrey, C. 1977. In search of Bella Abzug. *New York Times Magazine*, August 21: 15 ff.

GOVERNMENT DOCUMENTS

Rundquist, P. S. 1978. Formal and informal congressional groups. *Congressional Research Service*, Report No. 78–83 GOV, March 25.

Schwemle, B. L. 1982. Women in the U.S. Congress. *Congressional Research Service*, Report No. 82–37 GOV, March 9.

U.S. Congress. 1976. Joint Committee on Arrangements for the Commemoration of the Bicentennial. Women in Congress, 1917–1976, prepared by Tolchin, S. J. Washington: U.S.G.P.O.

UNPUBLISHED SOURCES

Smith, K. S. 1976. The characteristics of American women who seek positions of political leadership. Dissertation submitted to the Graduate Faculty of Political and Social Science of the New School for Social Research.

Stevens, A. G. Jr., Mulhollan, D. P., and Rundquist, P. S. 1980. Congressional structure and representation: the role of informal groups. Paper delivered at the 1980 Annual Meeting of the American Political Science Association, the Washington Hilton Hotel, August 28–31.

Index

About the Author

Irwin N. Gertzog received a B.A. in English from Union College, Schenectady, N.Y., and a Ph.D. in Political Science from the University of North Carolina, Chapel Hill. He taught at Yale University before accepting the Braun Distinguished Professorship in Political Science at Allegheny College.

Professor Gertzog is a specialist in Congress whose work has appeared in leading professional journals. He served as an American Political Science Association Congressional Fellow, later received a National Science Foundation grant to promote undergraduate research in Political Science, and subsequently returned to Washington for a year under a Social Science Research Council Fellowship. In 1982, Professor Gertzog received the Ross Excellence in Teaching Prize awarded by students, alumni, and faculty of Allegheny College. He spent 1983–84 conducting research and teaching at Rutgers University.